American Humor

By the same author

TRUMPETS OF JUBILEE

TROUPERS OF THE GOLD COAST
OR THE RISE OF LOTTA CRABTREE

American Humor

A Study of the National Character

Constance Rourke

Introduction and Bibliographical Essay
by W. T. Lhamon, Jr.

University Presses of Florida

Florida State University Press
Tallahassee

Library of Congress Cataloging-in-Publication Data

Rourke, Constance Mayfield, 1885–1941.
American humor.

Reprint. Originally published New York: Harcourt,
Brace, c1931.
Bibliography: p.
Includes index.
1. American wit and humor – History and criticism.
2. National characteristics, American. 3. American
literature – History and criticism. I. Lhamon, W. T.
II. Title.
PS430.R6   1986   817′.009   85-26428
ISBN 0-8130-0837-9

UNIVERSITY PRESSES OF FLORIDA is the central agency for scholarly
publishing of the State of Florida's university system, producing books
selected for publication by the faculty editorial committees of Florida's
nine public universities: Florida A&M University (Tallahassee), Florida
Atlantic University (Boca Raton), Florida International University (Miami),
Florida State University (Tallahassee), University of Central Florida
(Orlando), University of Florida (Gainesville), University of North Florida
(Jacksonville), University of South Florida (Tampa), University of West
Florida (Pensacola).

ORDERS for books published by all member presses should be addressed
to University Presses of Florida, 15 NW 15th Street, Gainesville, FL 32603.

Printed in the U.S.A. on acid-free paper

Again, for my mother

ACKNOWLEDGMENTS

GRATEFUL acknowledgments are offered to Mr. Clarence S. Brigham, Director of the American Antiquarian Society, who has given liberal assistance in the use of comic almanacs, pamphlets, periodicals, and songs in the collection of the Society; to Mr. Franklin J. Meine of Chicago, whose collection of American humor has been generously made available for this book; to Miss Mabel R. Gillis, Librarian, and Miss Eudora Garoutte of the California State Library, who have been helpful in discovering buried humor; to Mr. Edward B. Hall for assistance in the Widener Library; to officials in the Library of the University of Chicago, which contains invaluable comic material of the lighter stage; and to Mr. Samuel H. Ranck, Librarian of the Grand Rapids Public Library, who has patiently summoned books with which to make this book, and provided the support of a friendly interest. Permission to reprint poems of Emily Dickinson has courteously been given by Martha Dickinson Bianchi.

CONTENTS

FOREWORD

IN pursuing humor over a wide area, as in the nation, certain pitfalls lurk for the unwary. An antiquarian interest is likely to develop. An old piece of humor is discovered, and one turns it over like a worn carving or figurine, with mounting pride if one can name it as pre-Jacksonian, early Maine, late Arkansas, or perhaps not American at all but of doubtful origin, say neo-French. But other interests may transcend this beguiling pedantry, for humor is one of those conceits which give form and flavor to an entire character. In the nation, as comedy moves from a passing effervescence into the broad stream of a common possession, its bearings become singularly wide. There is scarcely an aspect of the American character to which humor is not related, few which in some sense it has not governed. It has moved into literature, not merely as an occasional touch, but as a force determining large patterns and intentions. It is a lawless element, full of surprises. It sustains its own appeal, yet its vigorous power invites absorption in that character of which it is a part.

Of late the American character has received marked and not altogether flattering attention from American critics. "It's a wretched business, this virtual quarrel of ours with our own country," said Rowland Mallett in *Roderick Hudson.* The quarrel seemed to begin in that period within which James laid his story, soon after the Civil War; traces of it may be seen even earlier. It has deepened; it has occasionally grown ponderous; it has often been bracing; at times it has narrowed to a methodical hilarity. Since the prevailing note has been candid, candor may be offered in turn. This book has no quarrel with the American character; one might as well dispute with some established feature in the natural landscape. Nor can it be called a defense. Some one has said that a book should be written as a debt is gratefully paid. This study has grown from an enjoyment of American vagaries, and from the belief that these have woven together a tradition which is various, subtle, sinewy, scant at times but not poor.

CONSTANCE ROURKE'S
SECRET RESERVE

W. T. Lhamon, Jr.

> . . . the very telling of it emerging shadowy
> and burlesque, ludicrous, comic and mad,
> from the ague of unbearable forgetting with
> a quality more dreamily furious than any
> fable behind proscenium lights
>
> — William Faulkner, "Old Man" (1939)

CONSTANCE ROURKE's *American Humor* has become a classic text of American scholarship, important in literary criticism, folklore, theater history, American studies, and popular culture. Since its publication in 1931, this quietly complex thesis has settled and survived constant dispute. In the critical community, histories, manifestos, economic interpretations, and apologies for a supposed national nonculture preceded her work. And in the creative circles Rourke analyzed, there were of course implicit, working aesthetics. But her *American Humor* was the first *theory* of American culture, conceived as such, for it shifted emphasis from simply historical questions to a fully dimensioned process with satisfying complexity. Where literary historians limited themselves to questions of when and whence, Rourke also wondered what, why, how, and what for.

The way she answered those questions ensured that her attention to American culture would remain uncommon. Even today, many books with "theory" in their titles actually refer to history (Jones) or to *"poetics"* (Perosa, xi) rather than to the nature and function of arts within a real cultural context. Even Henry James's famous prefaces to his novels were in this vein of poetics rather than theory and were surely not a theory of American literature, character, or culture. Relative to her predecessors and most of her successors, then, Rourke is distinct in professing a theory of mutual dependencies among the several domains of culture. This feature of almost ecological relationships connects Rourke always to cultural experience as we know it. That is why her theorizing has none of the sense of antiseptic removal from the world that has sometimes attached itself to literary study since the seventies. And Rourke's acute dealing in the familiar world has meant that more than a half century after their inception her claims are not disproved but confirmed. Her energy is not exhausted but still animates and defines America's central stories and forms.

American Humor has been, however, a classic without status. Its lucidity allows allies to take it for granted while antagonists ignore its insights. Now diffuse in the several disciplines it touches, and more referred to than read, Rourke's theory is nevertheless still more startling than staid. It illuminates work recently recycled into importance, like Twain's *The Innocents Abroad* (1869) and Melville's *The Confidence Man* (1857). And *American Humor* is indispensable to a full understanding of such seemingly antitraditional novels as the longer works of Jack Kerouac and Thomas Pynchon, as well as those of black writers from Ralph Ellison to Toni Morrison who most closely attend to folk and popular culture. Thus her range is broad and she anticipated perhaps even more than she summarily organized. Equally significant is that her strategy and style – if we may separate them from her conceptual contributions – continue to be calm exemplars of American criticism. They help Rourke sidestep critical jousting to pursue her true goals. In these as in so many other ways, *American Humor* remains a feminist landmark.

When no one else could find it, or even admit its existence, Rourke showed that America had a literary tradition and that it was specific. Out of all the regional tales that grew wherever people gathered around hearth or campfire, forge or barge, while the country pushed westward, she found three insistent figures that rose to national stature in the popular fancy. The first was the Yankee peddler, shrewd, protean, and laconic. Then the backwoodsman developed, a composite of buckskin hunter and river's raftsman, loud, giant, and earthy. And with these came the Negro minstrel, a motley song-and-dance man putting on white airs most often in blackface. These made the "comic trio" of her first three chapters. She discovered them in sources that earlier scholars deplored, thus ignored: the almanacs, songsheets, jokebooks, newspapers, melodrama, and accounts of vaudeville performances all rampant in the nineteenth century, early and late. (An exception that proves the rule here is George Lyman Kittredge's affectionate pot-pourri from the annual almanacs of Robert Bailey Thomas: *The Old Farmer and His Almanack* [Boston: W. Ware, 1904]. Kittredge's social history reveals the great bulk of chaff, however richly detailed, that surrounded the narrative grains that Rourke and her followers would later winnow.)

In her subsequent chapters, Rourke watches the trio and their formal retinue strut together across the American stage, crop up in Lincoln's speeches, incite Emerson's tropes, and amble before Whitman to show him the way. By midway in the last century, certainly before the United States was older than loquacious citizens might have lived, the young country had patterned its own structures of feeling to furnish American tale-telling, political rhetoric, and drama. This specific body of popular humor was the stuff that Hawthorne and Melville, Dickinson and Poe, Thoreau and Twain all used to make the first high tide of American literature. That was her thesis: there was very early in the land a lore on which American art built. "American vagaries," she believed, stated in her foreword, and proved throughout, "have woven together a tradition which is various, subtle, sinewy, scant at times but not poor" (x).

INTRODUCTION

If Rourke's position seems modest enough today, it was heresy at the tag end of the 1920s when she was developing and researching it. The Lost Generation was sitting around glasses of Pernod on the Left Bank, avoiding an America its members considered a cultural void. They were not alone in their conclusions; the prevailing criticism agreed. In his *Literary History of the United States* (1900), Barrett Wendell had described the brief American past as the "national inexperience" (153). Other critics allowed for cultured content in the country but believed it anarchic. Thus, in *America's Coming-of-Age* (1915), Van Wyck Brooks described the past as unusably split into "the peculiar dualism that lies at the root of our national point of view" (45) — "highbrow" idea-mongers versus "lowbrow" money-grubbers. "Dessicated culture at [one] end and stark utility at the other have created a deadlock in the American mind," he said "and all our life drifts chaotically between the two extremes" (14).

Widespread subscription to Brooks's criticism in the early years of this century shows that educated Americans truly anguished over such issues. But his poles made an inadequate, misleading rack for the display of any culture. Had the ethnic stereotypes promulgated in terms like "highbrow" and "lowbrow" not disqualified Brooks's diagnosis of the national root, then his invalid dialectic should have. True dialectical process generates synthesis, but Brooks's deadlocked because of two mistaken assumptions. First, his poles were insufficiently few, and, second, he inverted the implied flow of information between them. A nation has more than one set of tablets, and intellectuals on high rarely inscribe them alone or even dominantly. For the Brooksian elite or trickle-down account of culture, Rourke substituted a folk or welling-up theory.

Because Van Wyck Brooks was the leading American critic when Rourke wrote *American Humor,* his assumptions and model were surely two of her targets. Indeed, *American*

CONSTANCE ROURKE'S SECRET RESERVE

Humor is partly an answer to Brooks's plea in *The Dial* (11 April 1918) for Americans to discover, even invent, a "usable past." In that same piece he had also argued that America had "no cumulative culture." Rourke responded to both these terms. She showed that the comic trio was in use among American authors; thus in an explicitly cumulative process American authors were incorporating popular legends, and Rourke emphasized this as a "native tradition" with a "natural sequence" (301, 302). Perhaps Brooks's Brahmin blinders narrowed his outlook. Perhaps it took a midwestern progressive with something of a frontier ethic of her own to feel that America possessed and was already using its past, if one only knew where to look. Whatever the case, it was clearly not part of Rourke's strategy to waste much attention on Brooks's misconceptions. She characteristically knew that his ideas, too, were from a tradition, which she traced back toward its sources.

She found her cue, title, and most significant stimulation in that remarkable conjunction of American letters, Henry James's critical study, *Hawthorne* (1879). It was James's second book of criticism but, as Edmund Wilson remarked, "the first extended study ever made of an American writer" (Sale, v). Early in this volume, James noticed and then greatly elaborated a remark Hawthorne made in his preface to *The Marble Faun* (1860). "No author," Hawthorne had written, "without a trial, can conceive of the difficulty of writing a romance about a country where there is no shadow, no antiquity, no mystery, no picturesque and gloomy wrong, nor anything but a commonplace prosperity, in broad and simple daylight, as is happily the case with my dear native land." But Hawthorne did not invent the complaint because both the ideas and the cadences in his famous passage precisely echo those in James Fenimore Cooper's comments, made a generation before in 1828, that America provided "no annals for the historian; no follies (beyond the most vulgar and commonplace) for the satirist; no manners for the dramatist; no obscure fictions for the writer of romance; no gross and hardy offenses against decorum for the moralist; nor any of the rich artificial auxiliaries of poetry" (Leary, xi).

It was these continual American lamentations and the march of their rhythm that James syncopated in *Hawthorne*. Immediately apparent in hindsight, James had more humor than his predecessors. His increased verve, the exclamation point underlining the postcard-like trivialities he listed, and his extreme extension of the catalogue move James's third version of the set-piece toward parody of American self-flagellation:

> The negative side of the spectacle on which Hawthorne looked out, in his contemplative saunterings and reveries, might, indeed, with a little ingenuity, be made almost ludicrous; one might enumerate the items of high civilization, as it exists in other countries, which are absent from the texture of American life, until it should become a wonder to know what was left. No State, in the European sense of the word, and indeed barely a specific national name. No sovereign, no court, no personal loyalty, no aristocracy, no church, no clergy, no army, no diplomatic service, no country gentlemen, no palaces, no castles, nor manors, nor old country-houses, nor parsonages, nor thatched cottages, nor ivied ruins; no cathedrals, nor abbeys, nor little Norman churches; no great Universities nor public schools – no Oxford, nor Eton, nor Harrow; no literature, no novels, no museums, no pictures, no political society, no sporting class – no Epsom nor Ascot! . . . The natural remark, in the almost lurid light of such an indictment, would be that if these things are left out, everything is left out. (34–35)

While mocking his homeland, James's exaggeration also mocks its mockers – yet another dimension in his prose that

xviii

nearly every reviewer missed. Although James's comment continues importantly, all of Rourke's scholarly predecessors stopped reading right here to deliver verdicts prematurely. Noting the lurid indictment, they ignored the self-mockery and its ironic implications, just as they passed over the balancing remainder. That is why critics consistently read the passage even today as the *locus classicus* of American literary deprecation. Rourke acknowledged the indictment; had not her foreword nodded toward those negatives when it admitted the tradition was "scant at times"? But she based her theory on the humor in the cadenced passage, as well as on its next section, its remaining "good deal," its "wonder" at "what was left": "The American knows that a good deal remains; what it is that remains – that is his secret, his joke, as one may say. It would be cruel, in this terrible denudation, to deny him the consolation of his natural gift, that 'American humour' of which of late years we have heard so much" (35).

Constance Rourke meant exactly what Henry James did by "American humour" – it was their own, as well as America's, secret reserve. Certainly it was America's "joke," but it was also a "natural gift" in the way Ben Jonson meant ethic or "character" – the word Rourke stressed in her volume's subtitle. From this neglected part of James's famous passage came the book's title and its spirit of looking beneath the surface for the relative humor that foreign *partis pris* might miss.

A perfect example of this American secret reserve, the knowing what is left in comic terms, and in the same cadenced lamentation turned inside out, appears in the last two dozen lines of "Sounds," the third chapter of Thoreau's *Walden* (1854). When he went to Walden Pond, Thoreau abstained even from the comfort of domestic animals:

> I kept neither dog, cat, cow, pig, nor hens, so that you would have said there was a deficiency of domestic sounds; neither the churn, nor the spinning wheel, nor

even the singing of the kettle, nor the hissing of the urn, nor children crying, to comfort one. An old-fashioned man would have lost his senses or died of ennui before this. Not even rats in the wall, for they were starved out, or rather were never baited in, –*only* squirrels on the roof and under the floor, a whippoor-will on the ridge pole, a blue-jay screaming beneath the window, a hare or woodchuck under the house, a screech-owl or a cat-owl behind it, a flock of wild geese or a laughing loon on the pond, and a fox to bark in the night. Not even a lark or an oriole, those mild plantation birds, ever visited my clearing. No cockerels to crow nor hens to cackle in the yard. No yard! *but* unfenced Nature reaching up to your very sills. A young forest growing up under your windows, and wild sumachs and black-berry vines breaking through into your cellar; sturdy pitch-pines rubbing and creaking against the shingles for want of room, their roots reaching quite under the house. *Instead of* a scuttle or a blind blown off in the gale, – a pine tree snapped off or torn up by the roots behind your house for fuel. *Instead of* no path to the front-yard gate in the Great Snow, – no gate – no front-yard, – and no path to the civilized world! (emphases added)

The American secret that Thoreau tells is that true abstinence does not exist – there is always an *only* that becomes a long list; there is a *but*, an *instead of* or two, and an exclamation point ending it all.

Because Thoreau's book was so little known in its own time, it is unlikely Hawthorne had read it when he prefaced *The Marble Faun* or that James knew it as an example of his American joke. Nor does Rourke mention this passage in her discussion of *Walden*. What is important is that Thoreau's unremarked positive catalogue displays the general background for

James's teasing of the oft-cited negative catalogue. That Thoreau's passage exists, even unnoticed, indicates a structure of feeling established in the culture; it permitted then, and now confirms, the tropes and conceits covert in James and overt in Rourke. Thoreau's positive list exemplifies the secret reserve of American humor. The issue was in the young nation's air; there were many positions about it; this reserve was an American characteristic significantly more complex than Rourke's predecessors realized. Cooper considered these distinctions a deficiency, Hawthorne an instigation, Thoreau the means to novel exclamation, and James the native gift.

Rourke followed them all, but agreed most closely with James's rich clues in *Hawthorne*. Surely James taught her how the American's humor was an elastic equanimity that permitted enormous growth in experience at home and abroad. Only such poise under pressure might sustain the wonderful range of nineteenth-century American comic figures that peaks in those related characters of James's and Twain's fiction – fools but not fools, wisely winning innocents – when they faced the certain surprises of gilt drawing rooms and gold-rush tents. Recognition of this secret reserve allowed James to begin and Rourke to complete the negating of what Rourke called the American "series of negations" (156). Beginning to negate the negations, James turned American lamentation into the secret of American lore. Instaurating what James inaugurated, Rourke raised that reserve into the light of day.

That is why in the physical and conceptual center of *American Humor*, Rourke herself appropriated the issue and series for her own ends. The moment is significant in *American Humor* because during it she admits that American culture differed from European standards but insists on the worth of that variance. She sets it up by assuming, contrary to Brooks, a bottom-up cultural vector: "No society of cultivated men and women had supplied a subject matter, though it might perhaps be granted that such a society had sometimes formed an au-

xxi

dience" (156). Cultivated Americans had to watch their culture develop on its own before they could push it further.

But what was it they watched? That's where she quite consciously took up the Cooper-Hawthorne-James complaint, making the national problem her own critical dilemma and thus re-enacting their gambit: "For purposes of candor American comedy of the long period which stretched from the Revolution to the year 1860 may be described in a series of negations. Little of the purely human was contained within it, no deepening of the portrayal of character, nothing of a wide and interwoven web of thought and feeling where wit might freely play and the whole be gently lighted. . . . Little or nothing of the philosophical element had developed even in Lincoln's stories" (156–57). So much then for the unachieved values of English culture; American experience was not going to conceive a Jane Austen or George Eliot (whose discussion of English fictive character in chapter 17 of *Adam Bede* [1859] these cited phrases also evoke). Copying James's ploy of asking what remained, therefore, Rourke fulfilled her critical task by answering more specifically than did the novelist: "If they failed to exhibit subtlety, fineness, balance, [Americans] had created laughter and had served the ends of communication among a people unacquainted with themselves, strange to the land, unshaped as a nation; they had produced a shadowy social coherence" (157).

There can hardly be a better definition of lore than this "shadowy social coherence." Characteristically, modestly, Rourke has made the largest sort of point with her quietest phrasing. She has done it by compressing "shadowy" into a pun, meaning both darkly and incompletely binding. Certainly she disagrees with Hawthorne that the American "broad and simple daylight" of 1860 – the year preceding the Civil War – provided "no shadow." Her own "shadowy social coherence" recognizes that the land had its dark problems, its bruise points, well before then, that the national identity in fact derived from the social denials of the solitary Yankee, the danger of the frontier, and the dilemmas of a multiracial inheritance. America's peculiarly dark problems produced a specifically shadowy coherence evidenced not least, she would point out, in Hawthorne's own shadowy tales which she cited against his own phrase: "the older and more deeply established lore of New England was darkly tinged; [thus Hawthorne's] tales reveal a gamut of the more violent or terrible feelings, rage, terror, the sense of guilt, greed, strange regional fantasies, . . . witchcraft, ghosts" (187).

Quite apart from Hawthorne, however, Rourke in the first half of *American Humor* had shown that by the outset of the Civil War, America's popular writing was a packed house in which cavorted a mix of dark and light, evil and good, young and old, East and West, top hat and coonskin. The comic trio replayed and reinforced these contrary tendencies before rube and gent, all over this land and in Europe's capitals, too. By mingling more than opposing each other, they made fecund the mutual processes connecting the many parts of American life. In that sense, the other part of the shadowy pun emerges. The connections were not complete. Rube only partly colored gent, and beaver fur was not completely digested in becoming a felt top hat. The parts affected each other, yet remained discrete at their margins. Thus "shadowy" meant incomplete because Rourke knew that real lore is always in process and only as such can it be cohesive. Should the sequence ever complete itself, then its dynamic tensions would die and the constituent parts float off unusably toward the chaos Brooks had feared. In such ways the shadowy process is central to her theory, holding both it and American culture together. It opened up other new ground all around it.

This new territory included applying a Herderian theory of literary growth up from folk culture – and this in a land where there had been almost no folk scholarship. What notable exceptions existed traced survivals from the parent countries, as in

Francis James Child's study, *The English and Scottish Popular Ballads* (5 vols., 1882–98). Child exemplified the prevailing attitude in every American intellectual discipline from folklore to philosophy. That is, American culture was a worn remnant of baggage brought from Europe, whose own cultures were themselves distant descendants of a privileged, oral, and handcrafted past. Rourke broke with that approach. There was no way to follow it and at the same time believe in, understand, and interpret the American lore she was discovering.

This commitment to divulging America's positive shadowy coherence necessitated opening also another piece of new territory. She had to redefine what lore was and where one might find it. In that light it is more than coincidence that the year 1812, which Rourke postulates as the moment when peddler and gamecock emerged in almanacs and other printed sources, is the year the Brothers Grimm issued in Germany their first *Kinder und Hausmärchen,* or *Household Tales.* Folklorists have long thought this collection to be the first scientific collection of folktales. We now know, nevertheless, that the Grimms, much like the American journalists and publishers Rourke mined, were co-creators, sweeteners, and shapers of their tales (Ellis). The collaborative creation of fairy tales continued in Europe until Andrew Lang capped such collection in his twelve volumes of *Fairy Books* between 1889 and 1910. (Of course, the tales themselves have continued to circulate and change in talk, print, film, television cartoon, and comic book and to affect lives and literature.) This chiefly nineteenth-century European cycle of documenting and absorbing folktales into print therefore ran almost precisely parallel with the native legend sequence that is Rourke's subject in *American Humor.*

What the Germans were doing earnestly, what the French had been doing deftly (since Charles Perrault's *Histoires ou contes du temps passé, avec des Moralitez,* or *Mother Goose*

Tales, in 1697), what the Irish Celtic Revival was intending as a nationalist differentiation from the neighboring English, and what the English were doing as an integrating appropriation of international lore, Americans were performing with their own improvised, can-do slapdash. All the West was recording its oral legends and reshaping them for its new reading populations and their new needs, each nation in its own way, Americans openly, Europeans perhaps more self-consciously. *Avec des Moralitez*, plus the morals: the incipiently industrial society was starting the process of mediating its culture.

These successive scrims between legends and people changed the lore, for sure, and probably people's character, too. For instance, certain local and oral versions of songs, stories, and plays were blotted out by more dimensional (thus prestigious and powerful) printed and broadcast variants. But people still attended to and relayed some stories in preference to others, responding to and shaping their legends in pronounced ways. Journalists and Grimms might propose cultural paradigms, but audiences validated only what they bought, passed on, and embellished. In the late 1920s, none of this was very clear and would not become widely accepted for another forty years. That there remains division over the issue even now gives Rourke's early, working formulations the useful feel of tested tools—a balanced spade, a sharp paring knife—ready to the hand and sized for the job. She balanced and sharpened these implements working not in folk domains but in libraries' special collections with low-prestige printed sources. Rather than in the locally pristine tale or unadulterated ballad, she looked for common denominators that ran through each social class and geographic region in the thumbed and scuffed popular elements of American culture.

Therefore, "Since it had been produced on many levels," she wrote, "this comic poetry could not be called folk-poetry, but it had the breadth and much of the spontaneous freedom of a folk-poetry" (157). She developed this idea in the space of several pages at the end of her fifth chapter, "The Comic Poet." Despite the charge some folklorists raised in the 1970s that she confused "folklore with subliterature" (Dorson, 95), and the literary critic Daniel Hoffman's similar complaint of her "theoretical weakness" (12), Rourke is impeccable on these issues. "Through the interweaving of the popular strain with that of a new expression on other levels," she argued consciously and stated explicitly, "a literature has been produced which, like other literatures, is related to an anterior popular lore that must for lack of a better word be called a folk-lore" (161).

She did not confuse her comic trio with folklore, but there was not yet any other term to call it. Although Americans were not stereotyped folk—illiterate, oral, and rural—they nevertheless created lore that behaved like the folklore of traditional societies. She demonstrated this process and its sequential consequences for literature much more straightforwardly than did her European predecessors and peers (for whose odd hiding from the facts, self-deception, and misrepresentation, see Ellis). Thus, Rourke anticipated, if she did not invent, the entire study of popular culture.

Her remarks precede by half a century the present focus in studies of both popular and folk culture on lore itself, rather than on group or transmission, as the most significant factor in the three elements making up a mediated culture. Rourke assumed the independence and primacy of lore. It appears outside of primitive or illiterate groups. It provides more than a road back to some sacred past or privileged group. Therefore, more than being its product, she thought, lore is likely to define, and certainly to animate, its subscribing group or nation. One of the most significant implications in her work is that, for Rourke, lore is necessary. There will be lore in every culture no matter how urban or literate, for lore is what makes the group live as a group, providing the stuff by which constituents recognize their membership. Within the context of a national literary theory, particularly one proposed at the nadir of post-wasteland despair, the necessity of lore was a major boost. The concept provided a sense that everything is apt grist for the artist's mill, from Eliotian fragments to crude tales of the American West, from the flatboatman's boast to plantation frolics. When lore is necessary, one person's wasteland is another's special reserve. And when lore is necessary, one always has access to the character of the people who generate it.

What compelled Rourke's focus were the tales, figures, and forms that surmounted the regional and idiosyncratic to reach "the general view," that had "insistent status," that were "destined to capture the popular fancy" or become "a dominant figure" (78–79). Such phrases pepper her pages and irk those who cherish purely local quirks, but they were important for Rourke's exploration of a "shadowy social coherence." Still, her attention to common threads did not lead her to merge literature and popular culture, as some critics have done since Lévi-Strauss inclined that way in the mid-fifties. In that broad movement "literature" is the body of a people's expression which has its own ways of working an audience that differ in kind from a shaman's, tale-teller's, or journalist's workings but are not, prima facie, superior to them. To the structuralist, literature is not privileged beyond the functions and workings of other sorts of lore. Rourke stopped short of this; instead, she emphasized literature's distinctive completion of folk culture.

She thought that great literature completes lore absolutely, which is why she reserved superior status for Henry James: "As a great artist James had moved immeasurably beyond the simple limits of the original [backwoods] fable" (254–55). Obversely, Whitman was ultimately not great: "Like those popular story-tellers who had often seemed on the verge of wider expression, he failed to draw his immeasurable gift into the realm of great and final poetry" (175–76). This vertiginous axis in Rourke's theory clearly approaches the relativism of

xxvii

contemporary structuralist thought but just as decidedly veers away from that edge into the literary supremacism holding great literature apart at a premier "level" of achievement.

One may disagree with such judgments and still see how important was her connection between America's writers and their lore. To "enter the world of Whitman," she wrote, "is to touch the spirit of American popular comedy" (175). Such statements as this, which she multiplies with Hawthorne, Melville, Twain, Poe, and others, were truly radical and remain central truths of American literary theories. They are a main feature of what makes *American Humor* theory rather than chronicle. She was the first to know and show that "The same character was at work on both levels" (162).

A large pleasure in turning Rourke's pages comes from the small subtleties of her style. She subverted rather than confronted the critical conventions of her time. Her last sentence warned against "aggressive" stances opposing the sequence of culture, just as her foreword rejected quarrels and disputes. She hoped to manifest a tradition so clearly that argument would be unnecessary. And she succeeded. Therefore, when Van Wyck Brooks edited her posthumous *The Roots of American Culture* (1942), he simply capitulated: "these fragments, side by side with her other books, reveal the rich stores of tradition that lie behind us, the many streams of native character and feeling from which the Americans of the future will be able to draw" (xii).

Her noncombative tact topped a sack of strategies that promoted such generous reversals. Rather than arguing or girding her loins, Rourke vivified the lores she had uncovered, thus inserting criticism into the native sequence. The "difficult task of discovering and diffusing" (302) the land's significant stories was up to the critic, and so her book became a story in itself. In fact, *American Humor* is narrative criticism in which Rourke almost seamlessly segues between tales and analysis and frequently polishes insights indirectly, as if they were character traits or twists of plot. Readers catch these as they can. From the present participle in the vernacular, dangling modifier at the beginning of her foreword to the term "natural sequence" ending her last chapter, Rourke's style enacted her "enjoyment of American vagaries" (x).

Like the lores she diffused and the humor she studied, her tone was largely optimistic. While other intellectuals of her era, from Van Wyck Brooks to T. S. Eliot, pictured their setting as a cruel April of no renewal, Rourke discovered a ripe maturity. It is late in the day, she would write, and the season is the early harvesttime of midsummer night's eve, that magic moment when lore becomes art. Long ago, Americans had unconsciously sown seeds, which had long since sprouted. The cultural harvest was already ripening. Perhaps most important there were conscious reapers. "Toward evening of a midsummer day," she thus began her first chapter, "at the latter end of the eighteenth century a traveler was seen descending . . . into a fertile Carolina valley . . . his tall shadow cutting across the lengthening shadows of the trees. His head was crouched, his back long; a heavy pack lay across his shoulders" (3).

Every aspect of that opening contradicted the received truths current in 1931. The movement, mingling and multiple shadows, time and season; the traveler's distance from home (lore makers were supposed to be regionally isolated); even the audience implied in the passive verb (and described in her next paragraph) watching the peddler against the landscape – each detail in this only apparently casual prose indicated an ongoing process and the inevitability of lore. The orthodoxy through the twenties had been that there was no culture because the thinkers were split against the makers and shakers. But Rourke's first chapter looks back a hundred years to a welling cultural birth, recreating the legendary Yankee's arrival in the country-at-large, and lo! he's a peddling proto-moneymaker, already affectionately cartooned with a long back for a heavy pack. So, where is the split? The answer is that it was there, but also that the lore was already addressing and healing it "at the latter end of the eighteenth century."

Contrary to the oracular tone of her peers, Rourke's vernacular was a friendly accompaniment to American legends. So successful was she that her telling of the Yankee in Carolina announced his simultaneous arrival in critical consciousness. In like fashion, she also ushered in the gamecock gang – Daniel Boone, Davy Crockett, Mike Fink, and John James Audubon, whom she saw as a sharpshooter and tale-teller. Just widening the tradition to include these characters was a significant achievement. Moreover, she solved the problems in her topic for the so-called usable past school of critics – Brooks, Waldo Frank, Lewis Mumford – and instigated the more academic American Studies movement, as in the work of F. O. Matthiessen and Daniel Hoffman. But the minstrel portion of her theory, arguably its subtlest and most original feature, ran up against a closed door. Thus the minstrel's high position in *American Humor,* but low effect on the wake of Rourke's work, requires special attention.

Indeed, no other aspect of Rourke's theory has received less due notice than her claiming for the "Long-tail'd Blue," or Negro minstrel, a full third of American formative lore. Of scholarly work in her vein, only Bluestein's *The Voice of the Folk* (1972) directly attends to this claim for the centrality of black culture. Sometimes even the best specialized histories of American minstrelsy cite Rourke only in spare bibliographic references, suppressing her thoroughly challenging anticipation of their attitudes. And the most acute literary pursuants of her paradigms, like both Matthiessen and Hoffman, altogether ignore what she called Negro "portraiture" (79). Not until the last half of the 1950s, responding to the racial pressure of the times, did literary critics begin confirming what she had claimed. With Leslie Fiedler's "Come Back to the

Raft Ag'in, Huck Honey!" (1955) and Norman Mailer's *The White Negro* (1957), it was suddenly clear how prescient Rourke had been. Describing Dan Emmett's claim to have composed "Dixie" and other minstrel tunes – although his melodies, imagery, and lyrics were black commonplaces – Rourke had gently judged that "Negro melodies and fables . . . possessed his mind" (86). The understatement applies equally today to a range of contemporary culture performers, from Ralph Ellison's Sambo in *Invisible Man* (1952) to Flannery O'Connor's "The Artificial Nigger" (1955), from Norman Mailer to Elvis Presley, and from Mick Jagger to Bob Dylan ("Who's gonna throw this minstrel boy a coin? . . . Mighty Mockingbird, he still has such a heavy load" [Dylan, 232]). A highly stylized portrait of Negro culture, she correctly predicted in 1931, had possessed the American mind and would continue to do so.

Rourke herself did not extend her theory of black centrality into any of the literature she analyzed in the last chapters of *American Humor*. She must have considered the stiffly maudlin sentimentality in Harriet Beecher Stowe's *Uncle Tom's Cabin* (1852) opposed to the minstrel strain's loose burlesque. Nor did she comment on Joel Chandler Harris's Uncle Remus, thus missing the opportunity to cite Harris's confirmation of her central commitment – "nights with Uncle Remus are as entertaining as those Arabians ones of blessed memory" – which was, from the opening sentence to the famous Brer Rabbit tarbaby tale (1881), itself closely tied to the minstrel subject. And she was writing just too early to have absorbed either the Harlem Renaissance or William Faulkner's enduring Reverend Shegog, Luster, and Dilsey in *The Sound and the Fury* (1929). Faulkner's particularly consonant Joe Christmas appeared in *Light in August* (1932), the year following Rourke's study. She did not then know Carl Wittke's very early and still authoritative minstrel history, *Tambo and Bones* (1930). Because she saw little or no reinforcement of her convictions about the importance of minstrelsy in her early modern period, Rourke's belief that it would be a continual determinant of American humor was all the more remarkable, signal, and solitary.

Lonelier yet was the tack her perspective took. She would not claim that minstrelsy is the "travesty" of blacks that the conventional view has always made of it. Rather, she showed American minstrelsy stemming from a "tradition for faithful drawing" of blacks (80) which Edwin Forrest began in 1820 when he was evidently the first white to impersonate a southern plantation Negro on an American stage. The portrait that gradually emerged was true in the same sense that the pictures of the backwoodsman and the Yankee were: its broad features included ridicule as well as celebration, and its attacks revealed as much about its enactors as about its subject. True, some audience members responded naively, thinking that here was real black behavior. But the obvious burnt-cork masking signified to others, and clearly to Rourke, that the actual performance was of whites playing at artificial roles begun by blacks for complex reasons. The minstrel mask, then role, then show was a slowly built testing ground for the racial relations its actors inherited. Of course it was racist; of course its characters travestied human worth—just as Davy Crockett within the frontier tradition boasted of making a liar eat a cow's "confectionary." That is, the minstrel show had no corner on American crudity. What it did do better than other popular forms of its time was to indicate dynamically the vital position of blacks in the American imagination. In that way, it passed well beyond racist travesty. Rourke emphasized that the Negro's strength, not vulnerability, called minstrelsy into being: "The Negro was to be seen everywhere in the South and in the new Southwest, on small farms and great plantations, on roads and levees. He was often an all but equal member of many a pioneering expedition. He became, in short, *a domi-*

nant figure in spite of his condition, and *commanded* a definite portraiture" (79, emphases added).

The portrait began to take enduring shape in the 1830s. That was when Thomas Dartmouth Rice began his wildly popular impersonations of the black and crippled hostler Jim Crow, whose private dance Rice had glimpsed and copied along the Ohio River. Later, in the 1850s, well after the 1842 collaboration among Dan Emmett and three other white northerners in New York City, usually credited as beginning American minstrelsy, the minstrel show would develop its traditional tripartite structure. This predictable form both provoked and reined in runaway cross-hypings of miscegenated portraiture.

The elaborate minstrel form cordoned into the first part those particularly American takeoffs Rice had tapped during his Jim Crow routines. This wildest segment included audience-pleasing improvisation. But its main thrust went into volatile and increasingly complex interactions between the dandy and duped interlocutor, who put on white airs, and the fieldhand stereotypes of the endmen, named Tambo and Bones after their percussion instruments. The interlocutor grilled the endmen, who responded in turn with passively aggressive strategies and sly barbs of their own. Underlying this specific surface dialogue there was an abstract pattern whose implications Americans must have recognized as their own characteristic identity probe — white boss questioning black employee, rich man dressing down poor man, slicker querying bumpkin, European hectoring Yank. The issue of this grilling Americans have always known to be highly moot, winning depending on how you look at it and what you most prize. As it documented, built on, and made surreal such vernacular scenarios, the opening minstrel takeoff employed a multiply layered set of stereotypes. It showed white men in black makeup parodying black parodies of whites, just to mention the simplest sequences. Audiences enjoyed this complex negation of negations, but critics, finding it too complex to articulate, simplify it into "travesty." As we shall see, these simplifications are possible only in ignorance or suppression of the black folk origins of American minstrelsy. Rourke's strength, here as in relation to the Cooper-Hawthorne-James-Brooks issue of the putative American void, was to realize how much more richly complex the vernacular reality has been than the estranged accounts imposed on it.

The first part of the minstrel show ultimately exploded into the walkaround dance marking its traditional end, to be followed by the olio of vaudeville set pieces, then by a third section comprising the even more formulaic ensemble sketch of plantation life. This formal progression was from wild improvisation toward tamer entertainment: rouse 'em, then souse 'em. That is, the volatile queries into the politics of power and race went to such extremes during the opening section that they required a formal, stepped-down, cooling off. Mingling and mixing and holding it all together, the form cozened and contained the dangerous shadows that white and black traditions threw across the American character.

Rourke claimed Rice began the formal pattern when he extended Jim Crow's black dance into an afterpiece for his stage performances. Significantly, Rice put a Yankee body below the black facial makeup. He pranced on stage in red-and-white striped trousers and long blue coat with coins for buttons—which he grandly tore off and tossed to his audience. What was this but the enactment of a poor man's fantasy of a rich man's largesse? This costume became the subject of Rice's most popular song, "That Long Tail'd Blue," which in turn titled Rourke's chapter. She chose to name a third of America's self-laughter after the national propensity for miscegenation, which is after all what Rice represented. His greased face above the dandy Yankee coat perfectly emblemized both the fascination of Americans with blackness and the rapidly growing complexity in the way American culture imagined the

Negro. Black portraiture, she shows, was becoming increasingly dimensional.

This sense of the fundamental conflicts and complexity in American minstrelsy is Rourke's overlooked contribution to the subject. In the orthodox view, which must ignore Rourke's theory, minstrelsy ridicules stereotyped simplicities of blacks, thus carving out an acceptably safe niche for tamed Negro images in troubled white consciousnesses before and after the Civil War, when the mode had its heyday. However, there was considerably more to the phenomenon. For instance, what grew to be American minstrelsy had existed among blacks as folk play long before the early white practitioners of the form — Forrest, Rice, and Emmett — acquired it. Minstrel behavior among blacks had parodied whites from the start. Rice's long-tailed blue-coat costume and attendant behavior admitted, signified, and extended that parody. And Rourke's theory further extended his line. She was intuitively correct even though she then had no way to know that the folk roots went far deeper than Rice's glimpse of Jim Crow. However, later commentators failed to recognize or develop this folk origin and key feeling in the form. They ignored its core in an attempt to reduce it to a travesty of black behavior, which it was only in part.

A corrective step occurred in 1952 when the scholar Hennig Cohen reported the earliest known example of minstrel play in the slave community at Charleston. Cohen had found a white's hostile account of "'a Country-Dance, Rout, or Cabal of *Negroes*'" described in a letter to the *South Carolina Gazette* even before the American Revolution, in 1772:

> "The entertainment was opened, by the men copying (or *taking off*) the manners of their masters, and the women those of their mistresses, and relating some highly curious anecdotes to the inexpressible diversion of that company. Then they *danced*. . . . [S]uch assemblies *have* been

very common, and . . . the company has sometimes amounted to 200 persons . . . *are* frequent even in Town, either at the houses of *free Negroes,* [or] apartments *hired to slaves.* . . . Whenever or wherever such nocturnal rendezvouses are made, may it not be concluded, that their deliberations are never intended for the advantage of the white people?" (183–84)

Unlike orthodox theories of minstrelsy, which ignore Cohen's find, Rourke's account can gracefully absorb his confirmation of the historical disadvantage to whites in minstrelsy. The shadowy complexity of nineteenth-century American culture and its extraordinary seeking out of extremes, as in Rourke's theory, are entirely consonant with the idea that minstrelsy had at its historical root play "that was never intended for the advantage of the white people."

Rourke knew that not only high art challenged people. Both general cultural lore and literature encouraged people to know more by imagining new and strange relations. The national humor was "a fashioning instrument in America," she wrote toward the end of her book, that "engaged in warfare against the established heritage," allowing citizens to adapt to conditions in their new land (297). Therefore, she presented minstrelsy less as a travesty of blacks than as a cultural tool that changed Americans, making them as complex in character as their country necessitated.

The legendary Yankee had a "knack for making changes" (6). Rourke wrote that the "Masquerade was as common to him as mullein in his stony pastures" (6–7). Likewise the extremely boisterous backwoodsman embodied metaphor by becoming "the alligator or the racoon or the tornado" (76) that bedeviled his boondock home. And the minstrel portrait of the Negro in both black and white legends continued this need to break out of oneself into the other, the opposite, the free, and the extreme. Each of her comic trio, she insisted, equally "in a fashion of his own had broken bonds, the Yankee in the initial revolt against the parent civilization, the backwoodsman in revolt against all civilization, the Negro in a revolt which was cryptic and submerged but which nonetheless made a perceptible outline. As figures they embodied a deep-lying mood of disseverance, carrying the popular fancy further and further from any fixed or traditional heritage" (98–99). As figures they were American, thus more related to each other than to either African or European antecedents. This unification of blackface minstrelsy with other American forms is more satisfyingly complex, also certainly more provocative, than the competing analyses. It was not the first account of American minstrelsy, but it was early and it was the first to link the form into sequential connection with other American arts and the first to explore minstrelsy as an enduring national fascination.

Rourke's claim that Americans had created a rich new lore, in one generation, partly in the cities, and consonant with old folklores but particular to the new environment, was long thought impossible. But then Roger Abrahams collected toasts and dozens among Philadelphia black youths in the late fifties, concocting proof that corroborated Rourke's every dimension. Abraham's discoveries confirmed Rourke's natural sequence, "disseverance," radically new reworkings of transmitted patterns to accommodate new and particular group needs, sometimes identifiable authorship of legends and patterns – all these concepts – this time in oral culture rather than in Rourke's printed sources. Rourke's "theoretical weakness" had once more survived with surprising strength. She similarly survived Stanley Edgar Hyman's accusation, first in the forties, then reiterated in the mid-fifties, of not following the current orthodoxy on myth. Here, too, the orthodoxy fell away. Hyman argued that she failed to trace "*the relationship*" (emphasis added) of "American pseudo-folk-poetry" back to ancient rituals which the English Cambridge school was claiming underlie all important literature (116). In fact, Rourke drives far down that highway, writing that the minstrel "walkaround, with its competitive dancing in the mazes of a circle, was clearly patterned on Negro dances in the compounds of the great plantations, which in turn went back to the communal dancing of the African" (88). But she brakes before linking the African dance to any Ur-ritual dance, to the grove at Nemi, or to a privileged religious source. Therefore, to Hyman, she misses the single important relationship. But in this, as in all such instances of exclusivism, Rourke's moderation protected her. Claiming multiple relationships, granting an eclectic sponginess in American lore, and insisting on the significant differences in national experiences that make each generate its own varied lore, Rourke resisted the chic tendency to put all her eggs in one discreditable basket. (For a history of such discreditation, and verification of Rourke's understanding of lore as communal cohesion, see Hardin.)

Those then are Constance Rourke's features. She discovers a specific American tradition, emphasizes extant sequences of lore culminating in great literature, yokes literature and folk expression in a spectrum which a common character unites, and distinguishes criteria for excellence within that unity. Although she insists on the extremes in Americans and their life-shaping experience, her work is centrist, that is, interdisciplinary and commonsensical. It appears effortlessly unaggressive (though hardly passive), even while eradicating orthodoxy. As in her handling of the minstrelsy issue for which she could not claim a presence in the fiction of her immediate time, Rourke pushes her principles hard without overstating them. Her tone is strong understatement.

Sometimes she was too close to her topic to see its impact clearly, or to notice new legendary figures – the Horatio Alger, rags-to-riches legend, for instance – competing with her trio at the end of the nineteenth century. Indeed, she serves as a striking reminder of how very young American culture is and how its sequences continue. The hazards of such new fortunes are the obvious ones. One example is that after noting the great thematic contributions James made to American literature, she declared what hindsight proves to be indisputably wrong: James's "other great achievement, that of portraying the inner mind, cannot be said to have given any notable impetus to the American novel" (265). This inner mind is precisely what James did bequeath to the greatest examples of the American novel, from Stein and Faulkner to Ellison and Pynchon. That's why, despite this caveat, a reader's fascination with Rourke may peak in her chapter on James's *The American.* There she shows how America's most cerebral, apparently alienated, and ostensibly elitist author – the very one least likely to fit her theory – nevertheless understands the inner mind of his characters to be steeped willy-nilly in the lore of their national life, from washtubs on the West Coast to Wall Street finance on the East. The chapter demonstrates the unity of the American humor culminating in the dilemma of Christopher Newman.

Despite this special instance of James's *The American,* one rarely reads *American Humor* hoping for help with particulars in any one work or even one oeuvre. Rather, one reads Rourke to find out where American literature came from, where it is going, and why. One reads Rourke less to understand American characters than to watch the cascading American character. Americans read *American Humor* for the pleasures of recognizing themselves. Which is to say that beyond all its crisp theory and splendid prose *American Humor* is a fable of membership.

WORKS CITED

Abrahams, Roger. *Deep Down in the Jungle: Negro Narrative Folk-lore from the Streets of Philadelphia.* 2d ed. Hawthorne, NY: Aldine, 1970.

INTRODUCTION

Bluestein, Gene. *The Voice of the Folk: Folklore and American Literary Theory.* Amherst: University of Massachusetts Press, 1972.

Brooks, Van Wyck. *America's Coming-of-Age.* New York: B. W. Huebsch, 1915.

Child, Francis James. *The English and Scottish Popular Ballads.* 5 vols., 1882–98. New York: Dover, 1965.

Cohen, Hennig. "A Negro 'Folk Game' in Colonial South Carolina." *Southern Folklore Quarterly* 16 (1952): 183–84.

Dorson, Richard. *Folklore and Fakelore: Essays Toward a Discipline of Folk Studies.* Cambridge: Harvard University Press, 1976.

Dylan, Bob. *Writings and Drawings.* New York: Knopf, 1973.

Ellis, John M. *One Fairy Story Too Many: The Brothers Grimm and Their Tales.* Chicago: University of Chicago Press, 1983.

Ellison, Ralph. *Invisible Man.* New York: Random House, 1952.

Fiedler, Leslie, A. *An End to Innocence: Essays on Culture and Politics.* Boston: Beacon, 1955.

Hardin, Richard F. " 'Ritual' in Recent Criticism: The Elusive Sense of Community." *PMLA* 98 (1983): 846–62.

Harris, Joel Chandler. *The Complete Tales of Uncle Remus.* Edited by Richard Chase. Boston: Houghton Mifflin, 1955.

Hoffman, Daniel G. *Form and Fable in American Fiction.* New York: Oxford University Press, 1961.

Hyman, Stanley Edgar. *The Armed Vision.* 2d ed. New York: Vintage-Random, 1955.

James, Henry. *Hawthorne.* 1879. Ithaca, NY: Cornell University Press–Great Seal, 1956.

Jones, Howard Mumford. *The Theory of American Literature.* Rev. ed. Ithaca, NY: Cornell University Press, 1966.

Leary, Lewis. Introduction to *Home as Found,* by James Fenimore Cooper. 1838. New York: Capricorn, 1961.

Mailer, Norman. *The White Negro.* [San Francisco:] City Lights Books, [1957].

Matthiessen, F. O. *American Renaissance: Art and Expression in the Age of Emerson and Whitman.* New York: Oxford University Press, 1941.

O'Connor, Flannery. *The Complete Stories.* New York: Farrar, Straus and Giroux, 1971.

CONSTANCE ROURKE'S SECRET RESERVE

Perosa, Sergio. *American Theories of the Novel, 1793–1903*. New York: New York University Press, 1983.

Rourke, Constance. *The Roots of American Culture and Other Essays*. Edited by Van Wyck Brooks. New York: Harcourt, Brace, 1942.

Sale, William M., Jr. Prefatory Note to *Hawthorne* by Henry James. 1879. Ithaca, NY: Cornell University Press, 1956.

Wendell, Barrett. *A Literary History of the United States*. 1900. Detroit: Gale Research, 1968.

Wittke, Carl. *Tambo and Bones*. 1930. New York: Greenwood Press, 1968.

AMERICAN HUMOR

I. CORN COBS TWIST YOUR HAIR

TOWARD evening of a midsummer day at the latter end of the eighteenth century a traveler was seen descending a steep red road into a fertile Carolina valley. He carried a staff and walked with a wide, fast, sprawling gait, his tall shadow cutting across the lengthening shadows of the trees. His head was crouched, his back long; a heavy pack lay across his shoulders.

A close view of his figure brought consternation to the men and women lounging at the tavern or near the sheds that clustered around the planter's gate. "I'll be shot if it ain't a Yankee!" cried one. The yard was suddenly vacant. Doors banged and windows were shut. The peddler moved relentlessly nearer, reached a doorway, and laid his pack on the half hatch. The inhabitants had barred their doors and double-locked their money-tills in vain. With scarcely a halt the peddler made his way into their houses, and silver leapt into his pockets. When his pack was unrolled, calicoes, glittering knives, razors, scissors, clocks, cotton caps, shoes, and notions made a holiday at a fair. His razors were bright as the morning star, cut quick as thought, and had been made by the light of a diamond in a cave in Andalusia. He showed hickory cups and bowls and plates, and mentioned the haste with which people in a neighboring village had broken their crockery and thrown it into the street since crockery was

3

known to spread the plague. He told stories of the plague. In the end he invaded every house. Every one bought. The Negroes came up from their cabins to watch his driving pantomime and hear his slow, high talk. Staying the night at a tavern, he traded the landlord out of bed and breakfast and left with most of the money in the settlement.

A magnetized community watched his angular figure in butternut brown march steadily down the valley, climb a steep neighboring hill, and disappear over the top: the inhabitants then settled to a consideration of his singular character. He was said to have sold a load of warming-pans in the West Indies, and when he arrived in a Canadian village with a load of fashionable white paper hats and found no market because of cholera, he ground them up in a mortar and made them into pills. He always traveled alone; he declined to talk politics; he never drank or bet on cocks. When the barter was over he lapsed into an image as wooden as his ware, though he was prickly and local and could be roused to tart rejoinders. "Down east," said a Southerner to a peddler, "a cow and a calf and a calico frock is said to be a girl's portion, and that's the place you come from." "Well," said the Yankee, "an' you're from that place, ain't you? where a potato patch has cracks in it so wide the grasshoppers can't jump over, and that's the portion of the eldest son. My father told me," he continued, "that he was drivin' by one of your great farms, observin' the wretchedness of the land, and he said, 'The fellow that owns this must be plaguey poor.' 'Not so poor as you think,' said somebody

4

from the blackberry bushes, 'for I don't own but a third on't. My father give away one third to a man to take t'other.' "

Abreast of the frontier, through the widening settlements of the Mississippi, tramped this long-legged wizard, decade by decade, bringing a splatter of color to farms buried deep in the forests, providing the zest of the new tales and sharp talk. He was forever pushing into new regions, and could be descried down the years, walking to Oregon at the heels of the settlers or on the march across the plains to the gold of California. The farther he receded from view the more completely he changed into a sly thin ogre something greater than human size. He was a myth, a fantasy. Many hands had joined to fashion his figure, from the South, from the West, even from New England. What the Yankee peddler was in life and fact can only be guessed. Bronson Alcott was once a peddler. Peddlers may have been chock-full of metaphysics. Their secret has been closely kept. By the end of the eighteenth century the shrewd image had grown secure.

But the peddler was only one aspect of the Yankee myth. A many-sided Yankee had emerged at a stride during the Revolution to the tune of "Yankee Doodle," and soon was scattered in numbers over the earth. Scratch the soil in China or Tibet or North Africa, and up would spring a Yankee, exercising his wits. Before 1800 a tale was current in London of a Passamaquoddy captain who was coaxed into a low tavern by some sharpers. Unable to induce him to play, they drank three bottles of wine and departed. "Ah," said the landlord, wagging his head in mock sympathy, "I see you are not acquainted with our London blades. You must pay the reckoning." Jonathan looked discomfited, slowly drew out a handful of silver, gazed at it, and ordered another bottle. When the landlord left to fetch this, simple Jonathan ran to the mantelpiece, chalked the sum, scrawled, "I leave you a Yankee handle for your London blades," and ran out of the door.

The Yankee was often called practical, but in the bits of story and reminiscence quickly accumulating about him, his famed ingenuity often seemed less a practical gift than a knack for making changes. Some Yankees obtained the excitement of change by swapping. One Yankee swapped all the way to the Western Reserve, where he took up a claim, swapped in that region until he could swap no longer, swapped away his claim, and moved on from one piece of wild land to another, arriving at last on a sandy hillside with only the clothes on his back. The Yankee would often spend hours whittling; in his hands unexpected and fanciful shapes would emerge from white hickory, which added nothing to a practical existence. Nor was his favorite form of humor practical, though it bore that name. Elaborately prepared practical jokes consumed time, created enemies, brought into peril life and limb: yet the Yankee evolved a stock of these that amounted to lore and spread from Maine to Georgia.

Masquerade was as common to him as mullein in his

6

stony pastures. He appeared a dozen things that he was not. Long-backed, thin, "lank as a leafless elm," a New England coach driver might look as though a high wind would blow him away, yet he would wear nankeens and low shoes in winter weather, and was not fragile but lusty. Crowned by an old bell-shaped white hat, a tall lad in tow-linen trousers reaching halfway down his legs would appear at a tavern. Listless and simple, he might be drawn into a conversation with a stranger, and would tell a ridiculous story without apparent knowledge of its point. With no change of tone, out would leap an odd figure. "He walked away as slick as a snake out of a blackskin." "There we was amongst an ocean of folks and cutting up capers as high as a cat's back." A gulf often yawned between the large facts and his scanted version of them; as he marshaled the characters in a story he was an actor and a troupe.

He seemed cautious and solitary. Asked a question, he was likely to counter with another. One of the early wandering New Englanders who went to London soon after the Revolution wagered a friend that the first Yankee they met would answer any question with a question. They agreed to inquire the time and stopped a man from Salem, who pulled out his watch, gazed at it, said, "What time have you, sir?" Then, in reply to the stated hour, he asked, "Isn't your watch slow?" But this reluctance was only another form of masquerade. These bits of indirection were social; direct replies would end many a colloquy: questions

7

or evasions prolonged the talk and might open the way for more. The habit had a deep root and appeared in many forms. For years stories were told of transplanted Yankees who kept this pattern of conversation.

The plain, the practical, the saturnine and somber strains no doubt existed in the Yankee, but beneath these ran a surprising quickstep. "Yankee Doodle" was a jig; its innumerable versions told stories. One of them raced off into a runic rhyme—

> Corn cobs twist your hair,
> Cart wheels run round you,
> Fiery dragons take you off,
> And mortal pestal pound you.

The Yankee seemed an aboriginal character sprung suddenly, long-sided and nimble, from the gray rocks of his native soil. Surely he was no simple son of the Pilgrim fathers.

2

As a people the Americans are said to have had no childhood, and the circumstance has been shown to contain pathos as well as loss. But the Yankee stepped out of a darkness that seems antediluvian. Even the name Yankee abides in a thick early dusk, though a passionate research has been devoted to its origin, and numberless theories formed to fit private notions of the Yankee character. The air of "Yankee Doodle" may have come from Galway,

8

Germany, Spain, Hungary, Persia; it may have been a twelfth century church chant; in one stage it was probably a nursery rhyme. No one knows the lineage of the early words. In the matter of racial origins no greater stability has been reached. For many years in England the Yankee was compared with the yeoman of Yorkshire, who was also a wanderer, given to swapping. This ancient and inveterate practice among the northern Saxons was said to have driven hordes of invaders from the country. Many of the original Pilgrims came from Yorkshire, but the strain cannot be proved as determining the Yankee character, for numbers of others came from the south of England; and Ulster, France, Scotland, and Wales added their elements. Racial strains in the Yankee were well mixed.

As the texture of early Puritan life is examined, sources of Yankee strength become apparent, but not of Yankee humor: for humor is a matter of fantasy, and the fantasies of the Puritan, viewed with the most genial eye, remain sufficiently dark. After the abysses revealed by Cotton Mather had been skirted the New England imagination still ran boldly to witches and ghosts. Whittier said that some Irish immigrants settled in New Hampshire about 1820, bringing with them potatoes and fairies; the potatoes flourished, but the fairies died out. The native mind was not prosaic, but it perceived supernatural creatures of a large mold. Whittier wrote of an old strolling woman known as a witch through the valley of the Piscataqua, who once came to his grandfather's house and fell into a deep

9

sleep of several hours. During this time wild gusts of wind swept over the valley and down the river, upsetting wherries and market-boats on the way back from Portsmouth, and the old woman was thought to have cast a vengeful wind-breathing spell. Whittier also pictured a grotesque and hideous phantasm that appeared more than once on the white shore of a little lake that mirrored spray and leaf of pine and maple, and was fringed with orchards. A woman standing at a crossroad near by saw a horse and cart of a style used in New England a century before drive rapidly down a steep hillside and pass over a stone wall a few yards in front of her. The driver's countenance was fierce; behind the cart and lashed to it was a struggling woman of gigantic size, her face contorted by agony and fear, her arms and feet bare, her gray hair streaming. At the edge of the pond the noiseless cavalcade vanished.

Between these many shadows and the persistent humor of the Yankee the gulf seems wide. But humor bears the closest relation to emotion, either bubbling up as from a deep and happy wellspring, or in an opposite fashion rising like a re-birth of feeling from dead levels after turmoil. An emotional man may possess no humor, but a humorous man usually has deep pockets of emotion, sometimes tucked away or forgotten. If there were no index beyond these haunting shapes it would be clear that emotion was pervasive in New England. The exactions of pioneer life had deepened, yet suppressed, emotion. Again, emotion was stirred by the terror of the prevailing faith, yet caught within the meshwork of its tenets. Such compression with such power was bound to result in escapes and explosions. The result was a rebound; and frequently enough this occurred in New England, from the time of the revelers at Merrymount onward. A constant opposition existed between the dark emotions and an earthy humor.

The Revolution, with its cutting of ties, its movement, its impulses toward freedom, seemed to set one portion of the scant population free from its narrow matrix. The obscure dweller in the villages or on the farms—the Yankee —bounded up with his irreverent tune, ready to move over the continent or to the ends of the earth, springing clean away from the traditional faith, at least so far as any outward sign appeared in his growing portrait. He could even take the Revolution as a joke; most of his songs about it streamed nonsense. He had left the deeper emotions behind or had buried them.

Proof of his anterior experiences remained in his use of the mask. The mask was a portable heirloom handed down by the pioneer. In a primitive world crowded with pitfalls the unchanging, unaverted countenance had been a safeguard, preventing revelations of surprise, anger, or dismay. The mask had otherwise become habitual among the older Puritans as their more expressive or risible feelings were sunk beneath the surface. Governor Bradford had encouraged its use on a considerable scale, urging certain gay spirits to enjoy themselves in secret, if they must be convivial. No doubt the mask would prove useful in a country where the Puritan was still a power and the risks of pioneering by no means over. The Yankee retained it.

3

BOSTONIANS were and were not Yankees for many years. Sooner or later most New Englanders acknowledged themselves to be Yankees. Abroad, all Americans, even those from the South, were promptly dubbed Yankee. By the end of the Revolution the small United States had emerged as Brother Jonathan, an out-at-elbows New England country boy with short coat-sleeves, shrunken trousers, and a blank countenance. In the following years of inflated triumph the quiet, uncouth Yankee lad was often innocently put forward as a national symbol. The image was adopted in another of those half-lighted transitions which belong to Yankee history. No one can be sure how or when it was chosen. The name has been thought to derive from Washington's friend, Jonathan Trumbull of Connecticut, but that dignified figure hardly embodied the Yankee. Out of a past crowded with many dark passages, out of the travail of the Revolution, by a sudden, still agreement the unformed American nation pictured itself as homely and comic.

"The comic," says Bergson, "comes into being just when society and the individual, freed from the worry of self-preservation, begin to regard themselves as works of art." With his triumphs fresh and his mind noticeably free, by 1815 the American seemed to regard himself as a work of art, and began that embellished self-portraiture which nations as well as individuals may undertake. No one can say where or how these efforts might have ended if the American had been left to himself. He was not. Foreign artists insisted upon producing *their* portraits. After a few tours of observation the French, carrying the amiable light luggage of preconceptions derived from Rousseau, declared him to be a child of nature. The phrase gained a considerable popularity and had a long life, but it was difficult to graft the florid idea upon a Yankee base. The British schooling was more constant, and went deeper.

Notebooks in hand, British travelers poured across the sea; and while the onset was flattering the results were not, as these appeared in volumes that rose through many obscure writers to Captain Hall and the famous Mrs. Trollope and finally to Dickens and were echoed in British pulpits or in the august pages of the *Quarterly Review.* Perhaps the conscious or unconscious sense of an enduring tie between the two nations prompted this marked freedom of utterance. Accustomed to self-criticism of a quantity and stringency which the Americans and possibly no other people have ever attained, the British focused this talent without reserve upon the United States. In the intimate history of relations between the two countries these utterances played an important part; they were full of emotion and aroused emotion in return. The harsh accusations need not be repeated. Many of them were true. But the tacit sense of an alliance did not always make for British understanding. Irving, who surely cannot be accused of lack of sympathy for the British, discussed their extreme credulity in viewing American affairs. At the same time he indicated an essential flaw in the American armor. "Why are we so exquisitely alive to the aspersions of England?" he asked. He found the Americans "morbidly sensitive to the most trifling collision," and feared that the resultant sarcastic habit might ruin the national temper.

Irving's friend Paulding expressed the sarcasm and revealed the hurt in his *John Bull in America*, a highly popular allegory published in 1825 and many times reprinted. Paulding was acutely aware of a natural alliance between the two nations. With the familiar homely approach he said that Brother Jonathan "always wore a linsey-woolsey coat that did not above half cover his breech, and the sleeves of which were so short that his hand and wrist came out beyond them, looking like a shoulder of mutton. . . . He was a rather odd-looking chap, and had many queer ways: but everybody that had seen John Bull saw a great likeness between them, and swore that he was John's own boy, and a true chip off the old block. Like the squire he was likely to be blustering and saucy, but in the main he was a peaceable sort of careless fellow, that would quarrel with nobody if you would only let him alone." Because of his sense of a bond, British criticism stung Paulding sharply. Though he took many a neat pot-shot at the American character and scene he lapsed into confused and bitter anger when he saw shots coming thick from the British side. The outcome, however, was that he laughed, and turned his allegory into a trenchant broad burlesque of the British traveler in America, which had points of perennial application. The laughter spread, loud and confused, sensitive and satirical. A little sheaf of allegories similar to Paulding's were written, which made a running accompaniment for a wider and more emphatic assertion.

During the Revolution a fable had appeared on the stage called *The Contrast*, by Royall Tyler, whose theme was suggested by the exhortations and queries of its prologue—

Exult, each patriot heart!—this night is shewn
A piece, which we may fairly call our own;
Where the proud titles of "My Lord! Your Grace!"
To humble *Mr.* and plain *Sir* give place.
Our Author pictures not from foreign climes
The fashions or the follies of the times. . . .
On native themes his Muse displays her pow'rs;
If ours the faults, the virtues too are ours.
Why should our thoughts to distant countries roam,
When each refinement may be found at home?
Who travels now to ape the rich or great,
To deck an equipage and roll in state;
To court the graces, or to dance with ease,
Or by hypocrisy to strive to please?
Our free-born ancestors such arts despis'd;
Genuine sincerity alone they priz'd;
Their minds, with honest emulation fir'd,
To solid good—not ornament—aspir'd. . . .

Thus the prologue attacked a question referred to many years later in the title of Mrs. Trollope's famous book—the manners of the Americans, a subject, indeed, which was often to engage British attention.

The new American rejoinder was double: first that all refinements might be found at home; then that they didn't matter. On the whole the second view prevailed in the play and perhaps elsewhere. The contrast lay between an honest plain American and a silly, foppish, infamous Englishman. But it was a third character, the Yankee Jonathan, who gave savor to the notion that only a rough sincerity was of consequence in America. Introduced for the purpose of comic relief, he might easily have become a puppet; but his author hailed from Vermont, and Jonathan drew the breath of life. Astute and simple, gross and rambling, rural to the core, he talked "nat'r'l"—talked his way through the scenes, and became a presiding genius.

His appearance was dynamic. For a generation or more the fable and the portrait were worked over by many hands, until at last, from 1825 onward, when the British commentaries were in full swing, Yankee plays began to appear on the American stage all over the country.

Neat, small, and brightly colored, they repeated the original fable with a naïve and belligerent charm; each was sharply different from the others in scene and thread of story; in each the Yankee was a looming figure. He might be a peddler, a sailor, a Vermont wool-dealer, or merely a Green Mountain boy who traded and drawled and upset calculations; he was Lot Sapsago or Jedediah Homebred or Jerusalem Dutiful; sometimes he was a sailor. But he was always the symbolic American. Unless he appeared as a tar his costume hardly varied: he wore a white bell-crowned hat, a coat with long tails that was usually blue, eccentric red and white trousers, and long boot-straps. Brother Jonathan had in fact turned into Uncle Sam. Half bravado, half cockalorum, this Yankee revealed the traits considered deplorable by the British travelers; he was indefatigably rural, sharp, uncouth, witty. Here were the manners of the Americans! Peddling, swapping, practical joking, might have been national preoccupations. He burst periodically into song, with variations of "Yankee Doodle," with local ballads celebrating Yankee exploits, or chanteys. Some of the plays verged upon the operatic, and the prevailing high national pitch was repeated by casual allusions. A tavern was called "The Sign of the Spread Eagle." Beneath this aegis roamed the Briton, still wicked, still mannered and over-polished, either rich or nefariously seeking riches, and always defeated by simple rural folk to the accompaniment of loud laughter. Once indeed there was no contrast; rather the wistful contention of an alliance was repeated, and a gawky Yankee lad proved to be the son of an English nobleman.

This wry triumphant portrait was repeated again and again, up and down the Atlantic coast, over and over in the newly opened West, where its popularity had a quirk of oddity. Sectionalism had become rampant in the late

1820's; the western almanacs and papers were full of stories disparaging the Yankee. But of all portions of the country the West was smarting most acutely from British criticism; the emblematical Yankee was boisterously applauded there. He also traveled to England, where he was viewed with disapproval, not because of his derision of the British, which seems to have been received with equanimity, but because the character was genuinely disliked. Still, the Yankee was a novelty, and the Americans a favorite subject. With a sturdy disregard of pleasure London audiences continued to attend the Yankee plays.

Phantasmal conceptions may have sprung from this simple early stem, at home and abroad. Other national types had developed slowly, even through centuries, without close definition by themselves or by others. The American stepped full-length into the public glare, and steadily heightened the early yellow light. He gazed at himself in the Yankee plays as in a bright mirror, and developed the habit of self-scrutiny, which may have its dangers for the infant or youth, whether the creature be national or human.

4

THE image did not remain fixed; Yankee aptitudes took care of that. The local Yankee came into closer view. No one contributed more to this alteration than a now forgotten artist, Yankee Hill—George Handel Hill. Merry, improvident, unworldly, in his own character he offered

18

proof of Yankee variability. He liked fine clothes, good living, a pair of spanking horses with a brightly painted carriage. He was always deciding to give up the stage and adopt another profession; he studied half a dozen, but he remained an actor all his days. In New York he found that every touch of his native lingo brought applause even when he slipped into it by accident. He soon made Yankee portraiture his own, and went back to New England repeatedly to renew and widen his knowledge of the native character. His scribbled reminiscences abound in slight and charming New England sketches. He wrote of a fashionable dressmaker in a tiny village, with her faded blue and red swinging sign, her fondness for Byron, Bohea, and blushes. He pictured an old Revolutionary pensioner telling stories at a tavern over mugs of cider with the help of the villagers, who knew the stories all by heart.

Full of observation, full of affection, Hill's acting was pure in outline. Native traits were gently laid on—the stumbling security, the evasions that were social in intention, the habit of masquerade. His Yankees, quiet and low-voiced, wearing his own mild countenance, whittled a great deal and talked quite as much, but never very loud. They might have been evolved over hasty pudding and cider, at quilting-bees or husking-parties. They were deeply relished in New England. Hill was often invited to "come down our way and give a show." In Maine a Yankee from one of the farms was perturbed throughout an evening's performance because he thought that Hill had failed to arrive

19

and that the part was being taken by one of his own neighbors.

In England this racy quiet portraiture commanded a considerable enthusiasm. The Yankee—and in England the Yankee still invariably meant the American—was now warmly received, and understanding between the two peoples may have lightly teetered in the balance. But it was on native ground that Hill expanded and enriched his style. Stories had always been a Yankee habit. Hill increased their number until he bordered upon monologue, occasionally interrupted by the other players and by the progress of the action. Soon he adopted the monologue outright for some of his performances. Alone on the stage he could create an awkward young crowd of Yankees at a militia training, or a New England family in the midst of small affairs, with neighbors coming and going. His lecture called *A Learned Society* was a small comic monument to the New England thirst for abstruse discussion. He was full of simple satire, and gave many a sly thrust at New England pride before his native audiences, even touching on the character of the original Pilgrims, whom he appeared to regard with bored irreverence.

Yankee speech with its slow-running rhythms and high pitch—as if an inner voice were speaking below the audible one—was well adapted to the monologue. Its sound was subtly varied; the cautious drawl served to feel a way among the listeners. As Lowell pointed out some years later, Yankee speech was not so much a dialect as a lingo:

that is, its oddities were consciously assumed. It was another form of masquerade. Homely comparisons belonged to it—"strong as whitleather," "so thin you could pitch him clean *through* a flute." Hill used these sparely: "If you catch me there agin, you'll catch a white weasel asleep, *I* tell you." All his handling was narrow and thin; his lines rarely held of their own weight, yet they grew in texture.

Hill had drawn the native Yankee from the life, yet he sheered away from the highly individualized portrait. Though the monologue is essentially a personal affair, always verging upon soliloquy, he never turned it to individual uses. What came out was the group, the family, the little crowd. His portraits were generic; and in the end, for all the purely local emphasis, his Yankee was something more than Yankee. He was still the American. For the mock lectures as for the plays Hill continued to wear the flaxen wig, the red-white-and-blue costume, the high bootstraps and tall white hat of the nationalistic Yankee; and until his death in the late '40's he appeared in the fables of the contrast with their stress upon the nationalistic character.

Other players followed Hill in strengthening the local style and in maintaining the nationalistic outline. Silsbee and Marble, also Yankee born, disguised themselves as sailors or country lads and went to the villages and water fronts of New England to pick up new talk and new situations. They too centered upon the single character and drifted into monologues; they also kept the red-white-and-blue costume, and continued to act in the fables of the contrast. The Yankee had leapt into national stature, then had turned back, so to speak, to his native soil, but he again slipped outside the local character and became a national myth.

5

ABOUT the time when Hill first enlarged the Yankee portrait, in the late '20's, a lad traveled from a small village in Maine to Portland with a load of ax-handles, a cheese, and a bundle of footings. As his stay lengthened he grew reminiscent in letters home, writing of an old neighbor who sometimes drank a toast to the apple-trees in cider, and of the first arrival of the family in the Maine woods when they had all camped under a great oak, and of his Aunt Nabby, and of "making wall." He was not particularly successful in barter, though in Boston he got his watch off "pretty curiously." When he showed it in a barroom a man stepped up who offered to trade. "Says he, I'll give you my watch and five dollars. Says I, it's done! He gave me five dollars, and I gave him my watch. Now, says I, give me *your* watch—and says he, with a loud laugh, I han't got none— and that kinda turned the laugh on me. Thinks I, let them laugh that lose. Soon as the laugh was well over, the feller thought he'd try the watch to his ear—why, says he, it don't go—no, says I, not without it's carried."

The lad soon slipped away from trading; he had ambitions, and hoped to make "them are chaps that have been a sneering at me here stare at me like an owl in a thunderstorm." Presently he settled in Washington as adviser to President Jackson, "the old Gineral," as he called him.

This character was Jack Downing, whose author, Seba Smith, was born in Maine. The Downing papers were first printed in a Portland newspaper. They were as Yankee as the mock lectures of Hill, and read as though they were spoken or drawled; they were monologues. In them the Yankee emerged in a new rôle, as oracle. Downing was the President's friend in the unfolding situations, and this relationship was humanly drawn and kept: but beneath the placid stream of talk ran a drastic criticism of the Jacksonian democracy. The Peggy Eaton affair was satirized in an account of a similar scramble among the farmers' wives of Downingville. Nothing could have been more searching than the mild narratives that pictured the hordes of office-seekers and the extremes of land speculation. Leading Jacksonians were gently lampooned. According to one letter, when the President's bedroom window was found open a discussion ensued among his friends, who decided that a thief had come and gone that way. To test the possibility a long ladder was placed against the wall, and several of the gentlemen mounted, but were unable to reach the top. Van Buren almost reached it, then descended. "He turned right round to the Gineral calm as moonshine, and says he, 'Gineral, it wouldn't prove anything if I should get up to the window and I guess we may as well let it alone.'"

During the Mexican War Jack Downing reflected, "Some

think the business isn't profitable; but it's only because they haven't ciphered into it fur enough to understand it. Upon an average, we get at least ten to one for our outlay, any way you can figure it up—I mean in the matter of people. Take, for instance, the City of Mexico. It would cost us only two or three thousand men to annex it, after we got into the neighborhood of it; and we get at least one hundred and fifty thousand in that city, and some put it down as high as two hundred thousand. Some find fault with the quality of the people we'd get in this country, jest as if that had anything to do with the merits of the case. They ought to remember that in a Government like ours, where the people is used for voting, and where every nose counts one, it is the number we are to stan' about in annexin' and not the quality, by no means. . . .

"The long and short of it is, we fit our way into the City of Mexico and annexed it. Santa Anna cleared out the night afore with what troops he had left, and is scouring about the country to get some more places ready for us to annex. When he gets another place all ready for the ceremony, and gets it well fortified, and has an army of twenty or thirty thousand men in the forts and behind the breastworks, we shall march down upon 'em with five or six thousand men, and go through the flurry. After they have shot down about half of us, the rest of us will climb in, over the mouths of their cannons, and annex that place; and so on, one after another. It's pretty hard work annexin' in this way but it's the only way it can be done. It will be necessary for the President to keep hurryin' on his men to keep our ranks full, for we've got a great deal of ground to go over yet. What we've annexed in Mexico, so far, isn't a circumstance to what we've got to do. . . . It's dangerous standin' still in this annexin' business. It's like the old woman's soap—if it don't go ahead it goes back."

Later Jack Downing said to General Pierce: "Uncle Joshua always says, in nine cases out of ten it costs more to rob an orchard than it would to buy the apples."

The low-keyed satire, the faint masquerade, might have been rooted national habit, so snugly did these fit into the popular fancy. Here was the other side of cockalorum and bravado, swinging to satire and understatement, using a delicately edged weapon. There was irony in the situation, irony in the immense popularity which the Downing papers commanded. These monologues were spoken by a humble character who might have been expected to exalt rather than to puncture the workings of the democracy. This mythical oracle from a down east village had risen to his dominating position at the very moment when the power of New England appeared to be in decline, signalized by the reluctant departure of John Quincy Adams from the White House. Out of apparent defeat the legendary Yankee had risen like a jack-in-the-box, thriving on contention. He was still a national figure, however often he dipped into the life of Downingville or Portland; and he still belonged to fantasy rather than to actuality. He seemed a person; indeed Seba Smith considered his draw-

25

ing of the character of greater importance than the political satire. Truly enough in the first view Jack Downing makes the appeal of a genuine character. Yet as he is approached personal signs disappear. The tiny idiosyncrasies, the positive reactions, the many involvements which set off one character from another are never the focus of attention. He is lucid and large; he belongs with the Yankee of the fables.

The Downing papers continued for twenty years almost without a break, and were copied by newspapers throughout the country. They had an immense circulation in book form under the faintly satirical title, *My Thirty Years Out of the Senate*, and were shamelessly imitated by half a dozen prolific writers who signed themselves Jack Downing and often matched his author in wit. In fact Jack Downing had opened a sluice. Sam Slick, the Yankee clock peddler, would probably never have existed without the figure of Downing as a model. Never so clearly drawn as Downing, the creation of a Nova Scotian who hardly knew New England, Slick achieved a mammoth popularity that lasted for three decades or more, and in the end all but obliterated the reputation of the quiet original. After Slick came Hezekiah Biglow, who forsook subtle Yankee prose rhythms for rhyme, and who with all his timely challenges was somewhat rigidly governed by Lowell's theory that "true humor is never divorced from moral conviction." But lapses in drawing seemed to make little difference, so deep was the hold of the Yankee upon the popular fancy. For forty years or more after Jack Downing's first appearance, the country was never without a Yankee oracle or even half a dozen.

6

IN THE early '30's on the levee at New Orleans Audubon saw a Yankee in a wide flopping hat, a light green coat, flowing yellow nankeen trousers, and a pink waistcoat. From the waistcoat arose the billowing frill of a shirt, from the shirt a magnificent bunch of magnolia flowers, from the magnolias the head of a young alligator, "swinging to and fro amongst the folds of finest lawn." The Yankee, walking pompously, carried a bright silk umbrella in one hand, a cage of brightly plumaged birds in the other. He was singing "My love is but a lassie yet" in broad Scots, but his conversation proved his origin. He remains as a note—a brief wash-drawing—in Audubon's rapidly written journal. In letters, diaries, travels of the first half of the nineteenth century many similar jottings were made, which were seldom deepened or enlarged. In the main, the more abstract elements in the Yankee character commanded attention. John Neal's paper, *The Yankee*, founded in 1828, overflowed with generalized sketches from "about the middle of down east" and serious definitions of Yankee traits.

Something of a cult of the Yankee developed. "The word *Yankee* is no longer a term of reproach," said Neal defensively. "It is getting to be a title of distinction." "So far from being a talking boor," said Seba Smith, "he is on the contrary singularly wise, penetrating, and observant, reproducing in our day, from traditional use, the language of Shakespeare and Milton." Whether or not this was true, the Yankee had created a speech of his own with an abundance of homely metaphor; and his lingo was greatly relished even outside New England. "Coming on full chisel." "Saw my old hat in two if I don't do it." Such expressions were garnered in almanacs and joke-books that penetrated to all parts of the country. Small stories were told of how Jonathan climbed a greased pole by a trick; sketches were drawn of Jonathan sleighing in a pung. Occasional sea tales pictured him off for a "Nantucket sleigh-ride," and strange ghostly exploits in far parts of the world were added to the range of his accomplishments.

These tales were often full of circumstance, yet Jonathan remained, as in the beginning, an abstract figure. Even longer efforts to picture the Yankee proved no closer to the full character. From the '30's onward a small crop of Yankee novels appeared whose delineations almost invariably paused with a simple sketch, as though the writers found themselves unable to push beyond general outlines. It is true that one of them, *Jonathan Slick in New York*, by Ann Stephens, was full of fresh detail, so fresh indeed that it sparkled and glinted. In Jonathan's letters home some pretentious people in New York, their ambitions, their ways of living, their houses and furniture, appeared as in a bright-colored print; even the contours of the mahogany sofas and the silver on the dining-table and the chintzes at the windows were clear. Jonathan himself was there, talking—for the book is a monologue—in his native lingo. But with these accomplishments the line was drawn. Jonathan was still the old Jonathan; the story was the old fable of the contrast, slightly altered, now proving the superiority of the rural Yankee over the New Yorker.

In the middle '40's the fable was repeated again in Mrs. Mowatt's *Fashion*, which was almost a precise echo of the original *Contrast*, even to the prologue. Its Yankee was none the less Yankee for being a Cattaraugus farmer. Mr. Tiffany had been a peddler; the old consciousness of foreign criticism was still sharp. "In a word, madam," said the Count, "I have seen enough of civilized life—wanted to refresh myself by a sight of barbarous countries and customs—had my choice between the Sandwich Islands and New York—chose New York!" With the appearance of *Fashion* the fable had been maintained for nearly three-quarters of a century; and it was destined to endure many decades longer. Its repetition proved a lasting involvement with foreign opinion, just as the noisy assertion of American superiority suggested an underlying doubt that this superiority existed. The popular gaze was still fixed upon the homely and triumphant nationalistic figure.

The Yankee was never passive, not the crackerbox philosopher seated in some dim interior, uttering wisdom before a ring of quiet figures; he was noticeably out in the world; it was a prime part of his character to be "a-doin'." But though he often pulled strings, always made shrewd or caustic comments, though he often belonged to a family—

like the Downing family—he was seldom deeply involved in situations; even his native background was meagerly drawn. A fence, a bit of stone wall, or the remembrance of wild life showing in his talk—not too wild, recalling only the smaller creatures of the wood: these made his spare setting. Though he talked increasingly his monologues still never brimmed over into personal revelation. He was drawn with ample color and circumstance, yet he was not wholly a person. His mask, so simply and blankly worn, had closed down without a crack or a seam to show a glimpse of the human creature underneath.

A barrier seemed to lie between this legendary Yankee and any effort to reach his inner character. The effect was so consistent, so widespread, so variously repeated that the failure to see him closely must be reckoned not a failure at all but a concerted interest in another direction. He was consistently a mythical figure; he appeared in the forms of expression taken by myth, in cycles of short tales, fables, and plays. Plain and pawky, he was an ideal image, a self-image, one of those symbols which peoples spontaneously adopt and by which in some measure they live. Over-assertive yet quiet, self-conscious, full of odd new biases, he talked—this mythical creature: that was one secret of his power. A deep relish for talk had grown up throughout the country, on solitary farms, in the starved emptiness of the backwoods, on the wide wastes of the rivers. The response seemed an outcome of isolation; yet the same thirst existed upon the denser populations of the East. His slanting dialect, homely metaphor, the penetrating rhythms of his speech, gave a fillip toward the upset of old and rigid balances; creating laughter, he also created a fresh sense of unity. He ridiculed old values; the persistent contrast with the British showed part of his intention; to some extent he created new ones. He was a symbol of triumph, of adaptability, of irrepressible life—of many qualities needed to induce confidence and self-possession among a new and unamalgamated people. No character precisely like him had appeared before in the realm of the imagination. In the plays he may have stemmed at first from the Yorkshireman of early English plays; the framework of many a situation in which he appeared may have been borrowed; but he had existed in life outside all these; and his final character was newly minted. It was to survive in many fanciful manifestations as an outline of the American character; it has never been lost.

7

BUT again the character of the legendary Yankee was altered. The backwoodsman, rising in the West, was also destined to command the national horizon. It was not for nothing that the living Yankee brushed against him in his travels; by the middle '30's he had appropriated western tall tales in a spare gingerly fashion of his own.

"Did you ever hear of the scrape that I and Uncle Zekiel had duckin' on't on the Connecticut?" asked a peddler of an old Dutch woman who had let him spend the night in

31

her cottage in return for a new milk-pan. The story went the round of the almanacs.

"Well, you must know that I and Uncle Zeke took it into our heads one Saturday's afternoon to go a gunning after ducks, in father's skiff; so in we got and sculled down the river; a proper sight of ducks flew backwards and forwards I tell ye—and by'm by a few on 'em lit down by the ma'sh, and went to feeding. I catched up my powder horn to prime, and it slipped right out of my hand and sunk to the bottom of the river. The water was amazingly clear, and I could see it on the bottom. Now I couldn't swim a jot, so sez I to Uncle Zeke, you're a pretty clever fellow, just let me take your powder horn to prime. And don't you think, the stingy fellow wouldn't. Well, says I, you're a pretty good diver, 'n' if you'll dive and get it I'll give you primin'. I thought he'd leave his powder horn; but he didn't, but stuck it in his pocket, and down he went—and there he staid." Here the peddler made a perceptible pause. "I looked down, and what do you think the critter was doin'?" "Lord," exclaimed the old woman, "I don't know!" "There he was," said the peddler, "setting right on the bottom of the river, pouring the powder out of my horn into hizen."

II. THE GAMECOCK OF THE WILDERNESS

DURING the Revolution a small book appeared in London purporting to be a history of Connecticut. It was not quite historical. Its author, the Reverend Samuel Peters, was in fact disporting himself after a prolonged sojourn among the blue laws. He presented a highly irreverent view of the Puritans, and explained how they happened to be called pumpkin-heads. Passing from social habits to geography, he described the Connecticut River, whose narrows, he said, were so swift that a crowbar would float there. He pictured the monstrous march of the frogs of Windham, and dwelt upon a bird called the humility, which spoke its own name, had an eye as piercing as that of a falcon, and could never be shot as it skimmed the ground, for it always saw the spark in the flintlock before the powder was kindled and darted out of range. Connecticut also boasted of a little animal called the whappernocker.

The Reverend Samuel Peters had perhaps taken time to lay his ear to the ground and catch certain faint reverberations from the West, or it may be that such humor was destined to flourish on any new American frontier, and that he had heard snatches of it on the New England coast. But the stories were unrecorded; they did not flourish there; the Reverend Samuel Peters stands as something of a prophet.

33

for even in the West tall tales were not to come into abundant bloom for another generation or more. He was an artist as well, for he mixed the true with only slightly stretched and told his tallest stories with moderation. He was not appreciated in Connecticut. Perhaps the inhabitants saw more than met the eye in his study of the humility; examined closely, this might be taken as a tiny fable; the lines on pumpkin-heads were a broadside; and among the few woodcuts with which the book was adorned was one of an Indian woman in a canoe, not quite properly clad, sailing perilously down a narrow gorge and drinking a jug of whiskey. With all his accomplishments he was denounced by the Reverend Timothy Dwight as having created "a mass of folly and falsehood," and his little volume sank into oblivion.

For many years after his outburst tall talk and tall tales slumbered in New England. The Cape Cod sea serpent had its long day, and remained a simple sea serpent. At last, in the '40's, it became a caracoling monster that carried the crew of a schooner from the Straits of Magellan around the Horn; but by that time the western tall tale had acquired a considerable stature, and the story may have been a western fantasy.

2

IN 1822, at a theater in New Orleans whose pit and parquet were crowded with flatboatmen, an actor stepped out in buckskin shirt and leggings, moccasins and fur cap, with a rifle on his shoulder. He might have come from the audience. To a familiar air he sang a new song by the author of "The Old Oaken Bucket"—

But Jackson he was wide awake, and wasn't scar'd at trifles,
For well he knew what aim we take with our Kentucky rifles;
So he led us down to Cypress Swamp, the ground was low and mucky;
There stood John Bull in martial pomp: *but here was old Kentucky!*

With this he threw his cap on the ground and took aim. The response was a deafening Indian yell, and cataclysms of applause greeted each of the eight stanzas with their refrain—

Oh, Kentucky! the hunters of Kentucky,
Oh, Kentucky! the hunters of Kentucky!

Thereafter the song was sung at theater after theater in the South and West, sometimes half a dozen times in an evening. Sweeping eastward, it reached fame in New York with "symphonies" and accompaniments and elaborations—

We raised a bank to hide our breasts, not that we thought of dying,
But that we always liked to rest unless the game is flying;
Behind it stood our little force; none wished it to be greater,
For every man was half a horse and half an alligator.

Like the Yankee in the Revolution the backwoodsman had leapt up out of war as a noticeable figure—the War

35

of 1812; in the scattered western country his portrait had taken shape slowly. Once on the national horizon, however, he made up in noise what he had lost in time. He grew rhapsodic—about himself—and like the Reverend Samuel Peters betrayed a strong leaning toward natural history. He was not only half horse, half alligator, he was also the sea-horse of the mountain, a flying whale, a bear with a sore head. He had sprung from the Potomac of the world. He was a steamboat, or an earthquake that shook an enemy to pieces, and he could wade the Mississippi. "I'm a regular tornado, tough as hickory and long-winded as a nor'wester. I can strike a blow like a falling tree, and every lick makes a gap in the crowd that lets in an acre of sunshine." He was the most cunning of the creatures of the backwoods, a raccoon, "a ring-tailed roarer." Oddly enough, he was also a flower. "I'm the yaller blossom of the forest!" Heels cracking, he leapt into the air to proclaim his attributes against all comers like an Indian preparing for warfare. As a preliminary to a fight he neighed like a stallion or crowed like a cock. He was "the gamecock of the wilderness" and the "Salt River Roarer." "Down thar you go, war you a buffalo," he chanted in wrestling matches, with hands placed on the shoulder and hip of his opponent.

Strength was his obsession—size, scale, power: he seemed obliged to shout their symbols as if after all he were not wholly secure in their possession. He shouted as though he were intoxicated by shouting. He shouted in ritual, as

36

though the emotions by which he was moved were bending him to some primitive celebration. Leaping, crowing, flapping his wings, he indulged in dances resembling beast-dances among savages; his heel-crackings and competitive matches were like savage efforts to create strength for the tribe by exhibiting strength. They even appeared, in the fertile new country, like those primitive ceremonies to produce growth by which the sower leaps high to make the hemp grow high.

He not only created a bestiary; with the single digression to the floral he insisted that he was a beast—a new beast, and the records prove that in this contention he was often right. Gouging was his favorite method of attack in affairs not settled with a gun or knife. Men of the backwoods joined in mortal combat stark naked, strapped within a few inches of each other to a bench, armed only with bowie-knives. A steamboat captain, once a flatboatman, finding that one of his men had been badly treated in a house on the river near New Orleans, fastened a cable round the pier on which the house rested, and starting the steamer, pulled it into the river, drowning the inmates.

Horror, terror, death, were written large in the life of the rivers and forests. Yet the backwoodsman kept a comic oblivious tone; he seemed to possess "a certain jollity of mind, pickled in a scorn of fortune." A traveler floundering through the mire of a cypress swamp in Ohio saw a beaver hat lying crown upward in the mud. It moved, and he lifted it with his whip. Underneath was a man's head—a laughing head that cried, "Hello, stranger!" The traveler offered his assistance, but the head declined, saying that he had a good horse under him.

3

STRANGELY enough, the ancestry of the backwoodsman bore a close resemblance to that of the Yankee. His early faith had been the same, a rooted Calvinism, and he united similar racial strains, though the Ulster and Scots inheritance among the first inhabitants of Kentucky seems to have been stronger than among the New Englanders, and their history—also one of persecution—had been more violent. Some of them had sprung from that Highland stock which had been driven out of its mountain fastnesses in the eighteenth century; at an earlier date others had been forcibly transplanted to Ulster. Once again this migrant people had moved to Virginia, but the large holdings of the Cavaliers drove them from the Shenandoah Valley to seek land on the Yadkin; and even then it seemed that many of them were never again to take root. With an untouched wilderness on the horizon they moved onward and became the first explorers of the dark and bloody ground.

These many upheavals must inevitably have had a powerful influence upon a highly emotional people whose love of their own soil had once been possessive and deep. The new climate, lush and warm, was unfamiliar, and if the new land was rich its contours were strange. Heights of limestone rose sheer above the dark rolling waters of cavernous rivers. Canebrakes made impenetrable thickets where paraquets swarmed, and turkey buzzards. Always in the forest waited an enemy. Some of these people took on savage coloring as if for protection; others adopted savage modes with an avidity which seemed the outcome of deep-seated instinct. Renegades were plentiful; men like the Harpes plundered with no object, and like ogres in medieval fairy-tale slept with their victims in order to slay them, while creatures such as the Jibbenainosay haunted the land— half white, half Indian, monstrous and ghostlike, phantasms of terror to whites and Indians, moving through the forests on vengeful errands.

Indian legends seeped into the consciousness of the new settlers, turning this awry. After the harsher dangers were over, many a Kentucky pioneer was like the red-headed Pete Featherton, who one day crunched over dry snow for miles without a sign of game and at sunset found the streams running in the wrong direction, shadows falling the wrong way, and his own shadow traveling around him like the marker on a sun-dial, though much faster. A spell was laid upon his rifle that was relaxed only by Indian incantations and the appearance of a snow-white fawn. In these legends—which sometimes seemed to join with Gaelic fragments—white fawns often appeared, or white steeds of the prairies, or jet-black coursers. In one tale an Indian warrior was struck down in a storm and found a thunder-bolt beside him with a stallion on which he sprang, seizing the bolt; the stallion was the lightning, and the warrior crossed prairies, forests, rivers in an instant and was flung headlong upon the Rocky Mountains.

The backwoodsman conquered the Indian, but the Indian also conquered him. He ravaged the land and was ravaged in turn. Something of his prevailing hysteria was shown in his insensate habit of killing more game than he needed, or of shooting the hundreds of pigeons that blackened the sky from a blind wish to exhibit power or a blinder purpose to obliterate the wilderness. Yet he was often exuberantly, wildly light-hearted, and in the end, according to his own stories, he too bestrode the lightning, though not in the awed mood of the Indian.

Perhaps the bonds of strangeness and terror had been pulled overtight in his first period of conquest in the new country. Perhaps the soft climate released him. The French *voyageur* may have brought a different mood, who came by the rivers and kept to the rivers, who was livelier than the Kentucky scout and had the habit of song. As settlers arrived in the early nineteenth century the *voyageurs* were overwhelmed by numbers, and the backwoodsmen learned the art of steering the heavy broadhorns. But the habit of song persisted, as Negro oarsmen joined their number and broke into rowing-melodies. On the Ohio fiddles might be heard on the boats plying their way from Pittsburgh far down the Illinois shore, as soon as the dangers from savage attack were over.

At the great bends of the rivers where the horns sounded

their warning of the swift approach of the heavy boats, the
Ohio was like sheets of crystal, so clear that the eye could
see to a depth of twenty feet or more. In the early spring,
gum tree and locust, dogwood and redbud drifted. The
notes of the mocking-bird floated out: everywhere was the
fresh faint odor of wild grape.

> O, boatman! Wind that horn again,
>   For never did the listening air,
> Upon its lambent bosom bear
>   So wild, so soft, so sweet a strain!
>
> What though thy notes are sad and few
>   By every simple boatman blown,
> Yet is each pulse to nature true,
>   And melody in every tone.
>
> How oft in boyhood's joyous days,
>   Unmindful of the lapsing hours,
> I've loitered on my homeward way
>   By wild Ohio's bank of flowers;
>
> While some lone boatman from the deck
>   Poured his soft numbers to the tide,
> As if to charm from storm and wreck
>   The boat where all his fortunes ride!

The boatman's horn was heard by many travelers moving
into the West, and lingered in memory long after the steamboats had driven the broadhorns from the rivers.

The boatman blew his magic horn and improvised sentimental songs. As he "pulled upon the beech oar" he slipped
into a highly posed melancholy. He grew elegiac over lost

loves. But he was as hardy a rapscallion as ever drew breath. He "sang best to a mark," he said, and the broad prose of his rejoinders to taunts and queries echoed as widely as his lyrics. He had answers for every landing-stage, could provoke talk where none seemed to be forthcoming, and reënforced his repartee by muscular evidence. A prime wrestler and a crack shot, trained by Indian attack, from 1800 onward he lorded it over the Mississippi as well as the Ohio, and could easily be singled out by his arrogant bearing and tall figure in a crowd, all the way from Pittsburgh to New Orleans.

With the freer ways of the water the boatman perhaps emerged more quickly as master of his scene than did the backwoodsman. Well into the nineteenth century they seemed separate figures; yet in the long view they mingle. Even in the matter of music the two had been allied, for as terror receded from the forest, the sound of Scotch or English airs and ballads had arisen from the clearings. The hard ground was covered with corn bran for dancing; the backwoodsman played the flute, the fiddle, the flageolet; Negro slaves taught him the bones; the banjo came no one knows whence. Both the backwoodsmen and the boatman were lively dancers, mixing Negro breakdowns with Irish reels and jigs. The backwoodsman sang; his rough improvisations mingled with the older songs. He often had a cabin, but like the boatman he moved constantly. Boone's cry of "more elbow-room" was echoed for years by many others, and seemed the watchword of a host of men both restless and perplexed. "I don't like to be crowded," they said. Comic resilience swept through them in waves, transcending the past, transcending terror, with the sense of comedy, itself a wild emotion. They boasted and rhapsodized and made a rising clamor in the forests and along the great rivers. But they were full of sudden silences. They were curious, with the thirsty curiosity of the backwoods. Like all frontiersmen they possessed a gift for masquerade: they wore blank countenances. They were fond of costume, wearing bright fringes and many-colored coats. Each carried a gun, which was his dearest possession, his friend, his clown.

With these simple outlines the backwoodsman emerged into the general view during the early decades of the nineteenth century. Others entering the West might retreat to the mountain fastnesses of Kentucky to preserve there, as in amber, the speech and music and habits of an older world. Some chose the more stable life of the settlements. By the time the War of 1812 was ended Lexington had grown into a small city, with broad streets and a university; within or beyond its contours were deep lawns, fine gardens, chaste pleasure-grounds. But the men and women who followed these more ordered ways were etched sparely in the records of the time, or sank into oblivion. It was the huntsmen of Kentucky, the boatmen, the innumerable local figures of western legend, who commanded a wide and lasting attention.

4

IN THE blaze of light focused upon the American character by foreign travelers the backwoodsman came into full view; and he in turn considered foreign conclusions. Western newspapers and the primitive western stage were full of his responses. The French comments on western life were received with amusement because of their flattering romanticism. From these the backwoodsman culled the phrase "child of nature" and applied it coyly to himself. When he became a target for British criticism, indeed the very bull's-eye, western rejoinder was fairly neat. It assumed that the British traveler had gained his monstrous impressions of the West through western waggery. On many a small western stage Mrs. Trollope became a gross and gullible witch-woman who was stuffed with tall tales.

The backwoodsman also received critical commentaries from domestic sources. The opprobrium of New England was often as marked as that of Great Britain. Early in the century feeling in New England against the West became acute because of the steady drainage of migration to the new lands. Timothy Dwight declared that men left New England only because they were too disgraced or too unprincipled to remain at home; he pictured the West as a grand reservoir for the scum of the United States. In later years Whittier told a story that had come down to him, of a New England farmer who went to the Ohio country, where he married a western witch-wife, who inspired him with such terror that he was afraid to fall asleep for fear she would turn him into a horse, get him shod at the smithy, and ride him to a witch-meeting. He slipped away at last, returned to his native village, and married a New England maiden. But one day the witch-wife came riding up the street, and he was obliged to return with her to the West on a pillion and to stay there until she died. He then came back to his New England bride, and was thereafter often seen at the village tavern, old and stout and red-nosed, explaining over mugs of cider how little he had liked the rich bottom-lands of the West, and how much he had missed his father's pasture with butternut trees along the road.

In running reply to such aspersions the backwoodsman told of a long-legged cream-faced Yankee peddler who mistook a mud-turtle for an alligator, climbed a tree, found a knot-hole, and buried his head in it. Long strings of such brief hits were contrived, and the stories that riddled Yankee peddlers ran in cycles. "He wer hatched in a crack —in frosty rocks, whar nutmaigs am made outen maple, an' whar wimmen paints clock faces an' pints shoe-paigs, an' the men invents rat-traps, man-traps, an' new-fangled doctrines fur the aid ov the devil," said one story-teller of a Yankee.

But queerly enough, the backwoodsman indulged in conduct resembling that of the Yankee when under the fire of criticism, as if after all there were a tacit bond between them. He assumed in gross form the faults with which he was charged. He was considered uncouth, and he swaggered the more roughly. He was called a bragger and a liar: he gently retouched his exploits. He had begun early the social pastime of shooting cans on his comrades' heads as a proof of friendship, at greater and greater distances. About 1800 a traveler in the West had seen a bullet split at a hundred paces and the string of a flag cut at three hundred. He learned of a shot that enlarged the eye of a weathercock on a church steeple, and was told of a marksman in Kentucky who punctured a milk-pail carried on the shoulder of a maiden walking along a path on the farther side of the Ohio River. The backwoodsman's sight was like his aim. "I can see a bee a mile away, easy," he said. In Texas he had lassoed Comanche chiefs while galloping bareback on a stolen horse, and once flushed twenty of them from a bit of timber and shot them on the wing.

Probably the backwoodsman always kept a large blank gaze fixed upon the stranger as he polished his tales—or upon that hypothetical stranger and wary critic whom sooner or later he was sure to meet. He always demanded an audience: yet in the end, though he included the critic, though his self-consciousness grew noisy and acute, his finest efforts seemed mainly for his peers.

"You never did see anything rain like it did the fust day when we was floatin' down," said Bill Merriweather, telling of the disappearance of his Brother Joe on a trip from Georgia to Kentucky for a boatload of stone. "Near sundown we'd made a matter of twenty mile afore we went

46

ashore and tied up. We raised a rousin' big fire on the bank close to where she was tied, and cooked some side and possum, an' I was sittin' on a log talking to Brother Joe, who was standin' chock up agin the fire with his back to it. . . . Brother Joe allers was a dressy sort of chap, fond of the brass buttons he had on his coat and the flairin'est kind ov red neckerchers; and this time he had on a pair of buckskin breeches with straps under his boots. Well, as I was a talkin' to him ov the prospect for the next day, all of a sudden I thought the little feller was a growin' uncommon tall; till I diskivered that the buckskin breeches that were as wet as a young rooster in a spring rain, wur beginnin' to smoke an' draw up, and wur a liftin' Brother Joe off the ground! 'Brother Joe,' sez I, 'you're a going up.' 'Brother,' sez he, 'I ain't a doin' anything else!' And he scrunched down mighty hard, but it warn't ov no use, for afore long he wur a matter of some fifteen feet up in the air. 'Brother Joe,' sez I. 'I'm here,' sez he. 'Catch hold ov the top ov that blackjack,' sez I. 'Talk,' sez Brother Joe, and he sorter leaned over and grabbed the saplin' like as maybe you've seen a squirrel haul an elm switch on a June mornin'.

"But it warn't ov no use, fur ef you'll believe me it gradually began to giv' way at the roots, and afore he'd got five foot higher it split out'n the ground as easy as you'd pull up a spring radish. 'Brother Joe!' sez I. 'I'm listenin',' sez he. 'Cut your straps!' sez I, fur I seed it was his last chance. 'Talk!' sez Brother Joe, though he looked

47

sort of reproachful at me for broachin' such a subject, but arter apparently considerin' awhile he outs with his jack-knife, and leanin' over sideways, made a rip at the sole of his left boot. There was a considerable degree of cracklin' fur a second or two, then a crash sorter like as if a wagon-load of cordwood had bruk down, and the fust thing I knowed the t'other leg shot up like, started him, and the last thing I seed ov Brother Joe, he was whirlin' round like a four-spoked wheel with the rim off away down clost toward sundown."

Traveling actors seized such stories and commanded audiences on the stage or in the taverns. One of Barnum's companions on his early travels with a small circus through the Southwest was an accomplished purveyor. "Gentlemen," he would begin in a manner solemn and hortatory. "Gentlemen," he would repeat with a quiet pause as he approached a crucial circumstance. "That's a lie, by thunder!" some excited listener would cry as he unraveled the tale of a British Revolutionary officer recently found buried in snow at a high altitude in the Rocky Mountains, who had related his strange adventures when thawed out. Hawley went imperturbably on, joining story to story—matching himself in fact—until the bottom fell wholly out of reality and the final episode rose like a balloon with the string cut.

Half magnification, half sudden strange reversal, these tales were likely to culminate in moments of "sudden glory" that had a touch of the supernatural. Indian traces appeared in them with a comic movement upside down. Fragments of Gaelic lore brought by the earlier pioneers may have strengthened a sense of natural magic. Tall tales were often like wrestling matches or the rhapsodic boastings and leapings and crowings and neighings that prefaced a fight in the backwoods, with one tale pitted against another. A knock-down force belongs to many of them; the competitive purpose is plain in the unexpected thrust at the end. Almost always the listener loses a foothold or draws a sudden breath. It was the wilderness with its impenetrable depths, the wild storms of the West, the great rivers, the strange new wonders on every side, that produced the content of the stories—those natural elements, that had brought terror and suffering to earlier pioneers and still belonged to the farther, unknown West, but now were apprehended with an insurgent comic rebound and a consciousness of power.

Warmth sometimes infused some of the tall talk. "It was enough to make a young earthquake for the corn to grow as it did, an' as to the potatoes, I'll be skinned alive if ever I saw anything like it. Why, any one of them hot nights you could jist go into a little patch of fifty acres, clost to the house, an' hold your ear down, an' you could hear the young potatoes quarrelin', an' the old ones a-grumblin' because they didn't lay along and stop crowdin'. Why, one day one of our squash vines chased a drove of hogs better'n half a mile, and they ran and

49

squealed as if the old boy was after them. One little pig stubbed his toe and fell down and never was heard of afterwards."

Many of the tales and much of the talk verged toward that median between terror and laughter which is the grotesque; and some plunged into the monstrous, as in the stories about slavery contrived for traveling New Englanders with a bent toward reform. A crop of these horrors with a callous comic turn was grown, to produce a lasting bewilderment as to the condition of the Negro in the Southwest. The usual manner was impersonal—take it or leave it. A bright trail of fact usually fixed the attention of the listener; and this trail seemed natural. The look and feel of things became important in all the stories, as they had been habitually for the huntsman and scout and pioneer. A favorite approach was scientific, as though natural wonders were being expounded.

Audubon glided easily into this tradition, always the backwoodsman, the wanderer, and a prime shot. His massive achievement in painting the birds of America—"my beloved birds"—in their native habitat was an enlarged reflection of the expert huntsman's knowledge. He joined in the merrymaking of the backwoods, and played the fiddle and the flageolet. He had the western gift for opulent self-portraiture. He loved costume, was inordinately proud of his long thick hair, and appeared in London in his later years garbed in green and crimson. He loved disguise, and once on a journey dressed like a French sea-man, and thereafter insisted that he had grown up at sea. When Rafinesque, the eccentric naturalist, appeared in Kentucky, Audubon invented and described to him wholly unknown species of birds; for information as to the fishes of the Ohio, Audubon drew upon the rivers of an abun-dant fancy, and pictured fishes of such colors and strange shapes, such amazing habits and exploits, that they might have belonged to another world. Among them was the Devil-Jack Diamond-Fish that grew to be ten feet in length and was armored with large stone scales of diamond shape set in oblique rows, which were bullet-proof, and which when dried would strike fire with steel.

Rafinesque was also a romantic, and afterwards engaged in a scheme to induce the mussels of the Ohio River to make pearls: he should have capped Audubon's stories. But he let himself gaze at the flinty fish from a distance, and afterward declared that he had seen some of its scales. He accepted all of these stories, and was plunged into long and cumbersome toil in consequence, and suffered discredit as a scientist. Entranced, he even followed Audubon on a bear-hunt and was led a wild chase through densest cane-brake where fire suddenly lent fury to the scene, with the water in the jointed stalks exploding like shells and sug-gesting the advance of Indians with musketry. A bear lunged out; thunder broke and rain fell. Rafinesque, at-tempting to flee, became hopelessly jammed. The only mode of exit was to crawl, and such travel had terrors, for the canebrake was haunted by serpents and panthers and bears. "The eccentric was more than gratified by the exploit," Audubon mused afterward. "He soon left my abode without explanation or farewell."

"His words impressed an assurance of rigid truth," he declared pensively in later years of Rafinesque. "As he directed the conversation to the study of natural sciences I listened to him with as much delight as Telemachus could have listened to Mentor." Ulysses would have afforded a more appropriate comparison for himself, that other careless adventurer who possessed a gift for extravagant devices and achieved a wide pattern in wandering. Audubon showed the extravagant touch from time to time in the midst of the most faithful observation. In his *Ornithological Biography* he told of riding a wild horse through seven States, from Kentucky to Pennsylvania—a wild horse that had never known a shoe, waded swamps with docility, leapt fences like an elk, and was fond of pumpkins and eggs. He described Boone, whom he had known, as broad and tall and muscular, whereas Boone was slender and under six feet, always appearing smaller than he was. Even his scientific notes sometimes possessed an air of inflation: an uproar was caused among scientists by his description of a rattlesnake chasing a gray squirrel from treetop to tree-top and at last flinging itself upon its prey, killing it by constriction and swallowing the animal. The picture, somewhat diminished, fitted the habits of the blue racer but not of the rattlesnake.

In the controversy that followed, Audubon stubbornly added a further detail, saying that he had tapped the snake on the head as it was torpidly trying to move away, and that it had then raised its tail and rattled. He also insisted that he had taken the description from his journal, which he kept closely day by day; and it may be that even on the ground he saw the blue racer as a rattlesnake. Certain British scientists proclaimed him a new and greater Munchausen. "Sir," said one critic, "this is really too much even for us Englishmen to swallow, whose gullets are known to be the largest, the widest, and the most elastic in the world."

5

THE backwoodsman's fancy roamed over two figures of his own kind: Davy Crockett, the hunter and backwoods oracle, and Mike Fink, known in legend as the first flatboatman who dared to take a broadhorn over the Falls of the Ohio. Fink's frolics and pranks, his feats of strength, his marksmanship, became themes for endless story-telling. He had ridden a moose like a horse through wild country. In a canoe on the Mississippi he had grasped a she-wolf swimming to attack him, and had held her under water until she drowned. As an Indian stood on a hill proudly silhouetted against the sky with his scalp lock and hawk's feather etched clear, Fink—below him and many yards distant— raised his rifle: the Indian leapt high into the air and fell to the ground. The act was as cruel as deliberate murder, for Fink—as he intended—had severed the Indian's scalp lock. Many of the tales exhibited the broad, blind cruelty of the backwoods; yet many of them insisted that Fink was good. The abstract quality was habitually attached to shaggy backwoods heroes in later tales.

Mike Fink passed into legend not only because of his early exploits on the rivers but because he was the last of the boatmen—or so he was called—clinging contentiously to his broadhorn long after the steamboats came, when men could not be induced to travel in a low wooden ark. The tales about him became an elegy to wild days that were past or passing. "What's the use of improvements? Where's the fun, the frolicking, the fighting?" he cried in one of them. "Gone! All gone!" The sad noisy sentiment mounted through twenty years or more. The exploits of Fink were still being celebrated during the '50's by the western almanacs. He even passed into literary discussion: one writer said that if he had lived in early Greece his feats would have rivaled those of Jason, and that among the Scandinavians he would have become a river-god.

He was in fact a Mississippi river-god, one of those minor deities whom men create in their own image and magnify to magnify themselves. Gradually he grew supersized; he had eaten a buffalo robe, but New England rum had ruined his stomach. He became Mike Finch, Mike Finx, Mike Wing, in a hundred minor tales. Driven at last from the Mississippi, he moved into the unknown regions of the farther West, achieving the final glory of heroes, a death wrapped in mystery, indeed many deaths, for the true story was lost, and others sprang up.

Mike Fink embodied the traditional history of the hero, but he never attained the nation-wide fame of Crockett, nor did he embody so many aspects of life on the frontier, or slip—as Crockett did—into poetic legend. Crockett first emerged as a coonskin follower of Jackson; he later became Jackson's opponent, and was transformed into an oracle throughout the land, with a position similar to that of Jack Downing. Squibs and stories were contrived, purporting to reveal discussions between them—the legendary and the living figure. Crockett's philosophy was simple: he wanted to save the land from the speculator. In this early phase he was rather more the settler than the huntsman. In his autobiography, which seems to have been taken down as he said it, fragments of old dance and labor songs appeared— "Now weed corn, kiver taters, double shuffle!" He repeated other songs reminiscent of work in the fields and of old country games—

> We are on our way to Baltimore
> With two behind and two before,
> Around, around, around we go,
> Where oats, peas, beans, and barley grow,
>   In waiting for somebody. (*A kiss*)
>
> 'Tis thus the farmer sows his seed,
> Folds his arms and takes his ease,
> Stamps his feet and claps his hands,
> Wheels around and thus he stands,
>   In waiting for somebody. (*A kiss*)

55

The whir of the spinning wheel could be heard in this narrative, and the phrases of homely proverbs. "A short horse is soon curried." "If a fellow is born to be hung he will never be drowned."

But hog and hominy were soon mixed with air and thunder. Even in the autobiography Crockett's magnified exploits of marksmanship and strength were pictured—by himself. Soon still greater feats were attached to him. He had climbed a tree upwards of a hundred times that rose thirty feet without branches, sliding down and climbing up again to break the chill after a plunge into icy water. He was "shaggy as a bear, wolfish about the head, and could grin like a hyena until the bark would curl off a gum log." He had fiercely grinned at what he took to be a raccoon in the topmost crotch of a tree, but the beast failed to fall before his spell, and the striped circle proved to be a knothole from which his grin had stripped the bark. He was full of "quirky humors," and fought and neighed and crowed and proclaimed himself the "yallerest blossom of the forest." He could whip his weight in wild cats. "Gentlemen," the legendary Crockett boasted, "I'm the darling branch of old Kentuck that can eat up a painter, hold a buffalo out to drink, and put a rifle-ball through the moon."

Crockett became a myth even in his own lifetime. Other spurious autobiographies were offered as his own; he was made the hero of a hundred popular tales repeated by word of mouth and circulated in newspapers and almanacs.

After his death in 1836 he was boldly appropriated by the popular fancy. His heroic stand at the Alamo was richly described; and laments arose in the western wilderness. "That's a great rejoicin' among the bears of Kaintuck, and the alligators of the Mississippi rolls up thar shinin' ribs to the sun, and has grown so fat and lazy that they will hardly move out of the way for a steamboat. The rattlesnakes come up out of thar holes and frolic within ten foot of the clearings, and the foxes goes to sleep in the goose-pens. It is bekos the rifle of Crockett is silent forever, and the print of his moccasins is found no more in our woods."

Then Crockett reappeared in popular stories as though he had never died, assuming an even bolder legendary stature than before. The story of his life in one of the almanacs began by picturing him as a baby giant planted in a rock bed as soon as he was born and watered with wild buffalo's milk. Another declared that as a boy he tied together the tails of two buffaloes and carried home five tiger cubs in his cap. In another he wrung the tail off a comet, and announced that he could "travel so all lightnin' fast that I've been known to strike fire agin the wind." Lightning glanced through all the stories. By leaping astride the lightning Crockett escaped from a tornado on the Mississippi when houses came apart and trees walked out by their roots. He could make lightning by striking his own eye. He could make fire by rubbing a flint with his knuckles. On one of his adventures he was barred by an "Injun rock so 'tarnal high, so all flinty hard that it will turn off a common streak of lightnin' and make it point downward and look as flat as a cow's tail." Once he escaped up Niagara Falls on an alligator. "The alligator walked up the great hill of water as slick as a wild cat up a white oak."

For the most part Crockett was a wanderer, moving westward, to Texas, across the plains, to California, to Japan—for pearls—and to the South Seas. Diving there, he came to a cave, crawled until he reached dry land in the deepest depths beneath the ocean, made a lampwick out of his hair, soaked it in elbow-grease, and struck a light with his knuckles on a rock.

"Now I tell you what," people would say of some strange happening, "it's nothing to Crockett."

In the end he became a demigod, or at least a Prometheus. "One January morning it was so all screwen cold that the forest trees were stiff and they couldn't shake, and the very daybreak froze fast as it was trying to dawn. The tinder box in my cabin would no more ketch fire than a sunk raft at the bottom of the sea. Well, seein' daylight war so far behind time I thought creation war in a fair way for freezen fast: so, thinks I, I must strike a little fire from my fingers, light my pipe, an' travel out a few leagues, and see about it. Then I brought my knuckles together like two thunderclouds, but the sparks froze up afore I could begin to collect 'em, so out I walked, whistlin' 'Fire in the mountains!' as I went along in three double quick time. Well, arter I had walked about twenty miles up the Peak o' Day and Daybreak Hill I soon discovered what war the matter. The airth had actually friz fast on her axes, and couldn't

turn round; the sun had got jammed between two cakes o'
ice under the wheels, an' thar he had been shinin' an'
workin' to get loose till he friz fast in his cold sweat.
C-r-e-a-t-i-o-n! thought I, this ar the toughest sort of sus-
pension, an' it mustn't be endured. Somethin' must be done,
or human creation is done for. It war then so anteluvian
an' premature cold that my upper and lower teeth an'
tongue war all collapsed together as tight as a friz oyster;
but I took a fresh twenty-pound bear off my back that I'd
picked up on my road, and beat the animal agin the ice till
the hot ile began to walk out on him at all sides. I then
took an' held him over the airth's axes an' squeezed him
till I'd thawed 'em loose, poured about a ton on't over the
sun's face, give the airth's cog-wheel one kick backward till
I got the sun loose—whistled 'Push along, keep movin'!'
an' in about fifteen seconds the airth gave a grunt, an'
began movin'. The sun walked up beautiful, salutin' me
with sich a wind o' gratitude that it made me sneeze. I lit
my pipe by the blaze o' his top-knot, shouldered my bear,
an' walked home, introducin' people to the fresh daylight
with a piece of sunrise in my pocket."

6

As THE tall tale came into its great prime in the early '30's
a sudden contagion was created. A series of newspaper
hoaxes sprang into life in the East. The scale was western,
the tone that of calm, scientific exposition of wonders such

as often belonged to western comic legend. Explorations of the moon by telescope, voyages to the moon or across the Atlantic by balloon, were explained in the imperturbable manner of the tall tale, verging aggressively toward the appearance of truth and sheering away again. They were circumstantial, closely colored; yet they broke all possible bounds and reached toward poetry, making snares out of natural elements or even from the cosmos. No single character dominated them, and they went off at a long tangent from popular lingo; yet the alliance seems clear. Similar monstrous practical jokes were being played with the sun, moon, stars, winds, waves, and water in the tall talk of the West.

The new inflation crept into New England: and Uncle Zeke sat on the bottom of the river pouring powder from one horn into another. Improbable reverberations were heard in Philadelphia, which quickly became a fountainhead of American jokes. An old gentleman was so absentminded that he tucked his pantaloons into bed one night and hung himself on the back of his chair, where he froze to death. Another had whiskey so good that when he drank it he spoke broad Scotch. A man was so tall that he had to get up on a ladder to shave himself. There was the immemorial oyster, so large that two men were required to swallow it. Many of these tall tales in miniature have never died, and there was a reason for their sturdy continuance. Consciousness of native humor had dawned; and these little tall tales were pristine; they wore the lustrous air of new birth. They were therefore appropriated with loyalty and preserved as carefully as the old men hung up in bags in one of Hawley's Rocky Mountain stories. Again and again they were taken out, like the old men, and revived. Dry and wispy as they became, they continued for years to betray the sense of jubilant discovery.

With them came a long sequence of stories—chiefly hunting stories—in which the hunter killed or captured a bagful of game at a single stroke. In danger from the onslaught of a bear and a moose, he aimed at a sharp-edged rock; the split bullet killed both, and fragments of rock flew into a tree and killed a squirrel. The recoil knocked him backward into a river; swimming to the shore, he found his coat full of trout, and other fish flopped from his trousers. Such tales were told throughout the century and perhaps have never died. Their lineage is long; they appear in shy forms on the New England frontier of the eighteenth century. No doubt they have a far older ancestry, going back to fairy tales of Europe in which a hunter or a poor man wanders all day without finding game, and then encounters magical events in the forest. Touches of natural magic remain in the later inventions, but the excess belongs to the American frontier. It was in the West that these tales took on their final inflation; and from the West they spread over the country.

Not only the expansive effect but strange new words came rolling out of the West. The backwoodsman may have gained his freedom with language from that large era of the sixteenth or early seventeenth century out of

61

which many of his progenitors had stepped, passing so soon into the wilderness as to preserve their habits of speech, and to be uninfluenced, presumably, by the later stability of the English language. At least he was full of free inventions. "Absquatulate," "slantendiclur," "cahoot," "catawampus," "spyficated," "flabbergasted," "tarnacious," "rampagious," "concussence," "supernatiousness," "rumsquattle," and dozens of other ear-splitting syllables were among his novelties —sudden comic shouts or mock pompous words. Some of these passed into common use and moved eastward to join with the drawling speech of New England, mixing with the less marked vernacular.

Tall talk echoed from Florida to Oregon with whoops and boasting, and a larger verbal thunder rose to match it in the fantasy of western oratory. "What orator," said a Kentuckian, "can deign to restrain his imagination within a vulgar and sterile state of facts?" Said another, "The eloquence of the East is sober, passionless, condensed, metaphysical; that of the West is free, lofty, agitating, grand, impassioned. . . . The West defies and transcends criticism."

"The literature of a young and free people will of course be declamatory," said an oratorical writer in 1834, who was drenched in western ideas. "Deeper learning will no doubt abate its verbosity and intumescence; but our natural scenery and our liberal political and social institutions must long continue to maintain its character of floridness. And what is there in this that should excite regret in ourselves, or raise derision in others?" he queried—with remembrance of the parent critics across the sea. "Ought not the literature of a free people to be declamatory?" he reasoned. "Whenever the literature of a new country loses its metaphorical and declamatory character, the institutions which depend on public sentiment will languish and decline. . . . A people who have fresh and lively feelings will always relish oratory."

The American people relished oratory. With the beginnings of the Jacksonian democracy public speech burst forth in a never-ending flood. "And how, sir, shall I speak of him," said a member from Mississippi of Calhoun in 1840—"he who is so justly esteemed the wonder of the world, the astonisher of mankind? Like the great Niagara, he goes dashing and sweeping on, bidding all created things give way, and bearing down, in his resistless course, all who have the temerity to oppose his onward career. He, sir, is indeed the cataract, the political Niagara of America; and, like that noblest work of nature and of nature's God, he will stand through all after-time no less the wonder than the admiration of the world. His was the bright star of genius that in early life shot madly forth, and left the lesser satellites that may have dazzled in its blaze to that impenetrable darkness to which nature's stern decree had destined them; his the broad expansive wing of genius, under which his country sought political protection. . . . He stands beneath the consecrated arch, defended by a lightning shut up in the hearts of his countrymen—by a lightning that will not slumber but will leap forth to avenge even a word, a thought, a look, that threatens him with insult. The story of his virtuous fame is written in the highest vault of our political canopy, far above the reach of groveling speculation, where it can alone be sought upon the eagle's pinions and be gazed at by an eagle's eye. . . ."

This encomium was offered as "buncombe"—as burlesque. It sprang from a region where tall tales flourished. In similar set pieces every feather of the eagle was accounted for and magnified. Orators kept the bird so continuously in flight from the peak of the Alleghanies to the top of Mount Hood that its shadow was said to have worn a trail across the basin of the Mississippi. Niagara continued to roar; the inevitable lightning flashed. The thunderous echoes were heard in New England, and the Yankee as well as the backwoodsman learned the art of comic oratory. Barnum enjoyed it in his early years. Dickens regarded it with indignation. Serious oratory rose and fell in similar cascades, but so far-reaching was the burlesque that it was often impossible to tell one from the other without a wide context of knowledge as to the subject and the speakers. Popular declamation of the '30's and '40's has often been considered as bombast when it should be taken as comic mythology.

7

AN EXHILARATED and possessive consciousness of a new earth and even of the wide universe ran through this tall

64

talk and the tall tales; they were striated by a naturalistic poetry. Inflation appeared with an air of wonder,
which became mock wonder at times but maintained the
poetic mode. The Crockett stories even distantly approached
the realm of the epic, not merely because of the persistent
effect of scale or because of their theme of wandering adventure, but because they embodied something of those
interwoven destinies of gods and men which have made
the great epical substance. The tales were brief and scattered; the bias was comic; a perverse and wayward spirit
was abroad. The animistic might take the place of the
godlike presence, appearing in the spirit which sent the
squash vines chasing pigs or hoisted Brother Joe to the
skies through the medium of shrinking leather. But half-
gods had taken shape and walked the earth with a familiar
look in the later Davy Crockett and Mike Fink; and around
them faint shapes emerged of a similar large mold.

"I saw a little woman streaking it along through the
woods like all wrath," said Crockett in one of the almanac
stories. Sally Ann Thunder Ann Whirlwind Crockett wore
a hornet's nest trimmed with wolves' tails for a bonnet and
a dress of a whole bear's hide with the tail for a train; she
could shoot a wild goose flying, wade the Mississippi without wetting her shift, and stamp on a litter of wild cats.
Mike Fink had a huge daughter who could whistle with
one corner of her mouth, eat with the other, and scream
with the middle, and who had tamed a full-grown bear.
Another figure appeared as an occasional companion of

Crockett's, Ben Hardin, a well-known character in Kentucky who claimed that he had been a sailor on far seas and had consorted with mermaids. It was with Hardin in tow that Crockett performed some of his boldest exploits. The outlines of a supernatural hierarchy were sketched in these figures; and beyond them lay dim others belonging to local legend who might grow into a dynamic stature.

The whole history of these tales can never be traced, so transient were they, so quickly passed on and embellished, so rarely recorded. They belonged to that wide portion of the West known as the old Southwest, which spread from Kentucky and Tennessee in a broad encirclement through Georgia and the Gulf States to Texas and Arkansas, reaching beyond the Mississippi as the scout and huntsman and pioneer moved from his first base of the dark and bloody ground. The tales spread indeed over the entire country. The Crockett almanacs, widely circulated in the West, were reprinted in New England; and the stories which they contained were often caught up by other local almanacs and newspapers. Some of the almanac stories were clearly the work of sophisticated minds, but even when the hand of the skilled writer shows, a homely origin is usually plain. Many of them appear as direct transcriptions of tales current in the West. They were linked at times to make a consistent legend, but fragments were given place which sound like casual talk picked up first hand; and gross inconsistency in tone or handling was uncommon. The talk was that southern talk with a mellowed roughness which became the popular speech of the West.

Even on their own ground these tales took on finish, for they flourished not only among boatmen and backwoodsmen, but at the annual meetings of the bar in the West and Southwest, where the members, who often lived in remote isolation, joined in bouts of story-telling as after long drouth. The strangest, most comic experiences, quiddities, oddities, tales, and bits of novel expression were treasured and matched one against another.

These fabulous stories underwent the many changes to which popular legends have always been subject, but they never coalesced into large forms. The more extravagant of the Crockett legends were unattached to the older body of the Crockett story; they slipped into oblivion as the almanacs were scattered and lost. They exist now only in fragments. On the brink of a coherent wide expression, reaching toward forms that might have partaken of the epical, the popular fancy turned aside—turned to a theme which had always been dominant in the native mind—that of the native character.

8

THE TRUE tall tale with its stress upon the supernatural was laid against others of a prosaic grounding. Out of this new cycle would stride a man who rose six feet without surplus flesh, pantherlike, with a mouth like a wolf-trap and red-brown hair sticking up like the quills of a porcupine, who shook the rafters when he spoke and was bent on litigation; or a small stubby man in a calico vest with a cravat like a tablecloth, his head upheld by his shirt collar. Stories were told of such characters as Cave Burton, familiarly known as Blowing Cave, with observations on his Gargantuan feasts and the devices by which he was occasionally deprived of the spread banquet.

A scrupulous attention was devoted to well-known and accomplished liars. "Bolus was a natural liar, just as some horses are natural pacers, and some dogs natural setters. What he did in that walk, was from the irresistible promptings of instinct, and a disinterested love of art. His genius and his performances were free from the vulgar alloy of interest and temptation. Accordingly he did not labor a lie: he lied with a relish: he lied with a coming appetite, growing with what it fed on: he lied from the delight of invention and the charm of fictitious narrative. . . . The truth was too small for him. He adopted a fact occasionally to start with, but like a Sheffield razor and the crude ore, the workmanship, polish, and value were all his own. A Tibet shawl could as well be credited to the insensate goat that grew in the wool, as the author of a fact Bolus honored with his artistical skill could claim to be the inventor of the story. . . . He was fluent but choice of diction, a little sonorous in the structure of the sentences to give effect to a voice like an organ. His countenance was open and engaging, usually sedate in expression, but capable of any modification on the slightest notice. . . . Such a spendthrift never made a track even in the flush times of 1836. It took as much to support him as a first-class steamboat."

Scalawags, gamblers, ne'er-do-wells, small rapscallions, or mere corncrackers were drawn into a careless net of stories, against a background of pine barrens, sandy wastes, half-plowed fields, huts with leaky roofs. Their implements were rusty, their horses wall-eyed and spavined. They belonged to a rootless drift that had followed in the wake of the huntsman and scout, and they were not wholly different in kind. Sly instead of strong, they pursued uncharted ways, breaking from traditions, bent on triumph. Their adventures—of the rascally Simon Suggs, the worthless Sut Lovingood, the garrulous Major Jones, the characters in *Georgia Scenes* and *Flush Times on the Mississippi*—had to do with vast practical jokes, pranks played on ministers and camp-meetings and on settled respectable people generally, or on Yankees; their jokes on Yankees were perennial. These stories were as coarse-grained as poplar wood and equally light as timber. Grotesquerie and irreverence and upset made their center; caricature was drawn in the single line or phrase. "He drawed in the puckerin'-string ov that legil face of his'n," said Sut Lovingood of a sheriff. Another remarked of an ungenial adversary, "The feller looked as slunk in the face as a baked apple." "When he seed me," said Major Jones of Count Barraty, who had lectured on Greek art in a Georgia village, "he relaxed the austerity of his mustaches and walked out of the Square."

Within these tales character and custom in small sections of the Southwest were portrayed with such close and ready detail as to provide something of a record of the time and place. Dialect was differentiated with a fine gift for mimicry. Yet with all this steady seizure of the circumstantial these tales had little or nothing to do with a genuine actuality. They were rough fantasies cast into the habitual large outline. As in the tales of the deep backwoods, their odd local figures were generic, the events preposterous. These characters formed a regiment of small Tyll Eulenspiegels scattered over the West, upsetting remnants of the old order, hinting a new. This action and their triumph seemed the secret of the pleasure they induced—this, and their portraiture of new types in the new country.

Thin as much of their humor has worn, as mere upset is likely to be reduced to its barest outline by time, they were enormously popular in the quarter of a century during which most of them appeared, from 1835 to 1860. Longstreet's *Georgia Scenes* led the train; and scattered stories appeared in newspapers like the New Orleans *Picayune*, the St. Louis *Reveille*, the Louisville *Courier*, and in that prime sporting weekly and compendium of western humor, the New York *Spirit of the Times*. They were gathered in books and again widely circulated, adding a smutch of gross and homely color to the half-formed American portrait.

9

IN THE final and more poetic legends Crockett commanded the whole western world or even the universe. But in the early period of his vogue, in fact during his own lifetime, he appeared not as a half-god with a piece of sunrise in his pocket, but as a national figure. Like the Yankee he was drawn in a graphic stage portrait, under the name of Colonel Nimrod Wildfire in *The Lion of the West* and *The Kentuckian*. The author of the first play, Paulding, denied the identity, but the resemblances were many, and Wildfire was generally believed to be Crockett. The play was never a stable affair because it was always being altered by improvisation after the manner of western storytelling, and the original text has been lost; but there was no question as to its vogue. This early backwoodsman, leaping, crowing, neighing, boasting, dancing breakdowns and delivering rhapsodic monologues, traveled throughout the country and was enthusiastically received in the West; his reception in New York was uproarious. Other backwoodsmen of similar character soon appeared on the stage. For a brief time in fact the backwoodsman fairly matched the Yankee in the general view. He was appropriated; his eccentricities were considered not only western but American, and he was warmly applauded therefor.

This newest portrait of the American was taken to England, where it was scrutinized with care and considered "pleasing . . . open-hearted . . . childish." Discussions as to western humor were soon under way. "The muses of these curious phenomena are found in the wilderness . . . in dreary solitudes where the mind has no useful employment, and in the uncertain and extraordinary circumstances of a society so fast and loose that it has not and never had any parallel in the history of mankind," said one critic. He added, "The humors of our own Anglo-Saxon flesh and blood transported to America, and often located in wildernesses, are like nothing among the family which has remained at home." Precise Miss Mitford collected western tales, declaring that her purpose was "to promote kindly feelings between the two nations." "I have grasped at the broadest caricature," she said, "so that it contained indications of local manners; and clutched the wildest sketch, so that it gave a bold outline of local scenery."

The backwoodsman had emerged as a full-bodied American figure, but a curious circumstance became clear. A Yankee infusion appeared in many of these drawings. Nimrod Wildfire was made the nephew of a Yankee. In *The Gamecock of the Wilderness* the hero was clad in a buckskin shirt with a rooster for a cap, and his antics and talk were western. "The devil might dance a reel in my pocket 'thout dangerin' his shins 'ginst silver," he declared; and the inflation belonged to the backwoods. But his name was a composite of western strength and Yankee acumen, Samson Hardhead; and the double strain ran through the character. The part, moreover, belonged to a Yankee actor schooled in the Yankee fable, Dan Marble.

If the backwoodsman became Yankee, the Yankee of legend also absorbed the character of the backwoodsman. Sam Slick declared, "Many's the time I've danced 'possum up a gum tree' at a quiltin' frolic or huskin' party with a tumblerful of cider on my head and never spilt a drop." The song and the feat and the boasting belonged to the West, as did Slick's leap over three horses standing side by side. He even confessed that he was "a ring-tailed roarer." A Sam Slick broadside in London contributed to folk-talk and back-talk between the two nations, and stressed the double character. "It isn't every day that you see a genu-ine Yankee Doodle, I calculate! Oh, no. Now look at me. I'm cast iron all over, and pieced with rock. . . . I'm half fire, half love, and a little touch of thunder-bolt! . . .

> "So here I am, just down from South,
>   In everything a meddler,
>   Spruce and slick in everything
>   Is Sam the Yankee peddler! . . .

"We Yankees are a tarnation cute race; we make our fortune with the right hand, and lose it with the left. . . . We Yankees don't do things like you Britishers; we are born in a hurry, educated at full speed, our spirit is at high pressure, and our life resembles a shooting star, till death surprises us like an electric shock. . . . I am Sam Slick the Yankee peddler—I can ride on a flash of lightning and catch a thunderbolt in my fist. . . .

> "Oh, here I come before you all,
>   And reckon yourselves lucky,
>   That I have brought the news along,
>   From wonderful Kentucky.

73

"My mother from Virginny came,
My father was no noodle,
And 'twixt them both they brought me up
A regular Yankee Doodle!"

In the wake of Wildfire and Slick came Sam Patch, a spinner at Pawtucket with an aptitude for jumping, whose feats quickly passed into legend. He jumped over Niagara Falls but was unable to leap the Falls of the Genesee, and plunged through to the other side of the world and bobbed up in China—pure Yankee again though still jumping, and promising to take the shine off the sea serpent when he got back to Boston. He bobbed up in Paris. Plays were written around him, stories told, poems composed. An epidemic of jumping developed. Clerks called themselves Patch as they jumped counters, country lads as they leapt over rail fences; men traveled through village streets, jumping. Sam Patch became a symbol of quickness and power. Even today a small boy's red express wagon may bear the lineal name Dan Patch. "Some things can be done as well as others," said Sam Patch laconically. The character belonged to the backwoods, but the drawling tone and dry talk were Yankee.

"The leetle ends of the Yankee's coat-tails was soon standin' out toward sunset," concluded the story of a Yankee who pushed into the West with a pewter dollar. More and more frequently the Yankee was shown against the western background. The two figures seemed to join in a new national mythology, forming a striking composite, with a blank mask in common, a similar habit of sporting in public the faults with which they were charged, both speaking in copious monologues, both possessing a bent toward the self-conscious and theatrical, not merely because they appeared on the stage but because of essential combinations in mythical character. Both were given to homely metaphor. "A bear sat in the crotch of a tree looking at them dogs calm as a pond in low water," said a backwoodsman in one of the tales. Both figures had produced a strain of homely poetry.

Even on more prosaic ground some fusion appeared, drawn from life. Swapping was an ardent pursuit in the West and Southwest as well as in New England. "I am perhaps a *leetle*—jist a *leetle*—of the best man at a horse-swap that ever stole cracklin's out of his mammy's gourd," said a character in one of the southwestern stories. Those evasive dialogues by which the Yankee sought to learn everything and tell nothing and accomplish an expanded sociability were repeated by the backwoodsman. "What mout your name be?" asked an old Georgia cracker in *Georgia Scenes*. "It *might* be anything," answered the traveler, who knew his interlocutor's mode of conversation. "Well, what *is* it then?" "It is Hall, but it might as well have been anything else." "Pretty digging!" said the cracker; and when he was asked to give his own name, "To be sure I will," he replied. "Take it, take it, and welcome. Anything else you'd like to have?" "No," said the traveler, "there's nothing else about you worth having." "Oh, yes,

75

there is, stranger!" said the cracker, raising his rifle, shedding the Yankee, and becoming the backwoodsman.

In the mixed portrayals it was always possible to see where the Yankee left off and the backwoodsman began. The low key of the Yankee was maintained against the rhapsody of the backwoodsman. Yankee humor was gradual in its approaches, pervasive rather than explicit in its quality, subtle in its range. Backwoods drawing was broad, with a distinct bias toward the grotesque, or the macabre. Backwoods profusion was set against Yankee spareness. The Yankee might compare himself or another with a weasel or a blacksnake, but he never was the weasel or the blacksnake as the backwoodsman was the alligator or the raccoon or the tornado. And the Yankee as a figure stood alone or apart, a red-white-and-blue apparition which was still the dominant national figure. The backwoodsman was likely to appear in pairs, leaping or boasting or telling stories in matches with the background of a crowd. Yet a basic tie remained between them, even beyond effects of talk and masquerade, a tie which had been fashioned by the common mind out of which they sprang. Neither invited the literal view or the prosaic touch. The fantasies surrounding them might often be crude and earthy, but they were fantasies. These odd and variegated creatures were firmly planted in the spacious realm of legend.

III. THAT LONG-TAIL'D BLUE

TOWARD the end of the eighteenth century a genial foreign traveler told of some New York merchants who reached their counting-house by nine in the morning, donned aprons, and rolled hogsheads of rum and molasses around their wharves and were as dirty as their own porters, and could easily be mistaken for them. All day long they heaved, and hallooed, turning at intervals to scribble at their desks. At four they went home, dressed, had dinner, and were at the play at seven; after the play, which they vastly enjoyed, they went to supper, where they sang and roared and smoked and drank until dawn. At nine in the morning their lusty program began again. This sketch remained fresh and pertinent for at least two generations. But it was only a sketch. The outline was not filled in or given variations.

Soon after the Revolution certain other characters were thus briefly drawn—struck off like so many new coins in a visionary moment. The southern planter became a tall strolling figure with a fine presence, in a wide hat. In the *Knickerbocker History* and in *Rip Van Winkle* Irving created a comic mythology as though comic myth-making were a native habit, formed early; and these writings show the habitual playing off of one regional type against another. But his Dutch people were of the past, joining only

77

at a distance with the current portrayal of native characters. A few later Dutchmen with long pipes became foils for Yankee wit. They apparently faded before it. Except for Rip the Dutch character was lost to the general view; and other native types were only transiently considered. A little Frenchman in dimity trousers exclaimed over the restlessness of the Yankee in a few early burlesques and reminiscences, and then vanished. The transplanted Irishman was dimly though continuously drawn for thirty or forty years; he was in fact the most frequently attempted of all these figures. He was pictured in Brackenridge's early satire on the backwoods character, *Modern Chivalry*, and appeared in stories like that of *Banagher's Bassoon* on the Yankee stage: Banagher had come from Bangor. The Irish print was clear in airs and jigs and reels and in the language. A horn of hard liquor was known in the West as a little of "the creature" or of "the element." But the Irish character fused readily, it seems, with others, and was often impossible to trace. Within this early period the transplanted Irishman failed to emerge as an insistent figure.

Among this shadowy group there was one powerful exception, one type destined to capture the popular fancy: the Negro. "The blacks," said a traveler in 1795, "are the great humorists of the nation. . . . Climate, music, kind treatment act upon them like electricity." Negroes were remembered fiddling before a play at a Maryland tavern or in their cabins strumming banjos made of flat gourds strung with horsehair. Soon they had the tambo, bones, quills, fife, and triangle. A traveler on the Savannah River heard a mellow distant sound along the surface of the water that came nearer and nearer until it seemed to rise from under the very bow of his boat, when a primitive *bateau* slid from the shadows along the shore, carrying a tall old ebony Negro who stood erect "like some boatman of the Niger," playing on a long, straight wooden tube. Negro rowing-songs rose like barbaric chants on the watery highways of the West. Plantation owners on the Mississippi had crews of black oarsmen who sang as they rowed and improvised good-natured verses to match the occasions of the day. A few African creole melodies drifted down through the century. A western poet declared that "among the earliest original verses of the West were sundry African melodies celebrating the coon hunt and the vicissitudes of river navigation." The Negro was to be seen everywhere in the South and in the new Southwest, on small farms and great plantations, on roads and levees. He was often an all but equal member of many a pioneering expedition. He became, in short, a dominant figure in spite of his condition, and commanded a definite portraiture.

In the early '20's, at almost the precise moment when the backwoodsman appeared in legend with his "Hunters of Kentucky," the southern plantation Negro was drawn on the stage in Cincinnati by young Edwin Forrest. Made up for the part, Forrest strolled through the streets, where an old Negro woman mistook him for a Negro whom she knew; he persuaded her to join him in an impromptu scene that evening. This little sketch seemed unimportant, but Forrest had studied the Negro character; he inaugurated a tradition for faithful drawing. Other impersonations, now lost to view, no doubt followed, like tentative portraits; and punctually in the early '30's, when both the Yankee and the backwoodsman leapt to full stature on the stage, the Negro was also pictured in firm, enduring outlines.

The artist of course was Jim Crow Rice—who was white —the place any one of a number of cities along the route of western travel from Pittsburgh to Cincinnati or Lexington. Rice had heard an old crippled Negro hostler singing in a stableyard as he rubbed down the horses, and had seen him dancing an odd limping dance as he worked—"rockin' de heel." Rice studied the dance and learned the song, with its refrain—

> Wheel about, turn about,
>   Do jis so,
> An' ebery time I wheel about
> I jump Jim Crow.

These he used in a backwoods play, *The Rifle*, and the small interlude met with such instant success that he enlarged it to an afterpiece, weaving other Negro melodies and dances around the single impersonation. Presently he emerged—still in blackface—in the red and white striped trousers and long blue coat of the Yankee. The coat became the subject of one of his most popular songs, "That Longtail'd Blue," a ballad telling of the trials besetting the wearer of that garment. A later version was happy-go-lucky, as if the Negro were assured of his own nationalistic position.

This black-faced Yankee had in fact a confident breadth of impersonation. The buttons on his coat and vest were made of five- and ten-dollar gold pieces which he liberally tore off and flung to his audiences. For a time he was accompanied by a tiny comic *Doppelgänger*, small Joe Jefferson in red, white, and blue, who was tumbled out of a valise and danced the odd limping dance opposite him, joining in the plaintive melody. Soon Rice was drawing other Negro portraits, of a Negro dandy of the river towns, a Negro flatboatman, and a plantation Negro. Collecting cornfield dances and plantation melodies, he created a massed musical effect with a few others in blackface in his "O Hush" and "Bone Squash," which he called Ethiopian opera.

The vogue of this new entertainment was enormous. Rice enjoyed a popularity in the '30's and '40's which was said to be unmatched by that of any other American comedian of his time. He carried his impersonations to London, where he drew an extraordinary personal following. After these beginnings, in 1842, Negro minstrelsy was born. Four men gathered in a New York hotel, a rendezvous for show people. The leader was Dan Emmett, a backwoodsman of Irish descent who looked like a Yankee deacon. The other three were Yankees, and one of them had been an actor of Yankee parts. They played the fiddle, the banjo, the tambo, and bones. Emmett said afterward that they were all end-men and all interlocutors; and they all wore "that long-tail'd blue." Massed singing quickly became the core of minstrelsy, and in its wake came larger numbers in the choral dancing of the walkaround.

2

BLACKFACE minstrelsy has long been considered a travesty in which the Negro was only a comic medium. To the primitive comic sense, to be black is to be funny, and many minstrels made the most of the simple circumstance. This exploitation was deeply resented by the anti-slavery leaders of an early day, and in the end they went far toward creating the idea that the Negro lacked humor. After the Civil War it would still have been possible to reveal the many-sided Negro of the old plantations, but minstrelsy with its air of irreverence seems to have blocked the way. Because minstrels had sported with the Negro and had even sentimentalized his lot in a few songs, because of his tragic fate and a wish to prove that he possessed moral worth, dignity, and capacity, his friends collected and discussed and displayed only his religious pieces, the spirituals which have seemed his special creation. But Negro humor was always abundant, and from it early minstrelsy drew as from a primal source, keeping the tradition for direct and ample portraiture. Burlesque appeared, but burlesque was natural to the Negro.

Many minstrels had lived in the South and West and knew the Negro at first hand. One of them saw an old peddler of watermelons with a donkey cart in a Georgia town, followed him about until he had mastered his lingo, cries, snatches of song, as well as his odd manner. The portrayals, so freshly caught, were whole and rich. Emotion welled up in the small acts and through the olios in spite of crude stage contrivances. Forrest, who had long since become a tragic actor, declared that he knew no finer piece of tragic acting than the broadly comic impersonation of Dan Bryant as the hungry Negro in *Old Times Rocks*.

The songs and to a large extent the dances show Negro origins, though they were often claimed by white composers. Dan Emmett declared that he wrote "Ole Dan Tucker" as a boy of fifteen or sixteen, but this song of the older minstrelsy had a curious history for an independent piece of musical composition. The air resembles Negro airs; the chorus with its shouting dance refrain breaks away from the verses in the habitual manner of Negro choruses. And Emmett offered more than one version of the words in which appear those brief and cryptic bird and animal fables that have proved to be a consistent Negro creation—

> Jaybird in de martin's nest,
> To sabe his soul he got no rest.
> Ole Tucker in de foxes' den,
> Out come de young ones nine or ten.
>
> High-hole in de holler tree,
> He poke his bill in for to see,

> De lizard cotch 'im by de snout,
> He call for Tucker to pull 'im out.

In another version of the song, a touch of woe is mingled in an odd colloquy—

> Sheep an' hog a walkin' in de pasture,
> Sheep says, "Hog, can't you go no faster?"
> Hush! Hush! honey, hear de wolf a howlin',
> Ah, ah, de Lawd, de bulldog growlin'.

Most of these fables contained a simple allegory: the crow was a comic symbol for the Negro himself, though he might at times take the form of a sheep or a hog, while the master or the overseer or the patrol—the "patter-roller"—was the bulldog or sometimes the bullfrog. The jaybird habitually took a sinister part, descending into hell on Fridays; and other birds and animals were freely drawn in symbolical relations. In "Clar de Kitchen," one of Rice's most popular dance-songs, a fragmentary bird and animal fable appears with triumph for the Negro submerged and disguised.

> A jaybird sot on a hickory limb,
> He winked at me and I winked at him,
> I picked up a stone and I hit his shin,
> Says he, you better not do that agin.

> A bullfrog dressed in soger's close
> Went in de field to shoot some crows,
> De crows smell powder an' fly away,
> De bullfrog mighty mad dat day.

In all these fables touches of satire were present, directed toward the white man, or toward the Negro himself when he figured as the lumbering hog or sheep, or gave himself wit as a fox. Self-parody appeared in such dances with bird calls as "Turkey in de Straw," which Emmett claimed, but which surely went back to a common dance of the Negro.

Rice and Emmett can only have borrowed the fables, probably with their tunes. Apparently neither had a gift for imitation of the Negro mode of story-telling, for they mixed such stanzas with others of their own composition, or at least plainly not of Negro origin. Emmett offered at least two versions of "Ole Dan Tucker." The song and the character in fact underwent those possessive and affectionate changes and additions which mean that many hands have been at work upon them; the melody showed variations; and the character which they celebrated was likewise variable. Dan Tucker was pictured as a vagabond Negro who was laughed at and scorned by his own kind but who constantly bobbed up among them with outrageous small adventures. Since he consorted with the two sagest creatures in the animal world of the Negro, the fox and the jaybird, he was endowed with a comical magic; yet for all this he was an outcast, looming large as he combed his hair with a wagon-wheel, shrinking small and growing ridiculous as he washed his face in a frying-pan, and at last through the transformations of many years changing from black to white. Stories appeared about him as though he were a living figure; joke-books were named for him; one of them was ascribed to that "young Daniel" who is introduced casually in a stanza of one of the many versions of the song. No doubt tales and many other verses of the song appeared in improvisations and have been lost. Dan Tucker was a legendary figure, as long-lived as Crockett.

Emmett belonged to a family that had been among the early pioneers from Virginia; in later years his father's house in Ohio had become a station for the underground railroad. In the middle 1820's he was stationed as a fifer in Kentucky and later at a barracks on the Mississippi below St. Louis. He had traveled through the West with a small circus company; and these companies usually included at least one Negro dancer. For a time he played with Rice, who from the first had turned to the Negro for the direct portrait. Thus through his impressionable years Emmett had been brought into close contact with the Negro; indeed he declared that he had always confined himself to "the habits and crude ideas of the slaves of the South," even though in the next breath he insisted that the songs were of his own composition. Negro melodies and fables had possessed his mind. Plantation cries echoed in his walkarounds and choruses. Some of his songs were close to the spirituals, which are the acknowledged creation of the Negro. The opening stanza of his first version of "Dixie" contains a touch of the characteristic biblical picturing—

Dis worl' was made in jes six days
An' finished up in various ways—
Look away! look away! look away! Dixie land!

THAT LONG-TAIL'D BLUE

Dey den made Dixie trim and nice
But Adam called it Paradise—
Look away! look away! look away! Dixie land!

Here the verbal phrasing is unlike that of the Negro, whose habitual approach is swift and elliptical. Controversy has in fact gathered around the entire question of the composition of "Dixie," and Emmett has been denied even the smaller glory of transcription or adaptation. Whatever the circumstance, the traces of Negro origin remain in the biblical touch—never to be found in songs of lighter mood elsewhere in this time—in the cries of the chorus, and in the melody, which sounds like a fiddler's tune.

Similar traces appear elsewhere in the minstrel songs ascribed to Emmett, sometimes only in the words, sometimes in musical phrasing. He often used the Jordan theme recurrent in the spirituals. In his "Jordan Is a Hard Road to Trabbel" a fragment of the story of David and Goliath is joined with topical references to make a comic song. In his "Here We Are," or "Cross Ober Jordan," the river symbolizes another river of freedom, the Ohio—

I'll sail de worl' clar roun' and roun'
All by de railroad underground.
We'll cross ober Jordan, we'll land on tudder shore,
Den make room in de flatboat for one darkey more.

Here too was a vestige of the great western mode of travel belonging to an earlier day, in the mention of that great ark, the flatboat. And at least one spiritual, "Michael, Row

87

That Boat Ashore," was clearly a boat song. The rhythm and the remembrance of travel along the western rivers ran through many of the minstrel songs.

The spirituals were a source for Foster as well. He haunted Negro camp-meetings for rhythms and melodies; and his songs were immediately appropriated by the minstrels. Krehbiel has shown that "The Camptown Races" sounds like "Lord, Remember Me" with a quickened beat; and while he suggested that the Negro borrowed the "Races" for the spiritual, it seems equally probable that Foster was the borrower, since he used Negro airs and phrasing elsewhere. Many spirituals lend themselves to such transformations. Brought to a rapid stress, "Somebody's Knocking at My Door" could easily become a dance tune; and as it happens, a favorite minstrel song of this period was called "Somebody's Knockin' at Yo' Do'." The music bore no relation to that of the spiritual; only the salient phrase was repeated; but the whole body of this many-sided music is full of such phrases, turned ingeniously and restlessly, as by the Negro himself, to different effects.

The climax of the minstrel performance, the walk-around, with its competitive dancing in the mazes of a circle, was clearly patterned on Negro dances in the compounds of the great plantations, which in turn went back to the communal dancing of the African. The ancestry was hardly remote. Many who heard the minstrels in the Gulf States or along the lower Mississippi must have remembered those great holidays in New Orleans early in the century when hundreds of Negroes followed through the streets a king chosen for his youth, strength, and blackness. License ran high, and the celebrations ended in saturnalia of barbaric, contortionistic dancing. Often the walkarounds of minstrelsy were composed only of bold pantomime and matched dancing, accompanied by strident cries and the simplest binding of words, the words gaining their color from slave life—

> Darkies hear dat banjo ring,
> Yoe! Ha! Yoe!
> Listen to de fiddle sing,
> Yoe! Ha! Yoe!
> Dee dah doo dah dum
> Aha! Aha!
> Oh, massa sabe me, do!
> Aha! Aha!
> See dat nigger over dar,
> Yoe! Ha! Yoe!
> He's got de longest hair,
> Yoe! Ha! Yoe!

Plantation cries, wailing cries, stirring shouts with a tonic beat, ran through all early minstrelsy. Many of the choruses took up similar resounding notes with even greater breadth. The choruses with their open vowels and slurred consonants and rushing syncopated measures proved the reliance of minstrelsy upon Negro airs and chants even when the musical or verbal phrasing moved to another idiom.

89

3

Negro minstrelsy had arisen from the Southwest and from Negro life there; it showed many traces of regional origins. "Sugar in de gourd" and "honey in de horn" were heard in minstrel songs as well as in southwestern talk. The backwoodsman and the Negro danced the same jigs and reels; the breakdown was an invention which each might have claimed. In the '50's, a generation or more after the boatman had ceased to be a figure on the western rivers, rowing songs and boatman's songs and boatman's dances became a dominant pattern through minstrelsy; and they borrowed the fancy touch with which the flatboatman had often adorned songs about himself. Sometimes the songs were adorned with corals and dolphins and fireflies. Most of them kept the rolling choruses with a touch of nonsense.

De spring ob de year am come at last,
Winter time am gwan an' past—
Four and twenty boatmen, all in a flock,
Settin' by de seaside peckin' on a rock.
Dance de boatmen, dance!
O dance de boatmen, dance! dance!
Dance all night till broad daylight,
An' go home wid de girls in de mornin'!
Hi! Ho! de boatmen row,
Floatin' down de ribber on de Ohio.
Hi! Ho! de boatmen row,
Floatin' down de ribber on de Ohio.

THAT LONG-TAIL'D BLUE

Whether or not the tall tale was characteristic of the Negro or whether he took a touch of the art from the back-woodsman may never be known, since in an uncharted history the early improvisations have been lost; but magnification appeared in the early phases of minstrelsy with unmistakable stress. Dan Tucker combed his hair with a wagon-wheel. An animal song which belongs to the '40's and probably earlier celebrates a fabulous little black bull—

> He shake his tail, he jar de ribber,
> Hoosen Johnny, Hoosen Johnny,
> He shake his tail, he jar de ribber,
> Long time ago.

The encore verses of one of Rice's most popular songs, "Sich a Gittin' Upstairs," told of a "bone squash" captain who was cut in two in a fight, joined himself together with glue, finished his enemy, and lay down to sleep, only to find on awakening—the day was hot—that the glue had melted and that a thief had run away with his thighs—

> Dis being de case he saw no fun,
> An' having no legs he couldn't run,
> So he shied a stone at de old tief' head
> An' though seven miles off he killed him dead.
>
> A ball one day knocked off his head,
> De people all thought he was quite dead,
> But he picked up his head and ran away,
> And nebber was heard of since dat day.

Western myth-making was woven deep in early minstrelsy, so deep that it can hardly be counted an alien strain.

Another coloring was given by Irish reels, jigs, and lilts; the Negro seemed to pick up the Irish musical idiom with facility, and the composers often adopted fragments of the pleasing tunes. One of Emmett's Jordan songs moves to an Irish lilt; yet it contains biblical pictures in the fashion of the spirituals. Themes of English contradances occasionally broke through the Negro breakdowns and reels. No doubt the minstrel often bridged gaps in his knowledge of Negro music and lore by inventions of his own; the interjected pattern is often evident. Occasionally a fluent strain appears that seems drawn from popular songs of the day, in the mode of "The Old Oaken Bucket," with words that follow the inspiration of Tom Moore.

But the persistent stress was primitive; it was often sorrowful; the effect was exotic and strange, with the swaying figures and black faces of the minstrels lighted by guttering gas flames or candlelight on small country stages, or even in the larger theaters. And within this large and diverse pattern lay a fresh context of comedy. This was plain in the intricate and grotesque dancing, as the blackface minstrels "walked jaw-bone" or accomplished the deep complications of the "dubble trubble" or the "grapevine twist." Even in one of the spirituals "four-and-twenty blackbirds" cropped up with an air of satire as "four-and-twenty elders," and the minstrel songs were filled with such sidelong touches. The whole intention of the bird and animal fables was that of a delicate and shrouded satire. And a far bolder comic quality appeared which had hardly developed elsewhere in the American comic display—that of nonsense.

In an early "Yankee Doodle"—in "Corncobs Twist Your Hair"—the flavor of nonsense was unmistakable, but this seemed to spring from a brief extraordinary exhilaration, and almost no trace of the same feeling is to be found in other Yankee talk and stories. Strangely enough, with all his wild excess the backwoodsman never overflowed into pure nonsense. Perhaps the Negro did not invent the nonsensical narratives which appeared in his dialect, but the touch is akin to that in many of the Negro fables in song. Certainly nonsense in minstrelsy shows a sharp distinction from other humor of the day. The minstrel mode went off to a bold and careless tangent.

> Kentuck one night a party meet
> Who say dey goin' to have a treat,
> Dey come from Old Town, short and tall,
> To have a dance at de nigger ball.
> An' sich a gittin' upstairs,
> An' a playin' on de fiddle,
> Sich a gittin' upstairs I nebber did see,
> Sich a gittin' upstairs, an' a playin' on de fiddle,
> Sich a gittin' upstairs, I nebber did see.
>
> Mister Brown he come in his mackintosh,
> His head all frizzed like a punkin squash.
> He smoked cigars, the best Havan,
> An' a watch as large as a warmin'-pan,

93

An' sich a gittin' upstairs,
An' a playin' on de fiddle,
Sich a gittin' upstairs I nebber did see. . . .

Miss Rose come in her mistress' close,
But how she got dem nobody knows,
And long before de ball did meet
She was dancing Taglioni at de corner ob de street,
An' sich a gittin' upstairs,
An' a playin' on de fiddle,
Sich a gittin' upstairs I nebber did see. . . .

A little old man was ridin' by,
His horse was tryin' to kick a fly.
He lifted his leg towards de south
An' sent it bang in his own mouth.
An' sich a gittin' upstairs,
An' a playin' on de fiddle,
Sich a gittin' upstairs I nebber did see. . . .

The fling at the end was characteristic, and the song with its sibilant chorus all but pictured the gathering, hustling, dancing crowd in celebration. The satirical touch about Taglioni was possible for the Negro of the river towns.

Triumph was in his humor, but not triumph over circumstance. Rather this was an unreasonable headlong triumph launching into the realm of the preposterous. The triumphant note ran through the careless phrasing of most of the minstrel songs and was plain in the swift pulsations of the rhythms. Yet defeat was also clear—that abysmal defeat which seemed the destiny of the Negro. Slavery was

94

often imaged in brief phrases or in simple situations. Fragments of humble and cryptic work songs appeared—

Sheep shell oats, ole Tucker shell de corn.

Lines from forbidden devil songs were echoed—

O I'se sorry I sold myself to the debbil.

Defeat could be heard in the occasional minor key and in the smothered satire. Hitherto the note of triumph had been unmistakable and unremitting among American comic characters. The sudden extreme of nonsense was new, and the tragic undertone was new.

4

PRIMITIVE elements were roughly patterned in minstrelsy. Its songs, its dances, its patter, were soon set within a ritual which grew more and more fixed, like some rude ceremonial. Endmen and interlocutors spun out their talk with an air of improvisation, but this free talk and song occupied an inalienable place in the procedure. In the dancing a strong individualism appeared, and the single dancer might step out of the whole pattern; the jig dancer might perform his feats on a peck measure, and dancers might be matched against each other with high careerings which belonged to each one alone: but these excursions were caught within the broad effect. Beneath them all ran the deep insurgence of Negro choruses that flowed into minstrelsy for many years, even after its ritual grew stereotyped and other elements were added; and the choral dancing of the walkaround made a resonant primitive groundwork.

Within this ritualistic design certain Negro characters were permanently limned, little limping Jim Crow with his plaintive song the first among them, and Zip Coon, that "very learned skoler," rougher, simpler, and more humble, next in the early order. The third figure, old Dan Tucker, was perhaps the most enduring of all in spite of his many transformations; he was always the outcast—

> Git outen de way, git outen de way,
> Git outen de way, ole Dan Tucker,
> You'se too late to come to your supper.

All three of these characters were outcasts even beyond the obvious fate of the slave.

Following these or surrounding them were others of smaller appeal or lesser stature. They all revealed the Negro character: yet they showed that greater outline and more abstract drawing which reveals the world of legend. Magic was mixed with small events in these portrayals; and even real places took on the large and legendary air, as in the nostalgic lines of "Dixie." The biblical allusions heightened the air of legend.

These legends flowed into familiar patterns, these mythical characters slipped into familiar guises. Though the symbolical "long-tail'd blue" was seldom seen after the first few years of minstrelsy, its nationalistic promise was kept. The Negro in minstrelsy took a turn at playing oracle. Little Jim Crow talked comically on political affairs between dances and songs. Later Rice impersonated a bootblack with a bent toward philosophy: the axioms have been lost, but the drawing was said to be lifelike, and the figure occupied a considerable place in the popular fancy of the day. Zip Coon sang a crazy-quilt song with bits of animal fable edging toward politics.

O ole Zip Coon he is a larned skoler,
Sings possum up a gum tree an' coony in a holler,
Possum up a gum tree, coony on a stump,
Possum up a gum tree, coony on a stump,
Possum up a gum tree, coony on a stump,
Den over dubble trubble, Zip Coon will jump.
O Zip a duden duden duden, zip a duden day.
O Zip a duden duden duden, duden duden day.
O Zip a duden duden duden, duden duden day
Zip a duden duden duden, zip a duden day.

O it's old Suky blue-skin, she is in lub wid me,
I went de udder arternoon to take a cup ob tea;
What do you tink now, Suky hab for supper,
Why chicken foot an' possum heel, widout any butter.
O Zip a duden duden, duden, zip a duden day. . . .

Did you ever see the wild goose, sailing on de ocean,
O de wild goose motion is a bery pretty notion;
Ebry time de wild goose beckons to de swaller,
You hear him google google google google goller.
O Zip a duden duden duden, zip a duden day. . . .

97

Wandering lazily through the many further stanzas were satirical references to Jackson and the bank and Davy Crockett. Zip Coon was to become President of the United States and Crockett was to be Vice President.

Here was that legendary assumption of wisdom which had appeared persistently among American comic characters. This assumption had striking aspects, for the rise of the Negro minstrel coincided with a marked change in his place within the nation. Little Jim Crow appeared at almost the precise moment when *The Liberator* was founded; and minstrelsy spread over the land and grew in popularity as the struggle for emancipation gained in power through the '40's and '50's. The Negro minstrel joined with the Yankee and the backwoodsman to make a comic trio, appearing in the same era, with the same timely intensity. The era of course was the turbulent era of the Jacksonian democracy, that stormy time when the whole mixed population of the United States seemed to pour into the streets of Washington, and when many basic elements in the national character seemed to come to the surface. The Negro minstrel was deeply grounded in reality, even though the impersonators were white, even though the figure was a myth.

The three figures loomed large, not because they represented any considerable numbers in the population, but because something in the nature of each induced an irresistible response. Each had been a wanderer over the land, the Negro a forced and unwilling wanderer. Each in a fashion

of his own had broken bonds, the Yankee in the initial revolt against the parent civilization, the backwoodsman in
revolt against all civilization, the Negro in a revolt which
was cryptic and submerged but which none the less made
a perceptible outline. As figures they embodied a deep-lying
mood of disseverance, carrying the popular fancy further
and further from any fixed or traditional heritage. Their
comedy, their irreverent wisdom, their sudden changes and
adroit adaptations, provided emblems for a pioneer people
who required resilience as a prime trait. Comic triumph appeared in them all; the sense of triumph seemed a necessary
mood in the new country. Laughter produced the illusion of
leveling obstacles in a world which was full of unaccus-
tomed obstacles. Laughter created ease, and even more, a
sense of unity, among a people who were not yet a nation
and who were seldom joined in stable communities. These
mythical figures partook of the primitive; and for a people
whose life was still unformed, a searching out of primitive
concepts was an inevitable and stirring pursuit, uncovering
common purposes and directions.

But even in life the Negro was not wholly primitive; his
satire was often conscious; and the everyday comedy of the
Yankee and the backwoodsman almost invariably wore the
air of contrivance. Occasionally in practical jokes their
humor seemed only gross and physical; yet at best even
these contained a deliberate fantasy. As the three figures
were projected in stories or on the stage the effect of
consciousness was greatly heightened. With all their rude

poetry it was about a mind that these myths centered, a conscious, indeed an acutely self-conscious, mind. Masquerade was salient in them all. Minstrelsy was of course white masquerade; and the double use of the mask seemed to create a profound satisfaction for American audiences, as if the sheer accomplished artifice aroused an instinctive response among them. The mask might be worn as an inheritance or for amusement or as a front against the world in any of these impersonations, concealing a childish and unformed countenance: but it was part of a highly conscious self-projection.

Emotion seldom crept through this assumed disguise; none at all was shown by the Yankee characters or those who belonged to the backwoods, though the backwoodsman could indulge in a characteristic mock melancholy. In minstrelsy emotion was near the surface, surging obscurely through the choruses and walkarounds, but this was always communal, never individual. In all the array of popular comedy, which pressed close to circumstance and approximated many of the outer aspects of a common life, individual emotion was sponged out. Anger, love, hatred, remorse, were absent; fear alone was revealed, but only in a distant and fragmentary fashion, only to be cast away with laughter. If it created unities, the resilience of the comic spirit seemed a destructive agent, so blank were the spaces where emotion might have appeared.

Simple ties existed between this trio and the animal world. The Yankee looked there for swift, familiar comparisons in order to identify a human being, often satirically. The backwoodsman pictured himself as a savage and cunning beast and turned to the wilderness mainly for destruction. At the same time he evoked it. The Negro saw beasts and birds as emblems of himself and of others; his mood was that of companionship; and he kept to the gentle realm of the cotton-field, the meadow, the pasture, or the fringe of forest. In some sense wild creatures were seen in an alliance with man in all these glimpses; yet the unchanging stress was upon the human character, as if an absorption in character were primary.

Many minor evidences are at hand to show that the comic trio tended to merge into a single generic figure. The early "long-tail'd blue" was a lasting symbol. In stories and on the stage each took on qualities and even appearances of the others; they fell into many of the same roles. A hundred years after the emergence of little Jim Crow, tall talk was to appear in *Ole King David and the Philistine Boys*.

" 'What dat, ole King Saul?' say Little David.

" 'Dat's ole Goliar,' say old King Saul.

" 'Who he?' say David.

" 'De he-coon er de Philistines,' say King Saul.

" 'What do he want?' say David.

" 'Trouble,' say ole King Saul.

" 'Well, you de king, ain't you?' say Little David. 'Can't you ease his worries 'long dat line?'

" 'Who, me?' say Saul. 'I'm a married man. Cou'se I ain't skeered of him, but still and at de same time I got a wife and a family dependin' on me for s'port. So I don't see no reason how come I should git out and git hurted by no gi'nt.'

" 'He's a gi'nt?' say Little David.

" 'Twenty foot tall,' say King Saul.

" 'What else is he?' say David.

" 'Jest wait to he gits out in de clearin' and starts makin' his say-so,' say King Saul.

"So 'bout dat time ole Goliar stepped out in de clearin' and commenced makin' his say-so.

" 'I'm a cross betwixt a wild cat and de yaller ianders,' he say. 'I'm sired by Trouble and dammed by Sudden Death. I drinks nothin' but stump watter and a rattlesnake bit me and died. I breathes out forked lightnin' and I spits out thunder. When I laughs de skies pop open, and when I groans hit rolls up like a ball er yarn. I kills my friends and I makes hamburgers outer my enemies. Tornadoes and harrycanes follow me round like pet dogs, and lines and tigers is my playmates. I'm bad. I'm mean. I'm vicious, and jest natchally can't he'p it. When I gits sick hit takes nothin' less'n a Hebrew man's meat to cyore me. And I feel a buck auger comin' on. So look out! I'm reekin' wid meanness and I'm huntin' trouble.' "

The rhapsodic boasting of the backwoods had traveled down the century. But each of the trio remained distinct. None left a deeper print than the Negro in minstrelsy, even though his shadowy figure was the slowest to emerge, and though the minstrel never assumed the many distinct parts taken by the Yankee and the backwoodsman. The appeal of minstrelsy was insistent and enduring; minstrel companies multiplied quickly and spread all over the country; the minstrel songs were quickly appropriated by the nation. "The Ethiopian melodies well deserve to be called, as they are in fact, the national airs of America," wrote Bayard Taylor in 1849. "They follow the American race in all its migrations, colonizations, and conquests." Taylor was writing from California, where minstrelsy was heard almost as soon as the first gold-seeker set foot there, and where it grew as an accompaniment for that wild adventure. A minstrel song, Foster's "Oh, Susannah!" became a rallying-cry for the new empire, a song of meeting and parting turned to nonsense, a fiddler's tune with a Negro beat and a touch of smothered pathos in the melody. Fragments of familiar reels and breakdowns, of boatmen's dances and boatmen's songs, were often caught within the minstrel pattern: much of the pioneer experience was embedded there. No doubt the appeal of minstrelsy came from these draughts upon a common reminiscence, stirring some essential wish or remembrance.

Minstrelsy kept its Negro backgrounds until after the Civil War: then, if the Negro was set free, in a fashion his white impersonators were also liberated. Along with later blackface acting came a strong infusion of Irish melodies and an Irish brogue. German songs were sometimes sung on the minstrel stage; and much later the Jew occasionally emerged in blackface. Again in fantasy the Ameri-

103

can types seemed to be joining in a single semblance. But Negro music and Negro nonsense still prevailed; through years the old pattern was kept. The young American Narcissus had looked at himself in the narrow rocky pools of New England and by the waters of the Mississippi; he also gazed long at a darker image.

IV. STROLLERS

YOUNG Horace Greeley, walking into New York in 1830 in a short-sleeved coat and tow-linen trousers, was the very picture of the Yankee lad of the fables. He looked, in fact, like Yankee Hill. No one can know whether Greeley was conscious of the figure he cut in these years, but as he grew older surely his sense of masquerade became acute. With his old white hat and coat, his fringe of silvery-yellow whiskers, his ostentatiously uncouth manners, his drollery, he stressed his Yankee heritage in a few bold lines so that any passer-by might see.

Many bold self-delineations were appearing during these years. In New York or Baltimore or New Orleans the origin of strangers could easily be told by their dress, their bearing, even their physical type, as if all these effects had been consciously developed. Characters in this period often seemed larger than life. To match the rising grandeur of the Republic, heads of the antique Roman cast developed: then in later years the type vanished as though the animating conviction had failed. Even the more self-contained of these new Romans made grandiose gestures: Webster solemnly rose and bowed low to Jenny Lind when she had bowed in response to the applause of the audience in Castle Garden, as if he represented the entire aggregation. Characters in public life were indeed one of the great creations

105

of the time; and they often seemed to gain their emphasis less from a closely packed individuality than from bold and conscious self-picturization.

Tyrone Power, who traveled widely over the country in the '30's, found the mimetic gift singularly common in all phases of American society. The Americans had in fact emerged as a theatrical race. No doubt many obscure influences tended to create this bias of character. The new country made a strangely painted backdrop before which the American seemed constrained to perform; and every powerful force in pioneer life led toward outward expression. Self-consciousness had perhaps been induced early in the American by the critical scrutiny abundantly accorded him by the older races; and theatrical tendencies in the American character were heightened by a long intimacy with the stage.

"There is much discourse now of beginning stage plays in New England," Increase Mather wrote in 1686, at a time when the Puritan power seemed supreme. The restless interest in the theater worked slowly, with long gaps between its triumphs, but it was unremitting. By 1750 Bostonians were so eager to see a play at a coffee-house that a serious riot took place at its doors. Soon after the Revolution an exquisite theater was built in Boston, designed by Bullfinch and containing a chastely ornamented dancing-room, card rooms, and tea rooms. In eastern cities of the coast from New York to Charleston, playhouses were established; and as the migration from New England moved westward into upper New York, into western Pennsylvania and the Western Reserve, theatricals seemed to spring up in their wake. By 1815 small companies had reached Kentucky, and improvised theaters soon dotted the West. In the little town of Columbus in Georgia, timber that waved in the breeze on Monday was transformed into a theater the following Thursday. In Natchez a theater was built in an old graveyard, with dressing-rooms beneath the stage like catacombs, and bones in view. Ballrooms of plantation mansions were fitted up for performances, and plays were performed in taverns.

In the West at least, on the frontier, where the mixed elements of the American character were taking a pronounced shape, the results were hardly considerable as drama. The best acting—and many gifted players traveled over the country—could offer little more than sheer theatricals. With transient audiences and scratch companies and the hardships of travel there was small chance for intensification and depth; even the elder Booth concentrated only on single scenes. The pioneer theater was coarsened and haphazard. No drama came out of this broad movement: nothing can be clearer than the fact that drama as a powerful native form did not appear in America at this time or even throughout the entire nineteenth century. But the theatrical seemed a native mode. The Yankee first fully emerged in the theater; each of the trio of native characters was seen there. The theater took a place which in a civilization of slower and quieter growth might have been occupied

107

almost altogether by casual song and story; even the comic tale was theatrically contrived, with the teller always the actor, and the effect dependent upon manner and gesture and the stress of speech.

Now the theatrical, as opposed to the dramatic, is full of experiment, finding its way to audiences by their quick responses and rejections. On the stage the shimmer and glow, the minor appurtenances, the jokes and dances and songs, the stretching and changes of plots, are arranged and altered almost literally by the audience or in their close company; its measure is human, not literary. The American theater then, particularly in the West, was a composite of native feeling. It had significance, not because it might at some later time evolve into great national art, but because it was closely interwoven with the American character and the American experience. It marched with the forces of dispersal, essaying a hundred things by way of entertainment and revealing a growing temper.

2

Like gypsy crews, strolling actors moved over the country, following the trail of the pioneers, often abreast of them. At Olean one company bought a broadhorn and floated down the Alleghany, playing airs from *The Beggar's Opera* at solitary cabins, finding music in abundance wherever a few settlers were gathered. A troupe stopped at a double log cabin and discovered that a tiny theater had been contrived in a loft, with curtains and three large benches for boxes and pit. There with a few crude properties they offered the semblance of romance: but the world which they created for a few hours was no more fanciful than that which existed in the minds of their small audience. All around them lay shadowy sites of public buildings and wide ephemeral avenues and streets such as Colonel Sellers, a figure of later years, depicted at the breakfast table as he laid out a railroad line through Slouchburg and Doodleville, Belshazzar, Catfish, Babylon, Bloody Run, Hail Columbia, and Hark from the Tomb.

Many companies went into the West by way of the Alleghany, leaving behind them white flags flying on the banks of the river at places where those who followed might find a friendly reception. Pittsburgh, "sunk in sin and sea-coal," where pioneers had often been stranded for lack of money or had suffered strange adventures, was a difficult crossroads for actors. Not many of them could match the inhabitants in conviviality. One complained, "To see a Pittsburgh *bon vivant* under the table is a task few attempt who know them, and fewer succeed in accomplishing." And when debt was involved, difficulties in Pittsburgh were doubled. "The constables of Pittsburgh never forget an old friend," mourned the people of the theater. "What actor who has visited this city will ever forget it?" they cried satirically. As one actor was playing the gravedigger in *Hamlet*, he saw the bailiffs in the wings and popped into the grave, and was never heard of again. A whole troupe was caught on the wing for debt as they tried to leave town, and were obliged to hire themselves out as waxworks at a museum to raise the necessary money. A celebrated few succeeded in slipping away in skiffs down the Ohio at night.

On rafts, in broadhorns, companies traveled down the Ohio and the Mississippi, stopping at the larger cities, often playing in small villages. Some went on by wagon into the hills of Kentucky, where the roads were so steep that they were obliged to unload their properties and carry them, and where they often left their watches and chains behind as toll. A few passed through the Cumberland Gap and thus to Richmond, then coastwise to Savannah and farther south. One troupe ventured into Florida during the Seminole War, playing at forts and garrisons on the way, threatened by the Indians but continuing their journey until they were finally set upon, some of their number killed, and their wardrobe seized. Thereafter for a time the Seminoles galloped through the sandy lowlands garbed as Romans, Highlanders, and Shakespearean heroes.

Some companies deployed through Kentucky and Tennessee to the Gulf States, traveling down crooked little rivers in overladen steamers that took on cotton at every wharf, with Negroes pushing huge bales of cotton over the bluffs at night by the light of great fires and with a pit of fire roaring in the steamer below. Everywhere they found theaters, or theaters were improvised for them; every one came, black and white, children and their elders. Backwoodsmen rode up in their fringes and green blankets and fur. Flatboatmen could be distinguished by their rolling stride and implacable manner. Planters appeared in white Spanish hats of beaver on fine horses with bright saddlecloths, and farmers with their wives on pillions, and a host of Negroes.

Off stage the actors maintained an air of urban elegance, highly keyed, with coats of a lighter blue, green, or brown than was usually worn, and hats a little larger or smaller than was the custom. For the stage they brought baskets of faded velvet and silken finery; often their adornments were scant or contrived. One manager never permitted his actors the luxury of fleshings, but painted their legs and his own buff, red, or white for tragedy, with stripes and spots for comedy. Many an actor had for his theatrical wardrobe only a flaxen wig and a pair of comic stockings. The companies were small. Everybody doubled. Every one had precarious adventures.

In a theater at Mobile a slight noise was heard in one of the upper boxes, a rush, a bit of scuffle; the ladies in the box did not move; in the crowded pit there was almost no sensation, though it was soon clear that a man had been knifed. The performance and the applause proceeded without a break. Ambuscades were sometimes set on the roads for the actors; they were always dodging epidemics of cholera or escaping from fires. Yet they continued to join in that perpetual travel which often seemed the single enduring feature of the country. As processions of families and slaves moved from the Carolinas and Georgia to some new tract of forest or canebrake, the actors were close at their heels. The Chapmans, who invented the showboat, went up the Arkansas River to wild country, encountering ruffians, sometimes besieged, dealing out grape and canister in return, but inured to the life and continuing to ply the rivers for years.

By their own wish and in the fancy of their audiences these people of the theater remained a caste apart. The theater still savored of the black arts even though the ban upon it was broken. Changes of character on the stage seemed not altogether different from those which the devil was supposed to assume, changes of scene not far from black magic. These actors could change you "a forest into a front parlor, a desert into a dining-room, a stormy ocean into a flower garden, a palace into a den of thieves, all on the sound of a boatswain's whistle." Yet intangibly they joined with the people and the region, their bold accents of dress and posture heightening the native drift in that direction, their romantic language mingling with the stressed speech of the backwoods.

In an imaginative sense the audiences of the backwoods joined deeply with the players. Theirs was that intimate participation which means that acting has become reality. Out of the forest, groups would come riding at night who would talk with the actors as the play proceeded, or with each other about the characters. On a small stage in a Kentucky village a gambler's family was pictured as starving, and a countryman rose from one of the boxes. "I propose we make up something for this woman," he said. Some one whispered that it was all a sham, but he delivered a brief discourse on the worthlessness of the gambler, flung a bill on the stage with his pocketbook, advised the woman not to let her husband know about it or he would spend it all on faro, and then with a divided mind sat down, saying, "Now go on with the play."

Such participation often meant deep and direct drafts upon the emotions, and the black romantical plays like *Pizarro*, *The Iron Chest*, and *Venice Preserved*, popular at this time, with their themes of envy, hatred, remorse, terror, revenge, could evoke an emotional response with force and abundance. The bolder tragedies of Shakespeare—never his comedies in that early day—were staple pieces, with plays of the supernatural. *Hamlet* was frequently played for the ghost, the murder, the burial, and *Macbeth* for the witches, the sleep-walking scene, and the knocking at the gate, so strongly did the pioneer taste lean in this direction. Since lights were scarce the effects were eerie. One company acted a tragedy wholly in the dark before a Kentucky mountain audience. *The Spectre Bridegroom* was played by moonlight in a low-roofed opening like a hall-way between two cabins, and the ballet of *The Wizard Skiff* was danced before guttering candles. Hushed and startled, these audiences would watch and listen; then again the low murmuring talk would begin among themselves or with the actors.

Here in disguised and transmuted forms emotions which had been dominant in the early day of the pioneer lived again—emotions stirred by a sense of the supernatural, and those grosser feelings begotten of a primitive conflict between man and man, or of man and a rude destiny. With these came the wraith of the Indian.

As the Indian perished or was driven farther and farther from those fertile lands which the white invader wished to occupy, a noble and mournful fantasy was created in his place. After the Revolution, Indian plays and operas abounded. From the '20's onward Cooper followed with a spate of Indian novels. In the '30's, when the trio of popular American figures appeared at full length, the Indian assumed a still loftier stature and a more tragic mien. These were the first palmy years of Forrest's appearance in *Metamora, the Last of the Wampanoags*, a play whose vogue seemed unremitting, and which was copied in dozens of less conspicuous successes. Cooper's *Wept of the Wish Ton Wish* was dramatized and even became a ballet. The stage soon overflowed with Indian figures. Painted and decked, the dusky hero went his tragic way, fighting to be sure, full of "carnivorous rages" when Forrest played the parts, but most often declaiming. The Indian's pride, his grief, his lost inheritance, his kinship with the boundless wilderness, were made enduring themes. Talk flowed again, in Indian monologues, in oratorical outbursts, in rhapsodies.

This fantastic Indian was subjective, white beneath the war-paint, springing into full stature when pioneer life was receding. About his figure the American seemed to wrap a desire to return to the primitive life of the wilderness. It was not for nothing that he had appropriated Indian methods of warfare, Indian costumes, Indian legends: this borrowing had left a wide imprint. In the Indian plays he could drench himself in melancholy remembrance of the time when the whole continent was untouched. These plays were mournful elegies, and it would be easy to call them proof of national hypocrisy. But a whole people will hardly pore over books and drive themselves to the theater for more than thirty years in order to build up an effective attitude which no one is at hand to see but themselves; nor will they do so to smother a collective conscience. Like the novels of Cooper, the plays were immensely popular; and their elegiac sentiment surged up in a region where a more realistic view might have been expected to prevail, in the West. It was there that the legendary Indian strutted and declaimed and mourned with the greatest vigor, on small rude stages, before audiences of small farmers and back-woodsmen. He seemed an improbable and ghostly ancestor.

3

THE romantic ardor with which the American gazed at the Indian was in strange contrast with the chill or comic regard which he fixed upon the Revolutionary heroes. For the most part these were overlooked. Hundreds of patriotic plays were written from the Revolution onward; their considerable bulk forms a literature; but only a meager number were acted, and those that appeared had a way of becoming circuses or farces. Israel Putnam was a favored subject, and he seems to have been chosen less for his exploits in the Revolution than for his reputation for wry humor. During the French and Indian war, according to an almanac story, Putnam stirred the jealousy of a British officer, who finally sent him a challenge. "He came to Putnam's tent, found him seated on a small keg quietly smoking his pipe, and demanded to know what communication, if any, Putnam had to make. 'Why, you see,' said Put, 'I'm but a poor miserable Yankee, that never fired a pistol in my life, and you must perceive, major, that if we fight with pistols you will have an unfair advantage. Here are two powder kegs—I have bored a hole and inserted a slow match in each; so if you'll just be good enough to seat yourself there, I will light the matches, and he who dares sit the longest shall be called the bravest fellow.' " The matches burned slowly. Putnam—the "old wolf"—was imperturbable, the British officer distraught. Finally when the fire was within an inch of the kegs he dashed away. The kegs were filled with onions.

Such episodes embroidered the patriotic plays, crowding noble deeds off the boards. Putnam became a comic Yankee, when he was not astride a trick horse performing as in a circus. The equestrian play grew increasingly popular and

116

soon merged into the spectacle, employing Oriental tales of gorgeous coloring and picturing such fabulous characters as Timor the Tartar, Ali Baba, and El Hyder. As the scene widened the talk grew less, and the singing heroes of melodrama appeared. The Yankee, the backwoodsman, the minstrel, who had begun in brief interludes or afterpieces, now often usurped the larger part of a performance. Dancing was abundant. The theater became lighter and lighter in the late '30's and early '40's; and its whole mode was large and legendary. The staple characters in English low comedy, Dr. Pangloss, Mawworm, and Jeremy Diddler, were made to lean heavily toward the eccentric, even when drawn by accomplished English actors. They became fabulous figures, to match the American trio or the fantastic Indian.

"It was capital, but you must not be so quiet: give them more bustle," said a critic to Tyrone Power. "You must paint a little broader, my dear fellow," said another. "You're too natural for them; they don't feel it." Drawing grew broad, and steadily took on exuberance.

Theatricals swung into comedy as if under the direction of a popular impulse. Again emotion was submerged. Emotion had never been deeply grounded in this theater; the appeal had never been humanly comprehensive. The lyrical sweep was never included, the passion of love never revealed. The pitch of the dark emotions had been kept high; and this pitch was easily shattered.

Vicissitudes which naturally beset actors in a rude country furthered the movement into burlesque. When the hero of a tragedy fell in death with part of his body extended off stage so that he might play his own death music on the fiddle some of the audience was bound to see the double accomplishment. One company had a prompter who could both simulate a marble statue in *Don Juan* and dance hornpipes, and so great was the popularity of his hornpipes that, still a statue in Spanish white, he would come downstage in haste to dance. Inevitably the glamour of *Don Juan* diminished as the hornpipe progressed.

Crossing the Chattahoochee from Alabama to Georgia in the early '30's, a company found the streets of Columbus filled with Creeks, and the manager decided to employ twenty-four of them as the Indians of the Peruvian army in *Pizarro*, but the play did not proceed smoothly. When the company back-stage, the carpenters and scene-shifters, gave their customary shout at the advance of Rolla, the Creeks answered with a prolonged war-whoop, and raised this whenever the audience applauded, and again when Rolla addressed his army in the Temple of the Sun. When the high priest, followed by the priests and virgins, began the invocations, the Creeks responded with a low, mournful humming sound which speedily took on threatening undertones and rose to a war song. When the chorus began to sing the Creeks broke into a war dance in which the King and Rolla were constrained to join until the sweat poured off their bodies, while the virgins dashed from the stage and locked themselves in their dressing-rooms.

4

To sustain burlesque something more than grotesquerie is needed. Satire enters into its attentions; once a territory is invaded by burlesque, all its objects are likely to look puffed and stretched, pinched and narrowed. But pure satire stands aloof, while burlesque wholly possesses its subject and wears the look of friendship.

Through the '40's and '50's the spirit of burlesque was abroad in the land like a powerful genie let out of a windbag, finding a wealth of yielding subjects. The legitimate theater came to a standstill; and many reasons were found for this condition. The rise of Fanny Ellsler and of the dancers who came after her—Taglioni among them—was mentioned as causing a deflection. The lecture mania was cited, the panic of 1837, and the burning of the National Theatre in New York about the same time, which was to have brought a fresh theatrical inspiration from England. But while all these circumstances may have had their effect, while dancing became almost an obsession throughout the country, while the great cascades of oratory and talk in the lecture system seemed to flow for an endless popular delight, none of these could quite have thwarted the progress of the legitimate theater if any strong impulse had underlain it. The truth was that a vigorous burlesque had usurped the stage, turning the serious drama upsidedown, and joining with the comic array provided by the Yankee, the backwoodsman, and the Negro minstrel.

The pioneer in burlesque was William Mitchell, who had been a strolling actor in England, playing at fairs and country places. He established a neat and showy little theater in New York, the Olympic, at the end of the '30's, with red curtains at the windows and a balcony in front, and drew an audience which was almost wholly masculine. The performances took on the air of intimate parties; the audiences joined in all the choruses; every one knew the company. Mitchell collected about him a merry lot of actors who remained with him for years; and he led them off with his own funny faces and a gift for tragic acting that made a base for his burlesque of romantic tragedy and romantic opera.

Every popular opera found its way to the boards of the Olympic in squeezed and distorted form, every romantic play. *Lucia* became *Lucy Did Sham a Moor* and *Lucy Did Lam a Moor*. Dancers like Fanny Ellsler provided endless themes for entertainment. Mitchell usually impersonated them himself with mincing steps and an enormous bustle. Seizing upon the passion for Byron and the new vogue of minstrelsy at a single stroke, he produced *Man-Fred* in partial blackface, with a metaphysical Negro chimney-sweep for the hero, who may have been taken over from Rice's portrait of a philosophizing Negro bootblack, or who may have been created out of the extraordinary vogue of a Negro sweep song then popular in New York drawing-rooms. When the vogue of Dickens was at its height in the early '40's he produced *Boz; or, a Man Over-bored*. When

Dickens appeared on his lecture tour he concocted *Boz in America*, and travestied both the man and his writings. Yankee peddlers, the Cape Cod sea serpent, the Feejee mermaid, little Thumb, mingled with the distorted romantic figures of the operas and plays.

Mitchell caught and punctured every current wild obsession, romantic or merely comic, every theme which the current American fancy had taken up with its familiar extreme fervor. He revealed all the characteristic native capacity for plunging headlong into new enthusiasms. He was in fact burlesquing the American public as well as its preoccupations. And the American public responded with another headlong response, as if any extravagant romantic emotion could sweep it away, even though this emotion was changed into satirical grotesquerie, or as if after all its responses were fickle, and popular suffrages had been on the point of turning from these familiar obsessions. There could be no doubt of the new, destructive enthusiasm. Mitchell crowded his tiny theater for ten years. His burlesques became current coin of the theater all over the country; and when by one of those sudden changes frequently seen in theatrical history his career came to an end, the mode of burlesque was unshaken. It was freshly picked up by two other artists, Burton and Brougham, whose talents were joined at the Chambers Street Theatre in the late '40's.

Of the two Burton was probably the finer actor, losing himself in his portrayals and possessing a gift for satirical impersonation which left the original elements of character intact. But Brougham, who devised the sketches and plays, possessed that comic gravity which has been called the crowning conceit of burlesque. Each could improvise at random and at comical length, twisting a play to new effects offhand. Once they pretended to make a play before the audience, at the end gravely discussing what they should do to finish it off. When their leading lady suddenly failed them one evening they took turns playing her part, stepping out of their own, and adding extravagance to extravagance. Brougham added a strong Irish flavor, but Irish humor had already shown a way of becoming native humor; and both Brougham and Burton—who was English—had come to the United States as young men, and they remained for a long career. They counted themselves Americans; and their absorption of native themes and native modes seemed complete.

They produced a lusty, gay, and savage humor, full of barbs flung at the current scene, full of native extravagance. Through their incidental satire many of the cults of the day at last toppled into ridicule. They burlesqued the theories of free love which had appeared in some of these; they burlesqued the new woman's rights movement; they were always trenching upon the political scene. Their sharp sallies were often made in song, and set to familiar country tunes like "Wait for the Wagon" and "Rosin the Beau," thus wearing the guise of simple innocence.

Their great theme was the false romanticism of American sentiment for the Indian. Forrest's *Metamora* had already become a noisy *Metaroarer* on the lesser burlesque stage. Brougham used the violent declamatory style of Forrest and burlesqued it, but he produced a full-length satire on the windy Indian-worship, transforming the last of the Wampanoags into the last of the Pollywogs, and adding a mass of other characters, Whiskeetoddi, Anaconda, Tapiokee, and others who appeared

> With rifle, belt, plume, moccasin, and all,
> Just as you see them at a fancy ball.

An Englishman named Fitzdaddle entered the forest with a parasol over his shoulder, and Metamora slowly killed a bear to the tune of "Ole Dan Tucker." Metamora was in fact a ridiculous mingling of the trio of comic characters; and the artificial touch in American sentiment about the Indian was unerringly pointed.

This burlesque made only a tentative approach to a rich subject. In his *Pocahontas* Brougham handled it again with more driving satire. Said John Smith on meeting Powhatan—

> Most potent, grave, and reverend old fellow—
> To use the words of that black wight Othello,
> My very noble and approved good savage,
> That we came out here your lands to ravage
> Is most true: for this you see us banded.

Powhatan replied—

> I must confess, sweet sir, that you are candid.
> You'll probably excuse us if we doubt it.
> Pray how, sir, do you mean to set about it?

Smith—

> Easy enough: we have full powers to treat.

Powhatan—

> If that's the case we'll take some whiskey neat.

The pun widened to travesty, and Powhatan burst into song to the air of "Widow Machree"—

> O, wid a dudhien I can blow away care,
> Ochone! wid a dudhien!
> Black thoughts and blue devils all melt into air,
> Ochone! wid a dudhien!
> If you're short any day
> Or a note have to pay,
> And you don't know the way
> To come out of it clean,
> From your head and your heart
> You can make it depart,
> Ochone! wid a dudhien!

According to the prelude the play was derived from an antique Norwegian poem discovered in the vest pocket of a man in armor dug up near Cape Cod by a Chevalier Viking, Long Fellow, containing several square yards of

verse, a fragment of which was subjoined to show the peculiar Finnish—

> Ask you—how about these verses?
> Whence this song of Pocahontas,
> With its flavor of Tobacco,
> And the Stincweed—the Mundungus,
> With its pipe of Ole Virginny,
> With its echo of the Breakdown,
> With its smack of Bourbonwhiskey,
> With the twangle of the Banjo;
> Of the Banjo—the Goatskinnet,
> And the Fiddle—the Catgutto,
> With the noisy Marrowbonum.
> By one JONSMITH it was written,
> JONSMITH, the valiant Soldier,
> Sailor, Buccaneer, Explorer,
> Hero, Trader, Colonizer,
> Gent, Adventurer, Commander,
> Lawyer, Orator, and Author,
> Statesman, Pioneer, and Bagman.

Jonsmith became one of a peaceable crew of filibusters who
meant to take possession of the transatlantic region.

> Now the natives knowing nothing
> Of the benefits intended
> By this foreign congregation,
> Who had come so far to show them
> All how much they'd been mistaken,
> In what darkness they were dwelling,
> And how much obliged they were to
> These disinterested people

Who had journeyed to enlighten
Their unfortunate condition,
Through those potent, triunited
Anglo-Saxon civilizers,
Rum, Gunpowder, and Religion.

Now the natives, as I mentioned,
Didn't see the joke precisely
In the way it was expected,
They believing, simple creatures,
They could manage their own matters
Without any interference—
Thought the shortest way to settle
Those gratuitous adverses
Would be quietly to knock them
On the head, like Bulls of Bashan.

The action included many digressions of plot, and minor travesties. Showers of puns and *doubles entendres* fell, underlined in the text and no doubt sufficiently stressed as spoken, yet never appearing as palpable hits, for they came in enormous abundance, tumbling one over another; they effervesced and overflowed; they often chimed and were musical. Powhatan exclaimed, "Sergeant at arms, say what alarms the crowd? Loud noise annoys us, why is it allowed?" Powhatan was a musical monarch, opening before the arrival of Smith with a song to the air of "The King of the Cannibal Islands"; he was "a crotchety monarch, in fact a semi-brave," and at a crucial point in his trial Smith was bound over to a strong chord in the orchestra.

126

STROLLERS

When Smith and his companions were about to die some one cried—

> Hang on the outer wall, the interlopers!
> All: Hang them! Hang them!
> Smith: What fault have I committed? Halt!
> Powhatan: Ha! Do you falter?
> Smith: I fain would halt before I reach the halter.
> That cord is not my line in any sense.
> I'd rather *not* be kept in such suspense.

The major theme was never lost, and spread into a hundred timely ramifications. Toward the end, with a long view down the years, the predatory purpose of the American invaders was shown as continuing—

> Grab away
> While you may
> In this game, luck is all
> And the prize
> Tempting lies
> In the rich City Hall.
> Grab away
> While you may,
> Every day there's a job.
> It's a fact,
> By contract
> All intact you may rob.

A procession bearing glass ballot boxes was shown, and allusions were made to the Erie gamble.

In *Columbus el Filibustero*, the expedition to America

was made a gold-grabbing affair, and the Almighty Dollar figured largely, "in regal robes, promiscuously attended."

> And all will you see kneel,
> Oh, all will you see kneel
> Before the great and mighty dollar,
> All will *you* see kneel—

sang the chorus to the air of "Lucy Neal." When Columbus returned to Spain from his first voyage Ferdinand knighted him—

> That in stealing gold you may not cease,
> Receive the order of the Golden Fleece.

As a burlesque, *Columbus el Filibustero* was more cynically pointed than the others; it was also more human. Columbus was made a figure of dreams, then of pathos, as he went back and forth to America at Ferdinand's bidding. Yet this conception of the character was never unleashed from the satirical pattern; and the movement of the whole piece had the accustomed freedom and flow of all of Brougham's burlesques. When Columbus, old and tired, was told to kneel before Ferdinand—"The rules demand it"—he replied, "I can't, my constitution wouldn't stand it." Here too was a great cascade of puns. "The catbird's song must be the wild sea-mew." Columbus sang mock Italian bravura in pigeon Italian, and the tone of the opening chorus overflowed with easy urgency—

> Hail! oh, King of Arragon!
> Reign! oh, princely paragon!

128

Down upon your marrowbone,
  Long live the King!
Monarch mightier is he, sir,
Than Joe Smith or Julius Caesar,
Brigham Young or Nebuchadnezzar,
  Long live the King!
And hail to Isabella, too,
For she's a right good fellow too,
And a right good tune to bellow to
  Is long live the Queen!

In satirical quality and breadth Brougham's three major burlesques will bear comparison with the Gilbert and Sullivan operas, which they preceded by years. There were few national follies and foibles that remained untouched by this copious and candid art. Brougham lacked a composer with whom to work in duo; yet this was not altogether a disadvantage at the time, because the popular airs with which he threaded his pieces were fresh; they floated the unfamiliar satire, and afforded odd inflations and contrasts. It was in bulk and continuous purpose that Brougham failed. Beset by an abiding genius, versatility, he could write any kind of comedy well enough to win production; and along with this ease ran an uncurbed ambition. Brougham wanted to be a great manager as well as a great comedian and a great comic writer, and his fortunate alliance with Burton, who had a gift for management, was broken.

A thirsty public would have accepted burlesque after

burlesque of the satirical quality of *Pocahontas* and *Columbus el Filibustero*. In little towns along the Ohio, in the cloth and paper camps of California, the mingled songs, dancing, quips, and enveloping satire aroused riotous responses; and their spirit proved contagious. Briefer and less trenchant pieces were contrived by minor writers in the Mississippi valley. Blackface nonsense made the strain inevitable in minstrelsy. A blackface *Fra Diavalo* overflowed with plantation melodies and jigs and breakdowns. Wild oddities appeared in the phantom chorus of a minstrel *Somnambula*.

The great consistent theme through a decade or more of burlesque remained that romantic emotion which had belonged to the popular mind through its formative years, flowing far afield, as a sense of romance is likely to do. Romantic tragedy, romantic opera, and the ballet, penetrating even into the backwoods, had been a mode of expression and a sign. Scott, Byron, Dickens, had stirred the familiar romantic sense of the past and of distance. The melancholy wraith of the vanished Indian showed a crude romantic spirit at work on native ground.

American audiences enjoyed their own deflation; they liked the boldness of attack, the undisguised ridicule. Once again, as in the portraiture of the comic trio, the subject was essentially themselves. But their strange Indian-worship was so thoroughly riven as never again to enjoy popular consideration. Even the nascent romantic picture of the American as builder and colonizer was punctured.

This lawless satire was engaged in a pursuit which had occupied comedy in the native vein elsewhere. As if it were willful and human, the comic spirit in America had maintained the purpose—or so it seemed—to fulfill the biblical cry running through much of the revivalism of the time: to "make all things new." It was a leveling agent. The distant must go, the past be forgotten, lofty notions deflated. Comedy was conspiring toward the removal of all alien traditions, out of delight in pure destruction or as preparation for new growth.

Yet the burlesque of this long period could only have been created by a temper steeped in romanticism. If it punctured romantic feeling, it kept a breathless comic emotion of its own. Invading current fantasies, it employed fantastical forms. Indian myths might traipse across the stage in grotesque and balloonlike guises, but they only became mythical again with a broader and livelier look. It was not a realistic spirit that was abroad. The world of burlesque was still the familiar native world of phantasmagoria.

5

OTHER strollers besides those of the stage appeared in this long era, with an expression drawn in similar curves. These were the revivalists, the groups of millennium-seekers, the believers in cults. In a fundamental and not irreverent sense they belonged to the theater; they too followed the arc of romantic feeling; and they moved toward comedy, even toward burlesque.

In the West the first era of pioneering had lacked direct religious influences, and the backwoodsman had become subject to suggestions of place and of Indian *mores* which affected him deeply. At the end of the eighteenth century not a tenth of the population in Kentucky had religious affiliations. But the heritage of these people was profoundly religious, and their emotion knew no bounds when at last proselytizing began among them. They were of the race which produced the leaping, heel-cracking comic figures who proclaimed their identity with the lightning and the alligator. They joined in the orgiastic forest revivals on the Red River and the Gaspar River, shouting and pleading to be bathed in the blood of the Lamb, and bending, writhing, jerking, falling, barking, and creeping over the ground like the creatures of the wilderness. Periodic revivals sprang up; in these the cruder expression was left behind; and a free ritual developed with wailing and singing and approaches to the anxious bench and the massive pageantry of nocturnal baptisms.

Comedy was enacted there, a rude and violent form of the divine comedy. The restraining bonds were broken of that rigorous faith which seemed a solid American inheritance from the older civilizations. With its inner conflicts and cataclysmic formula of the human relation to God, Calvinism was profoundly dramatic. The individual was the least and meanest of all things, yet he found the weight of the everlasting wrath upon him and so gained stature. In the new resilient faiths now rapidly springing up this strict and somber drama was left further and further behind. Terror remained in the theme of death and in the prolonged anxieties which were often a prelude to peace, but the movement was away from creeds and close formulas, toward improvisation, rapturous climaxes, happy assurances, and a choral strain. In the revivals of Methodism and the other free new faiths all was generic, large, and of the crowd; in the end all was wildly hopeful. Rhapsody was common; the monologue in the experience meeting unfolded those inner fantasies toward which the native mind was tending in other, quite different aspects of expression, not in the analytic forms of Calvinism, but as pure unbridled fantasy and exuberant overflow.

The pattern of comedy appeared again in the innumerable cults which sprang up in the '30's and '40's as from some rich and fertile seeding-ground. Religious and social traditions were flung to the four winds. The perfectionists declared that the bondage of sin was non-existent and that the Millennium had already begun. At Oneida the bonds of earthly marriage were broken. Spiritualism proposed to break the bonds of death. The theme of death, which had been a deep preoccupation in the life of the pioneer, was repeated by these cults, with a fresh and happy outcome. Life was to be prolonged, the Millennium had arrived; in the state of perfection death might never come at all. Most of the new religious communities created almost overnight in the '30's and '40's agreed to release mankind from sin, poverty, or mortal care. They all possessed formulas, religious, economic, or social; and they all anticipated conclusions such as the world had never known. Triumph was their note. Biblical proof was adduced to show that the Americans were a chosen people, that the continent—even the Mississippi valley—was the predestined scene for the Second Coming and that the happy thousand years were to begin there. Mormonism with its legendary groundwork of Indian and Jewish history, stretching backward in magnificence, seized upon the conviction.

Hysterical, wrapped in a double sense of national feeling and religious conviction, the believers passed into moods of wildest exaltation. "New, new . . . make all things new." The enchanting cry resounded through all this ecstasy of faith. Many of the believers exemplified their conviction by singing, processions, and a continual migration. Many of them indulged in costume, the Millerites garbing themselves in heavenly white, the Shakers wearing dim colors which were dramatic in their negation, others in more varied uniforms. Some wore garlands. Some danced, in slow intense jerking steps, the Shakers on their way down the aisles of their churches, others more wildly in religious rites. Among the secular communities—with their infusion of a spirit which was basically religious—singing and dancing were almost a rule.

Among all these cults a latent humor broke out; this was clear in the names which they chose or accepted, such as the placidly humorous variations on Harmony and the grotesque nomenclature of the Shakers, Groaners, Come Outers, New Lights, Hard Shell Baptists, and Muggletonians. Brigham Young could thunder an assertion of his power one moment and the next with a twinkle declare that he was a prophet, as if he considered the title comic. A wide level of comic feeling had been established, sometimes infused with pliant hope, most often with exuberance. Frequently it was hard to tell when burlesque was involved, when fakery, when a serious intention. The basic feeling was romantic, but it crested into a conscious gaiety which raced beyond the romantic. Even in the most ponderous of these assertions there was something light-hearted.

Once again personal emotion was submerged in a coarse and crescent patterning of communal emotion; and the flight was toward legend. Around the simple outline of the divine comedy these people continually wove innumerable small new fables and beliefs. Once again, too, the movement was toward the theater. The orgiastic forest revivals with their pagan spirit and savage manifestations bore a not altogether distant resemblance to the Eleusinian mysteries out of which the Greek drama had developed. A fantastic basic ritual was often present in later cults, such as has been a prelude to the theater or the drama among primitive peoples. A minor religious theater could have been drawn from the celebrations of almost any one of these new sects. All their modes were outward, rhapsodic, declamatory, full of song, verging upon the dance, adorned with symbolic costume, moving toward that oratory which was half burlesque. Most of these effects were shaped for or with an audience: that is, they were theatrical. Among the Mormons a direct alliance with the theater was made. At Nauvoo, Joseph Smith encouraged dancing and theatricals, and Brigham Young played the part of the high priest in an early Mormon performance of *Pizarro*. After the hegira to Utah, Young introduced theatricals as a staple element in the Mormon scheme, and at the same time made a firm rule against tragedy, saying that his people had known tragedy enough, and thus following a sequence which had prevailed within American attitudes, that of flight away from oppressive circumstance into comedy.

In bands these strollers moved and moved again, traveling toward the West for the most part, like the clusters of home-seekers and the defeated Indian tribes and the people of the theater, until it seemed that the image of the processional must become the single lasting, significant image in the new country. Mixing with the greater migrations, they belonged almost consistently to that stratum of American life out of which popular legends and popular comedy had sprung. The early revivalism had arisen in the deep backwoods. In the Southwest the Negro had often joined in the revivals; in New England it was among country people that the new cults took shape; many may be traced to the hillsides of Vermont and New Hampshire. If a few were first shaped abroad, they all took on a native extravagance. Some had as brief an existence as a popular tale or a popular legend, some an even briefer span: but they joined to make a loosely striated underply of comedy which ran through the life and consciousness of the entire country through the first half of the century.

V. THE COMIC POET

FAR from having no childhood, the American nation was having a prolonged childhood, extended as the conditions for young and uncertain development were extended and spatially widened by the opening of wilderness after wilderness, the breaking down of frontier after frontier. The whole movement westward had a youthful illusory character, like one of those blind migrations of other peoples over the older continents. Popular expression had taken forms that have belonged to the childhood of nations: singing, dancing, brief story-telling, a ritualistic celebration. Humor had kept that prime resilience which is more than half physical. Character was drawn in simple and legendary outline, both on and off the stage, in and out of current story-telling.

This primitive drawing was maintained as though some essential search were under way for an intrinsic substance. Other characters were sketched beside the comic trio. The quicksilver talent of Tyrone Power had brought a handful of comedies into vogue in the early '30's, which were Irish in scene, glossy and romantic, and full of dancing and singing. In the '40's with the renewed movement for Irish freedom came Irish plays that were nationalistic and historical. Presently these were broken up into portrait sketches of the Irish boy and the Irish girl, set in America;

and a few slight stories and sketches drew them into happy conjunction with Yankee men or women, creating an emblem of that mergence of national types which had been seen elsewhere. Irish humor had always had a way of becoming American humor on American soil: it seemed that a new admixture might be on the way. But the effect was transitory; the Irish type—slow to appear—remained distinct, and was to be seen in many guises down the years, as Gallagher and Shean and a host of others offered new sketches. The character was not deepened or explored, but remained as a kind of puzzled, offhand experiment.

Still another figure emerged at the end of the '40's who was undoubtedly Irish in general ancestry but who soon merged with the riffraff of the New York streets and water fronts. This was the "b'hoy," known by his swagger, his soaplocks, his fireman's red flannel shirt. In the stage portraits he was Mose; he bobbed up everywhere like the Yankee, in California, in China, though he belonged unmistakably to New York. Impudent, full of racy and belligerent opinion, he appeared in the public view at a moment when national feeling had gone rampant with the outbreak of the Mexican War, with the acquisition of the far western empire of California, and the sudden discovery there of gold. In Mose was centered all the arrogance of an acute national self-esteem. He bragged, he was always on top, he waved a national flag whose texture was particularly coarse, and gained his constituency by this means and by a gutter wit.

Whether the "b'hoy" was drawn directly from characters on the New York streets or whether similar characters took on bolder outlines in life when they saw themselves egregiously celebrated on the stage can never be known. The diarists, the memoir makers, the writers of autobiographies, either had their heads in the air or their minds fixed upon their own portraits, or they feared the growing tendency to reveal the American as a common fellow. At least they did not trouble to notice city scalawags. But the living character existed, and rose to an acute self-consciousness. Perhaps because the theater had patronized the "b'hoys," the "b'hoys" patronized the theater, taking up posts in the galleries. Their hisses and outspoken comments were the terror of actors; their applause was a coveted guarantee of success.

Their devotion to the muscular histrionics of Edwin Forrest was particularly strong; in the Astor Place riots they took a cue from Forrest's jealousy of Macready and gave impetus to a current fury of anti-British feeling for which Macready was only the accidental stimulus. No doubt the riots were maneuvered for the benefit of an ambitious political group who saw an opportunity to bring themselves into the foreground, but the situation soon passed into the realm of hysterical popular fantasy. When Macready had been showered with eggs and the first act of *Macbeth* had been played in dumb show, when the theater had been cleared by the police and the militia stationed outside with orders to fire, the familiar consciousness of the British rose to monstrous heights; in the end thirty people were killed. "WORKINGMEN! Shall Americans or English rule this city?" ran an irrelevant query on hundreds of posters. "Fire!" yelled a grimy one who knelt with a stone between his knees. He tore open the bosom of his red shirt with an opulent gesture. *"Fire into this!"* he shouted. "Take the life of a free-born American for a bloody British actor! *Do it!* Ay, you darsen't!"

Theatricalism had run to a considerable extreme in the American character with this exhibition. But Mose was a transient figure; by the middle '50's he had ceased to exist on the stage. He had made one strong divergence from the accumulated American myth: he was urban. The Irishman of the stage gradually became urban. The comical German was soon drawn in the Hans Breitmann ballads and on the stage; and he too belonged to the cities. The Jew followed some years later, and was always urban. Popular portraiture seemed to move farther and farther away from the earlier characters. Yet all these figures possessed certain simple traits in common with the comic trio. Like the Yankee, the backwoodsman, the Negro, they sprang from humble life; like the trio they represented contentious elements in the American scene. They were all on the off-side; all were looked down upon or scorned by some one, often by whole sections of society, as the Yankee had been scorned by the backwoodsman and the backwoodsman by the Yankee. They were disparate characters, and warring;

141

they formed the hard and bony understructure of the nation.

The pioneer mythologizing habit remained unbroken. These new figures were no nearer the intimate and human than were the ritualistic figures of Negro minstrelsy. They wore the same air of masquerade; comic triumph was their creed. Though they never rivaled the original trio in scope or popularity or in long life, they made a cluster of small half-deities who embodied persistent obsessions.

2

WOMEN had played no essential part in the long sequence of the comic spirit in America. Sally Ann Thunder Ann Whirlwind Crockett could stand as a symbol: the women were gross counterparts of the men. An exception lay beyond and somewhat above these figures in the shadowy but persistent rise of the American bluestocking within the Yankee fables. The heroine of *The Contrast* was noticeably fond of reading; and against all tradition in that anterior English comedy which might have been an influence, this habit of hers was presented without ridicule. In the early American view ladies who read were not considered strange or amusing; they were in fact regarded with serious reverence.

In the Downing papers another bluestocking appeared in one of the rural cousins; and Aunt Nabby offered a plaintive remonstrance. "I don't believe you are happy for trying to no so much; ever since you took to study I see you don't laugh half so hearty as you used to, and you look sober three times as often. I'm afraid you'll be a spoilt girl for the country, Sarah." The reproach was unheeded; and the slight studious touch was repeated elsewhere. A few of the heroines of the later fables of the contrast exhibited a modicum of learning; and Gertrude in *Fashion* was a governess.

Feminine culture thus rose on the American horizon in a cloud no larger than a lady's book; and though this heroine was not comic she was placed in the realm of comedy. Those who believe that life copies art or that art is premonitory may perhaps find there intimations of a phenomenon which later was to come into enormous bloom, with a forecast of a division in the national temper: for the lady in these fables was lost in culture and the presiding masculine genius stood apart from it. The Yankee had little or nothing to do with these learned ladies. They belonged for the most part to a remote sentimental story in which he had but a small share.

Obviously social comedy could not develop when women remained shadowy, serious figures. Nor could social comedy develop among a citizenry of half-gods. Mythologies do not lend themselves to small or delicate comic intricacies. A human society is required for social comedy, and none had been imaged for the native view. No doubt societies existed in provincial towns like Salem or Newburyport or Lexington, or in such entrenched older cities as Boston and

Philadelphia and Richmond, but these were never drawn for the imagination; they remained at best few in number and widely scattered. Along the wide western trackways no social structure could be formed lasting and secure enough to hold an integrated group; there was neither time nor mood for that leisurely sinking of the plumb-line which yields a knowledge of the slighter human foibles and idiosyncrasies. In more than one sense the comic trio remained as emblems of the national life, since they appeared always as single figures, or merely doubled and multiplied, never as one of a natural group, never as part of a complex human situation, always nomadic.

So the English social comedy offered by James Wallack at the beginning of the '50's was a novelty. Wallack had cherished a vision through fire and flood and hardship as he traveled up and down the Mississippi like any gambling adventurer, taking chances with casual companies in ramshackle theaters, playing before flatboatmen and backwoodsmen and desperadoes drawn from the levee at New Orleans or Natchez-under-the-Hill. Suave and handsome, wearing fawn color and exquisite mustaches, a pattern of elegant manners, he was convinced even in these surroundings that others like him would come to life on the stage, creating a picture of charming amenities. He proved the worth of patience and fancy. In 1851 he found himself in New York with a theater of his own.

Probably no society was ever so finicking-finished as that which now existed on paper in the ready-made lines.

144

Bulwer-Lytton seemed the many-handed author of these plays: if he did not write them, he inspired them; they were already popular in England. They belonged to comedy because of an effect of high spirits and wit, and because of smooth triumph of the hero and heroine over adverse circumstances. Above all they pictured a fashionable society, self-contained and aloof, in which both men and women had a natural part. Women—unstudious and charming—flourished there. Many of them all but centered upon the character of women.

The whole array might have been expected to provoke ridicule in an American audience. *Fashion* was still being well received, with its broadside of satire directed against foreign civilizations and fashionable notions. The fine English creatures of Wallack's plays belonged to the group which had been touched with burlesque in every American portrayal from the early Dimple to Lord Fitzdaddle. But a complete reversal took place, one of those capricious reversals not uncommon in American feeling. These English ladies and gentlemen of an artificial world were received with applause and even rapture. Shabby minor actors played the parts in small rough theaters in the Mississippi valley. Revivals began of the older English social comedy such as *The School for Scandal* and *She Stoops to Conquer*, with their air of splendor.

Perhaps the tension created by British criticism was somewhat relaxed in this later day, though it had by no means disappeared. The basic tie had always been binding; now at last it seemed indirectly acknowledged. Yet the deepest reason for the warm reception of these pictorial plays may have come from the fact that they represented a society, when the American effort to achieve a society had been scattered and ineffectual. This effort had taken the crudest forms, in the amalgamation created by a gross comedy, in the communal associations of the revivals: it had been in the main ineffectual or transitory, but it had existed none the less. Here at last lay the happy semblance in easy patterns, offering a sense of completion.

The sequence initiated by Wallack was continued, as if the pleasure in completed outlines endured: but the plays were never again to have the pristine freshness of the first few years or to command so ardent an enthusiasm. The concerns of a vigorous comic spirit remained elsewhere. In the midst of Wallack's portrayals a portent arose in *Our American Cousin*.

The old fable of the contrast lived again in this play, transferred to an English scene. It had been tried out in London with the Yankee in the habitual blue coat, red-striped trousers, and bell-crowned white hat. The English characters announced that their American relatives were of enormous height, with long black hair reaching down to their heels and with a dark copper-colored skin; they were said to fight with tomahawks and scalping-knives. Again the composite Yankee-backwoodsman appeared: "I'm Asa Trenchard, born in Vermont, suckled on the banks of Muddy Creek, about the tallest gunner, slickest dancer, and generally the loudest critter in the State." He called the butler "old shoat" and "old hoss"; when asked for his card he said he had a whole pack in his valise and if the butler liked, he would play a game of seven up. "I'm dry as a sap tree in August," he exclaimed with American candor and the habitual simile. Shaking drinks, he discussed the relative merits of brandy smash, cherry cobbler, whiskey skin, and Jersey lightning.

Jefferson played the "long, simple, uncouth, shrewd Vermonter," but a caricature of the foppish Englishman captured the play, Lord Dundreary, a lineal descendant of Dimple in *The Contrast*. Touch by extravagant touch Sothern built up the portrait, mincing, tripping, lisping, stuttering, hopelessly silly: Dundreary was indeed the largest, the most complete, the most finished, of all the delineations in a long sequence. His figure submerged the action and the other characters; even the Yankee was all but lost. Jefferson used a far more human touch than had hitherto been seen in Yankee portraiture; perhaps for this reason his acting failed to carry against the archetypal drawing of Sothern. The mythological had the greater hold; and the obsessive interest in the British character came again to the fore with the familiar derision and the implicit American triumph.

The American fancy returned with immense gusto to these familiar figments. Few plays in America have had such a run; Sothern acted his famous part almost without a break for more than ten years. Others captured the play, keeping the original version, with the Yankee as the large and archetypal figure. In 1865 the original play with the Yankee stress could still be made an occasion which the President would attend. It was at Ford's Theatre, watching *Our American Cousin*, that Lincoln was assassinated. Lincoln seems to have enjoyed its early passages as these unrolled before him. He would have liked the talk and the Yankee character with its backwoods admixture, for his own humor contained many of the same elements. In that dark and bitter era something of solace may have been created for him and for the public by the broad fantasy, the effect of reminiscence, the familiar tang.

3

WITH the wealth of tradition wrapped about the trio of comic figures and the inevitable Englishman, they might have belonged to a latter-day *commedia dell' arte*, joining in an eternal or even only a richly local comedy as puppets. But this would have required a close sense of situation. Instead, these figures took on a large and lawless air, as in *Our American Cousin*, avoiding situation almost altogether. Character in terms of extravagance or even extravaganza was still the major concern.

In the '50's extravaganza appeared that was most often a colored fairy tale of vast proportions, half poetry, half burlesque, as in *The Deep Deep Sea*, which was filled with Yankee tars, Yankee jokes, Yankee monologues, as well as by semi-mythical characters. Few of these pieces were memorable; they were likely to bulge, to overflow, to mount in one direction or another regardless of any single situation. They were dominated by the monologue, the song and dance, the enlarged portrait or caricature. They captivated their public by these diversions and by their gaiety.

The theater was still a truant mode, an accidental form, full of humor, fragmentary stories, legendary figures, persistent fantasies. Nothing in the way of American social comedy was created, nothing of realistic native portraiture. The native theater had slight traffic with the real world; its medium was a rude and incompleted poetry. Even its portraiture belonged to poetry—a broad and experimental comic poetry.

The wayward form spread, reaching far beyond the stage, making an habitual approach to new and old experiences. From the '30's onward, in those prophetic handbooks of wind and weather, the almanacs, a long series of brief tales appeared whose theme was strange adventure at sea. Some in a fashion hugged the coast, like that of the Flying Island off Kennebunk, considered the Elysian Fields of the Indians, or the stories which had to do with the treasure of Captain Kidd. But for the most part these tales described wild adventures on farther seas. There was an account of a specter whaleman in a small boat, pursuing the captain, who had left him to drown. Many brief, strange stories of the whale fishery were told. A marked drift of interest was shown in the South Seas, as in the later Crockett legends, which during the same period were reaching farther and farther toward the western horizon. An early story was told of a ship's crew who buried their boatswain on an island in the South Seas and later saw the skeleton walking off with his head under his arm. The adventures of Crockett's companion, Ben Hardin, with a mermaid, were matched by the tale of a mutineer who escaped to a submarine cave with a girl of the Tonga Islands, where he lived for many years amid fine mats, flowers, and succulent food, behind the green and watery wall.

Most of these tales had Yankees for heroes—a "captain from Salem," "a whaler from Nantucket." Most of them had a strong supernatural strain; some were tales of cruelty and horror. But they were likely to appear in close relationship with grotesque and comic fairy tales, like that of wharf rats—monstrous creatures—that manned a ship in a French port. Indian tales of terror were told: but even these often contained a submerged comedy. The whole nexus was embedded in a broad context which heightened comic and grotesque effects. The illustrative woodcuts might have been devised to fit half-comic fairy stories and legends. Sometimes these cuts took on the mythological scale, showing great precipices, or snakes that were gigantic monsters standing on their tails. The adventurer of the story would be grotesquely tiny, swung from a limb and decapitating the snake with a deliberate security. Here and there a drastic burlesque of the tall tale was shown in illustration.

In loose alliance with these brief tales were innumerable stories of the sea, headed by those of Dana; they joined again with those told by the Yankee tar on the stage, and made a large, broken cycle that moved from moods of terror to burlesque. The Crockett legends were coming into their freest growth at the same time, likewise forming a loose sequence all but linked with these scattered sea tales, for Crockett, like the mutineer, explored the floor of the ocean and penetrated to submarine caves in the South Seas.

4

LIKE the later tales of Crockett or with them, these sea stories moved toward the epical in magnitude of fancy and in their persistent stress upon the animistic or supernatural; they were comic or embedded in a matrix of comedy; and they possessed a rude but authentic poetry. But the coalescence into some single striking outline which seemed imminent did not take place, at least on popular levels; they remained, like the fantasies of the theater, in brief and ephemeral forms. They were part of a national habit of story-telling which had grown in compass through fifty years or more, and was seen now mixed with the commonest preoccupations. The tale was told for its own sake; it was a mode of conversation, of rejoinder, of offering farewell, as limits were reached.

This invincible habit reached one high climax, in the familiar stories of Lincoln. Stories ran through all his talk; many of them have been lost; hundreds have been saved. They make no sequence; yet they draw together memories and fantasies of a whole region—perhaps more than one region—and yield a hardy comic poetry that has become part of a popular lore.

When "The Hunters of Kentucky" began to stir an exhilarated spirit in the West, Lincoln was a boy of thirteen. Before he was twenty he went down the Mississippi in a flatboat; Mike Fink was still on the waters, and Crockett was coming into his first fame. One of Lincoln's first cases arose out of the opposition of the flatboatmen to the building of a bridge across the Mississippi; he must have heard their lingo and their tales from his boyhood through many years; like most of them he was a prime wrestler. As a young lawyer he joined in those meetings of the bar where its members and the gathering litigants exchanged tall stories and offered treasures of odd expression gathered from the backwoods. He pored over old joke-books, relished the stories and songs of Negro minstrels, and liked such primitive sports as cock-fighting. He possessed, moreover, those strangely mixed emotions which seemed to make a groundwork for the humor of the time and place. Even in youth his was that melancholy akin to romantic feeling, which was otherwise evoked and revealed in this region by the black romantic plays. He had the characteristic rebound, and often the quick move into depression again.

As a story-teller Lincoln used the entire native strain; he was consistently the actor, the mimic, caricaturist, and even a maker of burlesque. He used stories as weapons, matching his gifts against those of his adversaries, to mow them down, to win an audience. In a political contest in 1840 he mimicked his opponent on the platform in gesture and voice and walk and the smallest idiosyncrasies of manner with so bitter a ridicule that at the end the man was reduced to tears. At the bar he used the same tactics; his famous "Skin defendant" meant an outpouring of personal satire. Personal ridicule belonged to Lincoln's armory throughout his career, and was usually offered with the favorite guileless air. He used it as an habitual form of reply to admonitory speeches made to him by pretentious citizens during the war. "Why, Mr. Harvey, what tremendous great calves you have!" he exclaimed at the end of one of these. He took a bottle from a shelf and gave it to another gentleman who had long outstayed his time, a bald-headed man, and told him it would grow hair on a pumpkin. Lincoln contrived many jokes and stories about pumpkins and pumpkin-heads, and applied the rude metaphor when Seward and Chase were finally induced to resign. "Now I can ride, for I have a pumpkin in each bag."

Lincoln belonged indeed to a hardy and contentious school of humor, even though his manner could become elaborately gentle, as in his well-known ridicule of Douglas. "I had understood before that Mr. Douglas had been bound out to learn the cabinet-making business, which is all well enough, but I was not aware until now that his father was a cooper. I have no doubt, however, that he was one, and I am certain also that he was a very good one, for"—and here Lincoln bowed gravely to Douglas— "he has made one of the best whiskey casks I have ever seen."

Often Lincoln's stories were drawn from a homely back-woods experience, as in the story of the little boy at a backwoods school who blundered over reading the names of Shadrach, Meshach, and Abednego, and later set up a wail as he saw his turn approaching again. "Look there, marster—there comes them same damn three fellers again!" As Lincoln told the story he stood at a window overlooking Pennsylvania Avenue. As he finished he pointed to three men on their way to the White House. They were Sumner, Stevens, and Wilson. The episode became a metaphor; and the three figures, after Lincoln's slow reminiscence, took on rather more than human energy and size.

In Lincoln two of the larger strains of American comedy seemed to meet. He showed the western ebullience, even in brief fragments. He was likely to call a bowie-knife a scythe. He told of a fight in which a man fought himself out of one coat and into another. But his economy of speech and his laconic turn seemed derived from the Yankee strain that belonged to his ancestry, and no doubt was strengthened by many encounters with Yankees in the West. In a debate against the Mexican War he mentioned an Illinois farmer who declared, "I ain't greedy about land. I only want what jines mine." The narrow phrasing was Yankee; the concealed inflation belonged to the West. No doubt the Bible had a deep influence upon Lincoln's style in speech and in writing; perhaps it was from the Bible that he drew his deep-seated sense of fable and figure. The Bible may have been an anterior influence for all western speech and western story-telling, as for that which came out of New England. But its traces seem to have altered and re-shaped. Those metaphors abundant in all American comedy—"slick as a snake out of a black-skin"—came from a native earth; often they belonged to special regions. The form and the substance of American story-telling seem derived from the life out of which it sprang.

Poetry belonged to most of Lincoln's stories—an earthy poetry; he used the fable, the allegory, the tale grounded in metaphor. The artist was often at work there: but with all the praise bestowed upon them, upon the Gettysburg speech and in a less knowledgeable fashion upon his other writings, Lincoln has rarely been described as a literary figure. Irony lurks in this relinquishment. Yet perhaps the uncertain view has fitness, for his alliance with the simple and primitive phases of American life remained strong.

5

MEREDITH declared that to produce the comic poet, "a society of cultivated men and women is required, wherein ideas are current and the perception quick, that he may be supplied with matter and an audience. The semi-barbarism of merely giddy communities, and feverish emotional periods, repel him." The long period out of which American comedy sprang might easily be called feverish and emotional; and surely the communities within which it was produced were often giddy and semi-barbaric. No society of cultivated men and women had supplied a subject matter, though it might perhaps be granted that such a society had sometimes formed an audience.

"They have the basis of the Comic in them: an esteem for common sense," Meredith said of the English. So far as their humor was a sign the Americans had singularly little regard for common sense. American comedy might be aggressive or competitive; it often tied hard knots: but these elements were transformed by extravagant purposes.

"To know comedy you must know the real world," said Meredith: but American comedy had stepped outside the real world into that of fantasy.

For purposes of candor American comedy of the long period which stretched from the Revolution to the year 1860 may be described in a series of negations. Little of the purely human was contained within it, no deepening of the portrayal of character, nothing of a wide and interwoven web of thought and feeling where wit might freely play and the whole be gently lighted. Lincoln had revealed a human touch, but not too frequently; and this was shown for the most part toward the end of his life. Little or nothing of the philosophical element had developed even in Lincoln's stories. Satire had persistently appeared, sometimes directed toward highly focused ends, often showing only the flare of quick attack. This humor was highly competitive even in its quiet Yankee turns. To look upon the comedy of this time was to conclude that the Americans were a nation of wild and careless myth-makers, aloof from the burdens of pioneer life, bent upon proving a triumphant spirit. Yet comic these fantasies were in spite of the strictures of Meredith. If they failed to exhibit subtlety, fineness, balance, they had created laughter and had served the ends of communication among a people unacquainted with themselves, strange to the land, unshaped as a nation; they had produced a shadowy social coherence.

No comic poet had arisen on these levels; yet comic poetry was present in abundance, keeping that archetypal largeness which inheres in the more elementary poetic forms, with the inevitable slide into figure and that compact turn with unspoken implications which is the essence of poetic expression. Since it had been produced on many levels this comic poetry could not be called folk-poetry, but it had the breadth and much of the spontaneous freedom of a folk-poetry; in a rough sense its makers had been the nation. Full of experiment and improvisation, it did not belong to literature; but it used the primary stuffs of literature, the theater that lies behind the drama, the primitive religious ceremony that has been anterior to both, the tale that has preceded both the drama and the novel, the monologue that has been a rudimentary source for many forms. It constantly hung on the verge of a wider or deeper expression; yet it had been drawn back, as if magnetized, to the primitive and archaic. Its largest movement had been toward the epical, the heroic, or as it might have turned out, the mock heroic on the epical scale.

"To make up a heroic age there must be two factors," said Jane Harrison, "the new and the old; the young, vigorous warlike people must seize on, appropriate, in part assimilate, an old and wealthy civilization. It almost seems as if we might go a step further and say that for every great movement in art or literature we must have the same conditions, a contact of new and old, of a new spirit seizing or appropriated by an old established order." But the American comic legends, retrospective though they often were, could hardly be called old. As by a concerted impulse the American had cut himself off from the older traditions; the natural heritage of England and the continent had been cast away so far as a gesture could accomplish this feat. Perhaps the romanticism of the pioneer in relation to the Indian was part of that instinct by which new peoples attempt to enrich themselves from old; the Indian possessed established tribal unities which the American lacked. Even the American absorption of Negro lore may have been an effort in the same direction. But the Negro could offer only the faint and distorted reflection of a primal culture; and the quest for that of the Indian had been abortive.

Nothing of fertilizing contact between new and old occurred in this long period; the comic spirit remained a restless spirit, constantly moving into new areas. Perhaps there could be no large fulfillment until all frontiers were broken and the far western movement ended, until the land was peopled and the long slow process accomplished by which a nation becomes genuinely coherent. The wonder was that with so little to draw upon except its own momentum the comic impulse had moved constantly toward large outlines. To have formulated the simplest of traditions in the midst of a continual and heedless movement was a triumph. Comedy had pictured significant elements in the American character and consciousness. If it failed to attain its own completion it had created a roughly homogeneous groundwork out of which a wider expression, even a literature, might spring.

Such preludes have existed for all literatures, in songs and primitive ballads and a folk-theater and rude chronicles. Great writers have often drawn directly from these sources; inevitably genius embraces popular moods and formulations even when it seems to range furthest afield. From them literature gains immensely; without them it can hardly be said to exist at all. The primitive base may be full of coarse and fragmentary elements, full of grotesquerie or brutality; it may seem remote from the wide and tranquil concepts of a great art: but it provides materials and even the impulse for fresh life and continuance.

6

Writing in his journal in 1834 on the cultural dependence of America on England, Emerson verged upon
prophecy. "I suppose the evil may be cured by this rank-
rabble party, the Jacksonism of the country, heedless of
English and all literature—a stone cut out of the ground
without hands:—they may root out the hollow dilettantism
of our cultivation in the coarsest way, and the newborn
may begin again, to frame their world with greater advantage." Though the American scene had been drawn, an
American literature was hardly definable in 1834. Twitter-
ing poetasters and essayists, pretty story-tellers and studious
novelists were springing up by the dozen as if to refute
the classic charge that the Americans were coarse. There was
a great effervescence of what may be called the false-
feminine; a thin sweep of genteel writing, dreary to read,
easy to destroy by a touch of satire, came on like a weedy
second growth when forests are cut. The dilettantism mentioned by Emerson was to continue for many years. In the
field of criticism and even in the general view that involvement with British opinion which had appeared in the
Yankee fables was repeated: the difference was that at last
the tie was openly acknowledged; it was in fact made the
single binding tie. English literature was accepted as the
single great American heritage; and American literature was
counted one of its provinces.

Gentility was assuaging; it was a convenient means

by which recognition of native literature could be avoided. The American strain was new, recognition was not easy. Emerson himself never saw the difficulties involved in the establishment of an American sequence. He never saw the problems created by the weight and pressure of the inherit- ance—the many inheritances—from across the sea. In the end the dissevering gesture might not serve; that mingling of old and new of which Jane Harrison has written might prove essential. Yet even as he wrote, the rank- rabble party had found a voice, and Jacksonism was prov- ing to be something more than political. Popular comedy had arisen in full force at the beginning of the Jacksonian democracy. The strain was coarse, "a stone cut out of the ground without hands," but it was strong: Emerson him- self belonged to it.

Scant, fitful, sporadic as American literature has proved to be, it has had roots in common soil. Through the inter- weaving of the popular strain with that of a new expres- sion on other levels a literature has been produced which, like other literatures, is related to an anterior popular lore that must for lack of a better word be called a folk-lore. No literal sequence followed from the comic mythologies, no simple, orderly completion. Extravagantly and willfully, as though it were possessed by the very essence of the comic spirit, American literature turned aside from these materials for the most part, and discovered others of its own. The wealth of a native mythology was left behind, except as Melville used this, and a few other writers. Yet the Yankee, the backwoodsman in minstrelsy—though the influence there was less direct—the strollers of the theater and of the cults and revivals, the innumerable comic story-tellers and myth-makers, had made a groundwork for this literature. Its forms were those which had been slowly channeled out by humor: they were the monologue, the rhapsody, the tale. Its color was drawn from comedy or from that other dark mixed mood from which comedy had arisen in relief. Comic lore had been but little concerned with persons; its great preoccupation had been with types or the crowd; it had never been embedded in societies. In the same fashion American literature in this primary phase was for the most part unconcerned with closely drawn individuals or a stable group, though it often turned toward legendary characters. Improvisation had been abundant on popular levels: it spread again through literature; this remained incomplete, like a first venture. The epical scope was again approached—and transiently attained; with this went that tendency toward the conscious, the self-aware, toward the inner view, the inner fantasy, which belonged to the American comic sense. Genius necessarily made its own unaccountable revelations. Many external influences were at work. But the basic patterns, those flowing unconscious patterns of mind and feeling which create fundamental outlines in expression, had been amply developed in a native comic lore. The same character was at work on both levels.

VI. I HEAR AMERICA SINGING

EMERSON, using the true tone of the oracle, began his oral and communal monologues about the time when that plain Yankee figure, Jack Downing, assumed the rôle. He used the familiar homely imagery, "the meal in the firkin, the milk in the pan." His "Hitch your wagon to a star" has been linked with western hyperbole; and indeed he showed western influences, but he kept ties with his own region, even with the country prophets there. The Yankee comedians had stressed the homely experience; in the Yankee portraits lay a first promise of that native, homely art which Emerson sought to encourage. "I ask not for the great, the remote, the romantic; what is doing in Italy or Arabia; what is Greek art, or Provençal minstrelsy; I embrace the common, I explore and sit at the feet of the familiar, the low." Like the Yankee of the fables he tended to stress the nationalistic when he touched upon the American strain. His *American Scholar* was not a pursuit of truths which might belong to the scholar or artist anywhere. A national literature—not merely an ample literature—was to be evoked. He spoke of "the sere remains of foreign harvests." "We have listened too long to the courtly Muses of Europe." "Our age is retrospective," he insisted in admonition, trying to create that disseverance from the past which had long been a dominant purpose in American comedy.

Broadly he touched this comedy again in an upswerving and resilient faith akin to that of the cults and revivals; his alliance with these was strong even while he noted them with detachment; he has even been considered a kind of wellspring for beliefs which in his time and later have been transmuted into extreme and absurd forms. A full philosophy, full persuasion, a critique of American life, Emerson never offered. His communications were broken, lyrical, rhapsodic; his writing and speech had the air of improvisation. Even his poetry has the same air of incompletion: it is that of a born lyrist struggling with a strange language in a new country of the mind, and unable to find an unpremeditated freedom.

The lyrical strain had sounded in the midst of the Yankee lingo; the air of wonder, the rhapsodic speech were appearing in western tall talk. There too incompletion had prevailed as if a world of the imagination were being invaded for the first time. There too the major scene, with all its approach to immediate circumstance, had been that of fancy. Emerson, in spite of his plea for the humble, the immediate, seldom touched the real world at all. "Reality eluded him," said Santayana. "He was far from being, like a Plato or an Aristotle, past master in the art and the science of life. But his mind was endowed with unusual plasticity, with unusual spontaneity and liberty of movement—it was a fairyland of thoughts and fancies. He was like a young god making experiments in creation: he blotched the work, and always began on a new and better plan. Every day he said, 'Let there be light,' and every day the light was new. His sun, like that of Heraclitus, was different every morning."

Emotion had a large place in Emerson's writing, but it was seldom a personal emotion, most often the revelation of some common happy mood. "I read with joy some of the auspicious signs of the coming days." He followed the form of the native monologue, in which the first person had been steadily used, the personal revelation of fact or feeling consistently avoided, which had moved toward the generic, including the many experiences rather than the one. So far as the shell of the monologue had been broken at all this was by some slight echo of the interior voice, brimming over in sound and rhythm rather than in direct statement, tending toward the soliloquy. Yankee Hill had verged toward this tone in his gentle drawling talks, Jack Downing in mild reminiscences. In Emerson the interior voice was heard unmistakably in reverie or soliloquy. He has often been linked with the Puritan divines by way of the pulpit, but these men attempted to unroll the voice of God; their own part was impersonal. In Emerson the personal inner voice spoke; and this belonged not to the realm of introspection cultivated by the Puritan, but to that other realm of the plain Yankee, who consciously listened to his own mind, whose deliberate speech had room for undertones and further meanings. Emerson was aware of the tendency: he even saw it elsewhere. "Our age is bewailed as the age of Introversion," he said in 1837. "Must this needs be an evil?"

Thoreau carried the inner tone even further. "In most books, the I, or the first person, is omitted," he declared in the opening passages of *Walden*. "I should not talk so much about myself if there were anybody else I knew so well." The monologue remained his persistent form even though he expressed a contradictory theory as to literary quality. "In writing," he said, "conversation should be folded many times thick." Thoreau seldom or never attained that delicately balanced consideration of other thought and feeling which produces conversation. Dimension belongs to his writing, but this came from a mind closely bound within itself and woven with the filaments of its native surroundings—the mirroring pond, the lichen, the swamps, the green plumes and white heart of pine.

In his *Yankee in Canada* Thoreau revealed the direct flavor of the native monologue, grown a little drier. "I fear I have not got much to say about Canada, not having seen much; what I got by going to Canada was a cold. . . . I will not stop to tell the reader the names of my fellow-travelers; there were said to be fifteen hundred of them. . . . It would indeed be a serious bore to touch your hat several times a day. A Yankee has not leisure for it." In the lingo of the time Thoreau was "quirky," that is, obstinate and headstrong and full of notions. With all his aversion to distant movement he was not unrelated to the mythical figure of the Yankee peddler; he made the same calculations, many of them close and shrewd, often in the area of bargaining. He had that air of turning the tables on listeners or observers which had long since belonged to the Yankee of the comic mythologies; he used a wry humor in slow prose argument; he kept the habitual composure. Whoever might be his companion Thoreau seemed always alone, like the legendary Yankee. His tough and sinuous reveries were unbroken. "In any weather, at any hour of the day or night, I have been anxious to improve the nick of time, and notch it on my stick too; to stand on the meeting of two eternities, the past and the future, which is precisely the present moment; to toe that line." Here was the essence of self-consciousness, revealed in Yankee speech. Yet this always verged toward the abstract, slipping aside from personal revelation, and moving with increasing frequency toward another theme which had engrossed the Yankee, the land. That sense of wild land which had infused the Yankee monologues, creating a spare imagery and metaphor, was pressed by Thoreau back to its source until he obtained a whole subject.

Thoreau greatly deepened the figurative Yankee speech, and soared occasionally into allegory. "I long ago lost a hound, a bay horse, and a turtle-dove, and am still on their trail. Many are the travelers I have spoken to concerning them, describing their tracks and what calls they answered to. I have met one or two who had heard the hound, and the tramp of the horse, and had even seen the dove disappear behind a cloud, and they seemed as anxious to recover them as if they had lost them themselves." This beautiful and cryptic poetry was cast into Thoreau's discourse a little awry: he suddenly stopped, as if unable to pursue further the theme or its implications. It has the partial and fragmentary air which has been seen elsewhere in native fable and figure, rising as from hidden sources, then pausing as though the underlying inspiration were insecure or incomplete.

Whole passages of Thoreau's writing will have an unmistakable native authority, the true sound of native speech; others follow that are close and studied, narrow and purely literary. He produced no philosophy, though he obviously intended to construct a philosophy. His experience at Walden remains a singular experience; he is read for the aphorism or the brief description, for the Yankee character inadvertently revealed, for the shadowy impersonal soliloquy sounding even through the more prosaic talk like water underground.

2

WHITMAN stressed the personal intention, insisting that it belonged to all his poetry. *"Leaves of Grass* indeed (I cannot too often reiterate) has been mainly the outcropping of my own emotional and other personal nature—an attempt, from first to last, to put a *Person*, a human being (myself, in the latter half of the nineteenth century of America) freely, fully and truly on record." Yet Whitman's emotion was rarely the personal emotion; it always included others who swiftly become the subject or even in a sense the singer. The "I" or "Me" of Whitman is no more personal in final content than was that of the rhapsodic backwoodsman: it has the urgency of many people. The gesture is open-handed, the framework that of autobiography: yet this poetry constantly slips into another realm. Once he acknowledged this escape or evasion.

> Before all my arrogant poems the real Me stands
> yet untouch'd, untold, altogether unreach'd.

In the end Whitman went far beyond that transcending of the merely personal which must occur if poetry is to be created. For the first time in American literature, perhaps for the first time in all literature, he created a generic and inclusive "I" who embraces many minds and many experiences.

Passage after passage in his poems begins with the personal experience or mood only to drop these for the generic. In the first few lines of *Starting from Paumanok* Whitman is briefly himself: he then quickly becomes that being who was his great subject, that mythical American who had not only known Manhattan but had been a pioneer in Dakota and a miner in California, who had roamed the entire continent and had comprised all its typical experiences.

> I am of old and young, of the foolish as much as the wise,
> Regardless of others, ever regardful of others,
> Maternal as well as paternal, a child as well as a man,

Stuff'd with the stuff that is coarse and stuff'd with the stuff
that is fine,
One of the Nation of many nations, the smallest the same
and the largest the same,
A Southerner soon as a Northerner, a planter nonchalant
and hospitable down by the Oconee I live,
A Yankee bound my own way ready for my trade, my
joints the limberest joints on earth and the sternest
joints on earth,
A Kentuckian walking the vale of the Elkhorn in my deer-
skin leggings, a Louisianian or Georgian,
A boatman over lakes and bays or along coasts, a Hoosier,
a Badger, a Buckeye—

He was a Yankee sailor aboard a clipper; he was a farmer
in a country barn, among the dried grasses of harvest-time.
Whitman was not only full of this great theme but aware
of queries which might arise in relation to it, often humorously aware—

> Do I contradict myself?
> Very well then I contradict myself,
> (I am large, I contain multitudes).

His inclusions might be grossly made: but by the scope
of his view and the urgency of his consideration he evoked
a large and comprehensive figure not unlike that inclusive
character toward which the types of popular comedy had
seemed to merge.

Often this figure went beyond the bounds of nationalism,
as in portions of the *Song of Myself* and in *Children of
Adam*. Whitman could leave the nationalistic for the purely

human. Yet the body of his thought was nationalistic: his iterated theme was the American—was the nation. "The ambitious thought of my song is to help the forming of a great aggregate Nation," he declared, frankly leaving the purpose to transcribe a *Person* altogether. With an exuberance like that of the fable of the contrast he shouted, "I chant America the mistress, I chant a greater supremacy." His notions of the older countries were closely linked with those of the fable. Whitman's warmest conception of the older nations was that of pity. "Once powerful," he called them, "now reduced, withdrawn or desolate." In a less temperate mood he could talk of "Europe's old dynastic slaughter-house, Area of murder-plots of thrones, with scent yet left of wars and scaffolds everywhere." In a nobler measure he queried—

Have the elder races halted?
Do they droop and end their lesson, wearied over there
    beyond the seas?
We take up the task eternal, and the burden and the
    lesson,
            Pioneers! O Pioneers!

He carried the theme into a hitherto untouched sphere, the consideration of poetry—

Shrouded bards of other lands, you may rest, you have done
    your work.

He passed to a visionary scheme for perfection which America was to crown—

And thou America,
For the scheme's culmination, its thought and reality,
For these (not for thyself) thou hast arrived.

Whitman was filled as well with themes which he might
have caught from those strolling exponents of the divine
comedy who reached a crest of their ecstasy in the decade
before he began to write. Like them he declared that he
meant to "inaugurate a religion." They had often denied
evil, announcing that perfection was at hand. "I say in
fact there is no evil." He declared that "only the good is
universal," and that he meant "to formulate a poem whose
every thought or fact should directly or indirectly be or
connive at the implicit belief in the wisdom, health, mystery, beauty of every process, every concrete object, every
human or other existence. . . ." He was constantly occupied with the theme of perfection—

> In this broad earth of ours,
> Amid the measureless grossness and slag,
> Enclosed and safe within its central heart,
> Nestles the seed perfection.

In America he expected to find "a world primal again."
From America "in vistas of glory incessant and branching"
he expected perfection to spread.

Some of Whitman's convictions may have been gained
from austere statements of similar themes by Emerson: but
his large impetus seems to have come from popular sources,
particularly in the West. In that highly sensitized period

172

just before he began the writing of *Leaves of Grass* Whitman went over the Cumberland Gap by the wagon-road which many pioneers had followed, and down the Ohio and the Mississippi by boat. The physical imprint of the West appears throughout his poetry. Even in that long soliloquy in which he considers the place of his birth on the Atlantic shore he is soon "singing in the West," singing "chants of the prairies, chants of the long-running Mississippi. . . ." He mentions the mocking-bird again and again. "Flatboatmen make fast toward dusk near cotton-wood or pecan-trees." He wrote of soft afternoon airs that blow from the southwest. "I saw in Louisiana a live oak growing." "O magnet South!" he cried—the South which was the old Southwest. The imagery in the phrase *Leaves of Grass* may have come from the prairie lands and great meadows of the West. His stress upon physical prowess and strength was western, as was his resilient good humor. "Henceforth I ask not good fortune, I myself am good fortune."

At times Whitman achieved a serene and ineffaceable and tender strain of feeling which seemed a final residuum of humor; this belonged to his finest poetry. At others he followed only the wildest of western comic boastings—often with unconscious comedy. The rhapsodic, leaping, crowing backwoodsman had long since come into the popular view, adopting the phrase "child of nature." Whitman in turn celebrated "spontaneous me," or described himself as an acutely self-conscious "child of nature" under the title *Me Imperturbe—*

Me Imperturbe, standing at ease in Nature,
Master of all or mistress of all, aplomb in the midst of
    irrational things—

His famous "I sound my barbaric yawp over the roofs of
the world" might have been shouted by the gamecock of
the wilderness, even though the image belongs to the cities.
In his early *Boston Ballad* Whitman joined in the classic
comic warfare between the backwoodsman and the Yankee.
Half gravity, half burlesque, in its swift slipping from the
foothold of reality the poem is not far from the pattern of
the tall tales or from the familiar extravagant form of
mock-oratory.

In later years Whitman could fall into that rough-hewn
grotesquerie of language which the backwoodsman had exhibited in moments of exhilarated comedy. "In fact, here
I am these current years 1890 and '91 (each successive
year getting stiffer and stuck deeper) much like some di-
lapidated grim ancient shell-fish or time-banged conch (no
legs, utterly non-locomotive) cast up high and dry on the
shore sands, hopeless to move anywhere—nothing left but
to behave myself quiet." He noted the Negro dialect, and
found there hints of "a modification of all words of the
English language, for musical purposes, for a native grand
opera in America." He theorized about language. "In
America an immense number of new words are needed," he
declared. "This subject of language interests me—interests
me: I never quite get it out of my mind. I sometimes think
the *Leaves* is only a language experiment—that it is an

attempt to give the spirit, the body, the man, new words, new potentialities of speech—an American, a cosmopolitan (the best of America is the best cosmopolitanism) range of expression. The new world, the new times, the new peoples, the new vista, need a tongue according—yes, what is more will have such a tongue—will not be satisfied until it is evolved." He freely used plain words, "farmer's words," "sea words," "the likes of you," and much of the jargon of the time. Whitman, in short, used language as a new and plastic and even comical medium, as it had long since been used in native folk-lore.

To enter the world of Whitman is to touch the spirit of American popular comedy, with its local prejudices, its national prepossessions, its fantastic beliefs; many phases of comic reaction are unfolded there. Nothing is complete, nothing closely wrought; often Whitman's sequences are incoherent, like sudden movements of undirected thought or feeling. "No one will get at my verses who insists upon viewing them as literary performances," he said. The scale was large; Whitman possessed that sense of a whole civilization which must belong to the epic; his sweeping cadences could have held the heroic form; and though he lacked the great theme of gods and men his awareness of the country had a stirring animism, and his prototypical American was of far greater than human stature. Yet Whitman did not achieve the heroic, or only rarely, in broken or partial passages. Like those popular story-tellers who had often seemed on the verge of wider expression, he failed to draw his immeasurable gift into the realm of great and final poetry. For the most part he remained an improviser of immense genius, unearthing deep-lying materials in the native mind, in a sense "possessed" by the character of that mythical and many-sided American whom he often evoked. He was indeed the great improviser of modern literature. He had turned the native comic rhapsody, abundant in the backwoods, to broad poetic forms.

Whitman achieved the epical scale; at the same time he remained within a sphere which, along with a movement toward the epical, had been defined in popular comedy— that of the acutely self-aware. At the end of *Me Imperturbe* he uttered a brief prayer that the supreme naturalness which he desired might be achieved, as if he knew that the shadow of himself stood in his way. Elsewhere he was revealed as acutely self-conscious, when like any backwoodsman on the rivers and levees he picturized himself in a costume conspicuous by its negation of color. He was self-aware in the promotion of his own work, in his summaries of purpose. But with all this, with all his forced awkwardness and flamboyance, he achieved an ultimate culmination of the conscious in the richness and fullness of his finer soliloquies. The free mind was there, turned inward, truly conscious and indwelling, yet flowing naturally into speech. That movement toward the soliloquy which had appeared in popular modes and again in the writings of Emerson and Thoreau reached a culmination in Whitman. His finest poems are cast in the deep and delicate form: *When*

I HEAR AMERICA SINGING

Lilacs Last in the Dooryard Bloomed, the rhapsodic *Crossing Brooklyn Ferry*, the long and sometimes cryptic *Starting from Paumanok*, the reflective songs in *Children of Adam*. The monologue or rhapsody was turned inward, without analysis or introspection: moods, shades of feeling, fragments of thought, pour out in an untrammeled stream which is often not far from the so-called stream of consciousness. Whitman anticipated by many years the modern mode of inner revelation with its broken sequences, its irrelevant changes, its final move into the realm of soliloquy.

It was on this level that Whitman touched the great theme which had so deeply underlain the experience of the pioneer, the theme of death, touched it with an emotion that belongs to the finer aspects of comedy. "And to die is different from what any one supposed, and luckier," he said. "And I will show that nothing can happen more beautiful than death." *When Lilacs Last in the Dooryard Bloomed* is a poem of reconcilement with death of profound tenderness, embracing the widening theme of the farm-lands and the cities, "the large unconscious scenery of my land with its lakes and forests," as if there in warmth and sunlight and a common life lay an ultimate answer. The simplest flow of feeling is kept, like that of some archaic ceremonial—

O what shall I hang on the chamber walls,
And what shall the pictures be that I hang on the walls,
To adorn the burial house of him I love?

Always this feeling deepens, so that the poem becomes a poem of reconcilement not only for the death of Lincoln but for all death within a beloved land.

Whitman had circled from the generic and inclusive and nationalistic "I" to the realm of inner feeling; and the inner world which he discovered was that which had been opened by comedy; it was of the mind; that is, it was reflective rather than emotional. Sorrow occupied him greatly only once, in *When Lilacs Last in the Dooryard Bloomed.* The verses in *Drum Taps* were written less in sorrow than in tenderness or assuagement. Emotion in Whitman most often meant deep tenderness; its quality was indwelling. With all his direct improvisation and outpouring the simple emotions were far from belonging to him. His most ardent feelings were those which he could share with a crowd; his sense of identity with other human beings seemed to stir him more deeply than any other experience. On the theme of sexual passion he was sometimes direct, but the emotion which he expressed was likely to be strange and inverted, or to move quickly outside the realm of feeling altogether into a consideration of the many divergent forms of passion, or to sweep into argument. Again the conscious superseded the emotional.

In literature the scope was new and strange which could include the epical scale in free expression and at the same time reveal the conscious and indwelling mind. To these biases, which had belonged to American popular comedy, was added another, likewise of that province. Neither

Whitman—nor Thoreau—for all their inclusions of the outer world was primarily concerned with outer circumstance. Thoreau stood, as he said, at the meeting of two eternities; Whitman's true world was wholly visionary even when it included the touch and color of earth.

3

OF ALL American writers Poe has become a symbol for the type of genius which rises clear from its time, nourished mainly from hidden inner sources. Poe himself would have delighted in that theory, for he fostered the conviction that he ranged over only the rarest and most esoteric materials. But Poe came from that Scotch-Irish stock with its heritage of unsettlement from which were drawn the scouts and myth-makers and many strollers of the West; the theatrical strain that had been strong among them was his by birth; and he began to write at the end of the '20's when American myth-making was passing into its great popular diffusion. Essential foreign influences on Poe have been discovered, but in general the influences which weigh most with any writer are those which are akin to his own feeling and purposes. Poe drew upon German and French romanticism: but a homely romantic movement of native origin was making itself felt nearer at hand; and Poe both by temperament and environment was susceptible to the native forces.

The impact of popular comic story-telling in America

must have reached Poe. At his foster-father's house Negro
legends were surely current among the slaves; he must have
heard the exploits of those adventurers by land and sea
who drifted into the office of Allan and Company. Since
this firm were agents for subscriptions to newspapers Poe
no doubt had access to the current almanacs, which even
in an early day were beginning to print compact stories of
wild adventure. He may have seen tales of buccaneering
and of buried treasure there, preparing him for *The Gold
Bug*, or of hazards at sea, which suggested *Arthur Gordon Pym*. At the University of Virginia a few of his
companions were accomplished in the western art of biting
and gouging; probably story-telling was exhibited as another form of prowess. Poe himself gained a reputation as
an amusing story-teller in these years. At Baltimore in 1831
and 1832 he could hardly have missed echoes of western
story-telling, for Baltimore was a point of convergence for
travelers from all that wide circle known as the Southwest;
they came on horseback or by stage over the mountains, by
boat from Savannah or New Orleans. Their appearance
was striking: their talk and tales were caught fragmen-
tarily by many observers. At the theaters the backwoodsman was being portrayed in the semblance of Crockett; and
the new stage character was creating a highly novel sensation.

That broad grotesque myth-making which had to do
with corn-crackers and country rapscallions Poe surely encountered, for in 1835 he reviewed Longstreet's *Georgia*

Scenes, with enthusiasm. When Poe went to Philadelphia, always a center for the comic theater, the larger pattern of native figures must again have moved before him, and surely his association with Burton on the *Gentleman's Magazine* gave an impetus to his sense of native comedy, for though Burton's alliance with Brougham lay in the future, he had long been a comedian and had compiled comic joke-books and song-books. Poe possessed besides what Woodberry has called "a contemporaneous mind." He quickly turned to matters of current interest, exploration, treasure-hunting, mesmerism, Masonry, balloons, topics that crowded the newspapers and were being discussed by popular lecturers. He turned to comedy; as by instinct he turned to the hoax. His early *Journal of Julius Rodman* purported to give a literal account of a western journey and was essentially a hoax, as was his *Arthur Gordon Pym* with its studied effort to produce an effect of truth. His *Hans Pfall* was in the vanguard of a long sequence of hoaxes, anticipating by only a brief space Locke's famous Moon Hoax, which made a great stir in 1835. With its carefully prepared verisimilitude even to effects of costuming, with its intense stress of all outward sensation, *Hans Pfall* bore a close resemblance to the more elaborate and finished tall tales of the West, which were scrupulous as to detail, and which often gave—as it happened—a particularly keen attention to costume. His *Balloon Hoax* in 1844 had its brief day of acceptance as fact. One of Poe's last stories, *Von Kempelen and His Discovery*,

181

was essentially a hoax; and his talent for comic fantasy was shown in still another form in a topsy-turvy extravaganza, *The Angel of the Odd*.

Poe never used native legends directly except perhaps in *The Gold Bug;* yet in creative bent he was perhaps one of those major writers who instinctively turn toward long-established traditions. Unrooted in any region—if indeed any American of those years could be called rooted—he found no long and substantial accumulation of native materials, even though the comic myth-making faculty was abroad in force during his later youth. None the less Poe followed a course habitually followed by traditional writers and myth-makers: he did not invent, he borrowed and re-created. His *King Pest* was built upon a scene from *Vivian Gray;* he borrowed indeed at every turn.

Even if native legends had been strewn about with unmistakable richness one cannot be sure that Poe would have used them. That restless impulse which had driven other story-tellers farther and farther afield might have moved him. But the patterns, if not the substance of his tales, were those of a native story-telling. The gamut of his moods might have been drawn from the West, plumbing horror, yet turning also to a wild contrived comedy. Because of his own dark fate, and because Poe himself often stressed the *frisson*, terror has overtopped comedy in the general apprehension of his tales. His designations of "grotesque" and "arabesque" and his later "tales of terror" have created a further submergence of the comic. Yet

King Pest, with its background of the plague and the night, is one of the most brilliant pure burlesques in the language, transmuting terror into gross comedy, as it had often been transmuted in the western tall tales.

According to Poe's original plan for the *Tales of the Folio Club* each member of the Club was to be satirically described; after the telling of each tale they were to criticize it, their comments forming a burlesque of criticism. The tales run through a wide range of humor, from the sheer absurdity of *Lionising* to the hoax of *Hans Pfall*. The Duc in *The Duc de l'Omelette* bore some relation to those derisive portraits of foreigners which were steadily gaining American favor; he was even given a not inharmonious touch of diabolism. Poe's command of verbal humor was uncertain; his puns often fall below tolerable levels. Yet these too are part of the mode of the time—a time when language was being carelessly and comically turned upside down and even re-created, as if to form a new and native idiom.

His laughter was of a single order: it was inhuman, and mixed with hysteria. His purpose in the hoaxes was to make his readers absurd, to reduce them to an involuntary imbecility. His objective was triumph, the familiar objective of popular comedy. To this end, in his burlesques and extravaganzas, he showed human traits or lineaments in unbelievable distortion, using that grotesquerie which lies midway between the comic and the terrible; with Poe the terrible was always within view. There are touches of chilly barbarity even in *Hans Pfall*. The fantasy-making of the West had swung from an impinging terror to a gross and often brutal comedy; Poe also stressed black moods and emotions, embracing a dark and ghostly melodrama, employing themes bordering upon those in the romantic tragedy of the day. In the midst of burlesque in *Tales of the Folio Club* he reached an antithetical horror, in *Berenice*.

Western story-telling had often been callous: in callousness Poe could pass beyond human limits, in the *Facts in the Case of M. Valdemar*. He used the magnified scale in rooms, corridors, draperies, in the accumulation of detail, in sensation. He enjoyed mystification; his tone and level throughout were those of legend; and if his scope in story-telling was brief he verged toward larger forms. His *Tales of the Folio Club* were made to follow in a prismatic sequence, and other stories fall into loosely united cycles.

Poe entered another area marked out by the popular comic tradition: that of the inner mind or consciousness. Not only Emerson approached this, or Thoreau in the delicate exemplification of inner states, or Whitman in his outpourings. Poe—and also Hawthorne, and even Melville—invaded this area and in some measure conquered it. Poe used the first person continually, adopting it in part perhaps to gain an impulse toward an exploration of states of mind or feeling which were often undoubtedly his own. Beyond direct transcriptions, which may have been unconscious, he clearly attempted to explore the character of the inner, even the sub-conscious, mind. In *The Black Cat* he dwelt on "the spirit of PERVERSENESS. . . . Yet I am not more sure that my soul lives than I am that perverseness is one of the primitive impulses of the human heart— one of the indivisible primary faculties or sentiments which give direction to the character of Man. . . ." He mentioned the "unfathomable longing of the soul *to vex itself*—to offer violence to its own nature." He made notations on small crises of the mind, speaking in *Ligeia* of the endeavor to recall to memory something forgotten when "we often find ourselves upon *the very verge* of remembrance, without being able in the end to remember." These fragmentary touches and others like them scattered through Poe's tales culminated in his story of double identity in *William Wilson*, in which memory—its obscure envelopments, its buried treasures—made a recurrent theme. Half symbolical, half factual, filled by intimations of a complex and warring inner state, *William Wilson* stands as a fresh creation in an almost untouched field, a prelude to the so-called psychological novel, and a further revelation of a native bias.

In critical theory the psychological strain has sometimes been linked with the Puritan influences; but surely no tie with the Puritan faith and its habit of introspection can be found for Poe. By birth and upbringing and sympathy he was wholly alien to the Puritan strain. Nothing remotely moralistic can be found in his observation, no identity with religious feeling, no judgments. Instead, Poe seems near those story-tellers of the West who described wild and perverse actions with blank and undisturbed countenances, and whose insistent use of the first person brought them to the brink of inner revelation.

4

HAWTHORNE, like Poe, was a writer who would naturally have worked best within a thoroughly established tradition; his predilections are shown in his care for style as well as by his choice of themes that were at least partially worked over and defined. His natural inclinations seem to have been toward comedy; his notebooks provide a singular contrast with his tales. They contain, it is true, many notes outlining poetical or abstract themes: but side by side with these are acute linear sketches of individuals, of groups, caught with immediacy and the fresh daylight upon them, seen with no veil of distance or of time. Throughout most of his years Hawthorne was on the outlook for odd and salient characters; he often enveloped them with humor in his brief notes; he had a gift for slight inflation in drawing, and even for the touch of caricature. From his boyhood at Salem when he was near the wharves with their changing crew of seafaring men, he had seen something of the rough fabric of a common and immediate life. As a youth at Bowdoin he had been on the fringe of the eastern backwoods with its inevitable small filtration of adventurers. Even in later years he betrayed a tie with this popular and common and often comic existence by his alliance with the invincible Peter Parley.

But that uncouth, unassimilated life about him, those casual aggregations of seamen and day-laborers and vaga-bonds—what after all did he know of them? His igno-rance was not his alone: what did any one of his time know of them? Even his brief notes were adventures in recognition. Close elements of the native character had re-mained unstudied except for scattered and casual sketches, outlined mainly by unconcerned travelers impressed for the moment. Only prototypal drawings existed, of a few of the larger figures in American life, and in Hawthorne's forma-tive years these provided no rich accumulation upon which to draw, which he might use for intensification.

Hawthorne turned toward a form which comedy more than any other native impulse was shaping within the pop-ular consciousness, that of legend, which permitted a fan-tastic or narrow or generalized handling of character. The materials which he found were not comic; the older and more deeply established lore of New England was darkly tinged; his tales reveal a gamut of the more violent or ter-rible feelings, rage, terror, the sense of guilt, greed, strange regional fantasies, like that in *Ethan Brand*, witchcraft, ghosts. The scarlet letter was said to glow in the dark; Haw-thorne suggested that the tale had come to him as lore; cer-tainly much of *The House of the Seven Gables* came to him as tradition. In such works as *The Wonder Book* and *Tan-glewood Tales* he again found the remote and legendary.

Even when his narratives were lengthened their scope was the brief scope of the tale; and though they did not join in cycles the tales were loosely linked. In his preface to *The House of the Seven Gables* Hawthorne disclaimed the purpose to write a novel, declaring that "the latter form of composition is presumed to aim at a very minute fidelity, not merely to the possible, but to the probable and ordinary course of man's experience." He called his narrative a romance, and insisted upon the right to mingle "the Marvellous" in its course, even though this might be only as "a slight, delicate, and evanescent flavor." Again, he spoke of the story as "a legend . . . from an epoch now gray in the distance . . . and bringing with it some of its legendary mist." Writing of some scenes from *The Scarlet Letter* which had been performed as an opera in New York, he said, "I should think it might possibly succeed as an opera, though it would certainly fail as a play." *The Scarlet Letter* had indeed the bold and poetic and legendary outline which may belong to opera; and the same qualities inhered in all of Hawthorne's finer work.

Though he drew upon a traditional material, Hawthorne could not rest at ease as the great English poets have rested within the poetic tradition that came to them through the ballads and romances, or as the great English novelists have drawn upon rich local accumulations of character and lore. The materials at his hand were not rich or dense or voluminous: time had not enriched but had scattered them. The effort to create imaginative writing out of such a groundwork must inevitably have been disruptive for an artist like Hawthorne; it was making bricks with only wisps of straw. The scantness of his natural sources may account for the meagerness of his effort, rather than some obscure inner maladjustment of his own; indeed, for a highly sensitive and traditional writer the constantly thwarted search for a richly established material could have caused a fundamental disarrangement of creative energy.

Yet if the result was small, Hawthorne's writing had freshness of accomplishment. In *The Scarlet Letter* a woman was drawn as a full and living figure for the first time in American literature. The semblance of a society was depicted; the Puritan settlement becomes a protagonist in the tale. This attempt toward a new and difficult portrayal was still slight and partial; the society appears mainly as a mob under strong emotion; and in *The House of the Seven Gables*, where a small group is imaged, its members filter one by one out of the shop door or are mentioned from a distance. Hawthorne entered an even more difficult area. In *The Scarlet Letter*, for the first time in an American narrative, emotion played a prevailing and simple part, restrained though it was by barriers which seemed persistently set against the expression of deep feeling. There can be no doubt of the love that existed between Dimmesdale and Hester; yet this is never expressed in a word, scarcely by a sign: it is shown only by a kind of running emotional shorthand in their brief exchanges. Their meeting in the wood was the first scene created by the American imagina-

189

tion in which emotion is all but overwhelming; some may call it the single great scene in American literature where love is dominant: but even here there is no direct revelation.

Hawthorne was deeply engaged by the consideration of lost or submerged emotion. In *The Scarlet Letter* this makes the basic theme: it was Dimmesdale's concealment of the bond with Hester which appears as his great wrong. It was warmth of affection, mingled with grief, which at last gave humanity to the elfin Pearl. Again and again in Hawthorne's briefer tales—sometimes only by allusion—he makes clear his conviction that the sin against the heart is the unpardonable sin. That suppression of individualized feeling, conspicuous in the American temper, was in a sense his major subject. Yet except in the one instance he seemed unable to reveal a deeply felt and simple emotion. The feelings which Hawthorne portrayed were for the most part complex or distorted; they were indeed, as in the writings of Poe, and in the romantic tragedy abroad in this period, mirrorings of those harsher feelings which had often belonged to a pioneer existence.

But these—rage, greed, terror, the sense of guilt—are only half lighted in Hawthorne's writing; they no longer take on the full fury which they had exercised on the frontier. He too plumbed the inner mind; he too was concerned with "introversion." For the most part his discoveries appeared in terms of pure fantasy; Hawthorne even transmuted regional legends into inner moods. Again and again in *The Scarlet Letter* the flow of the tale seems sensitively adapted to the flow of inner and secret feelings. In the passage describing the minister's impulses as he passes among his people after the meeting with Hester in the wood, Hawthorne reached a final and even prophetic discernment: here was a brief and effortless exposure of a grotesque inner license. Poe may have surpassed him in the discernment of subtle thoughts or impulses or in the definition of these: but Hawthorne portrayed the natural movement of a mind in a form which was to develop in modern literature, as direct revelation. No doubt Puritan influences created something of the bent toward inner scrutiny in Hawthorne. The Puritan element of judgment was often clear in his writings, though, as he said, it was sometimes deliberately added. But Hawthorne at his finest never used the abstract formulations of the Puritan: he chose the direct and earthy mode, as in the passage on Dimmesdale's fantasies: and there at least he slipped into an irreverent rude comedy far from the conscious Puritan habit. With all the delicacy of his approach, with all the invention which fairly transformed style into a means of revealing phases of buried thought or feeling, Hawthorne like Poe was close to the rude fantasy-making of the pioneer.

5

INSTEAD of moving against the American temper in his greater works Melville moved with this temper and was supported by it. Without those lusty undirected energies which had persistently maintained the sense of legend he could hardly have created *Moby-Dick* at all, for the primitive legend-making faculty lies at its base, with something conscious and involved that was not primitive inwoven with it, that had also appeared on popular levels. Popular comedy had run a long course when Melville began to write in the late '40's; its characters, its temper, even its verbal ingenuities, were established. Tall tales of the West had overspread the entire country; the abundant sea-lore which had grown up at the same time was fully created. These would have reached Melville not only through the common channels of the almanacs and popular journals but through primary adventures of his own. On the wharves at New Bedford and as a sailor to far seas he must have known characters who overflowed with such stories; he would have heard them, for he was himself a master of oral story-telling: the art inevitably draws forth examples in kind.

In *Typee* and *Omoo* Melville was close to a simple sea-lore: the fate of the mutineer who escaped to a submarine cave with a girl from the Tonga Islands roughly suggests that of the heroes of these tales, even though Melville's sources for his stories were his own. He was linked with the native comic temper of the time, particularly that of the West, with its strong bias toward a naturalistic existence, its lyricism, its continual revelation of the movement toward the farther West and the western sea. Comedy appears in the idyllic temper of these two tales, a comedy

192

temperate and sweet, like that which had sometimes seemed an underply for popular humor, shown in the more idyllic passages in the life of the cults, with their wreaths and garlands. But in the midst of a rich light-heartedness, Melville was aware of a latent dynamic emotion which had also found expression in the West, either shooting up geyserlike into wild travesty or plunging into dark emotion, full of brutal natural force. "He must be possessed by a devil," said Mohi of the young prince Tribonnora in the later *Mardi*. "Then," said Babbalanja, "he is only like all of us." Diabolism raised its head in the midst of the idyll with comic gusto; the narrative is a fairy-tale plumbed by the opposing spirits of comedy and terror.

In *Moby-Dick* this many-sided diabolism reached an ultimate culmination. Its concern is with one of those illusory marked creatures of the natural world, magic and powerful, which had often appeared in western legends of the jet-black stallion or the white deer. In one of his descriptions of the whale Melville spoke of the White Steed of the Prairies, "most famous in our Western annals and Indian traditions." Among the tall tales of the West was one which ran close to the main outline of *Moby-Dick*, describing the comic adventures of a backwoodsman who sought a fabulously large bear, the Big Bear of Arkansas, in revenge for depredations. Legends concerning Mocha Dick were known before Melville used them. As early as 1839 J. B. Reynolds, to whom Poe turned for strange material, had written an account of this white whale of pro-

193

digious size, strength, and cunning. For the rest Melville used the familiar method of the legend-maker, drawing an accumulation of whaling lore from many sources, much of it from New England, some of it hearsay, some from books, including stories of the adventures of other ships encountered at sea, or further tales suggested by episodes within the main sequence of his story.

Tragic though the theme was, comedy mapped the outlines of *Moby-Dick* and shaped its forms. Passage of comic fantasy are strewn through the narrative. The first encounter of Ishmael with Queequeg is pitched to the key of hilarious comedy, though penetrated by the gruesome and terrible. The comic touch is repeated again and again. "Fishiest of all fishy places was the Try Pots, which well deserved its name; for the pots there were always boiling chowders. Chowder for breakfast, and chowder for dinner, and chowder for supper, till you began to look for fish-bones coming through your clothes. The area before the house was paved with clam-shells. Mrs. Hussey wore a polished necklace of codfish vertebrae; and Hosea Hussey had his account books bound in superior old shark-skin." There are passages that echo the comic interchanges of the current joke-books and of the stage, as in the talk about the harpooneer, with its punning on "being green" and being "done brown," underlined as was usual in printed puns of the day. "A clam for supper? a cold clam; is *that* what you mean, Mrs. Hussey? But that's a rather cold and clammy reception in the winter time, ain't it, Mrs. Hussey?" A series of chapters on

194

fish is headed "Schools and Schoolmasters," "Fast-Fish and Loose-Fish," "Heads or Tails."

Comedy belonged to such names as Hosea Hussey and to the liberal designation of other characters by the names of the prophets, a comedy that was close to the use of biblical names in the Yankee fables, though here the implication was often ironical or tragic. Names like Stubb and Flask were frankly comic. "This imperial negro, Ahasuerus Daggoo, was the squire of little Flask, who looked like a chessman beside him." "Don't whale it too much a' Lord's days, men," said Bildad, in the Yankee vein, "but don't miss a fair chance, either, that's rejecting Heaven's good gifts." The ship seemed to contain representatives of all those major characters who had figured largely in American comedy. There were Yankees from Ahab down; the teller of the tale was one of those wanderers over the globe who had told and dominated many a Yankee story. There was a Negro, an Indian, and a mountaineer six feet tall with "a chest like a coffer dam," in the shadows of whose eyes "floated some reminiscences that did not seem to give him much joy." A member of one of the cults appeared on board the *Jeroboam*, a sailor who had been a Shaker prophet. Captain Ahab is described as though he were a comic, elementary creature of the sea. "Over his ivory-inlaid table Ahab presided like a mute maned sea-lion on the white coral beach, surrounded by his war-like but still deferential cubs."

Comedy remains in *Moby-Dick* like the strong trace of

an irresistible mood. Even the movement of the narrative is that of comic travesty: it soars, circles, and rises to the persistent native form of rhapsody. But this primary resilience is stripped to its core. Humor becomes sardonic; that terror and sense of evil and impending death which had often been part of the comic legends of the country are relentlessly uncovered. Melville broke through the mask of comedy to find its ultimate secret, and gave to *Moby-Dick* the final element which creates the epic: an encounter between gods and men. In that vast and prototypical creature, the white whale, evil is concentered—"that intangible malignity which has been from the beginning; . . . all that most maddens and torments; all that stirs up the lees of things; all truth with malice in it; all that cracks the sinews and cakes the brain; all the subtle demonisms of life and thought;—all evil, to crazy Ahab, were visibly personified, and made practically assailable in *Moby-Dick*. He piled on the whale's white hump the sum of all the general rage and hate felt by his whole race from Adam down; and then, as if his chest had been a mortar, he burst his hot heart's shell upon it." Animistic fantasy infuses *Moby-Dick*, even at the Inn with its heathenish array of clubs and spears set with glittering teeth, adorned with knots of human hair—weapons with legends attached to them. The *Pequod* was "a cannibal of a craft," tricked out with the bones and teeth of her chosen enemy, the sperm whale; *Moby-Dick* was said to possess supernatural powers, and inspired the strange legend of an underground sea passage through the world. Strange sights were seen, the great white squid, and the "spirit spout." "Stricken, blasted, if he be, Ahab had his humanities!" said Peleg; but for the most part Ahab moves outside the human and becomes a prototypical figure, engaged in a titanic and inhuman struggle. The basic physical struggle was age-old; it had reappeared in fresh forms as small schooners set out from the Atlantic coast bent upon wresting treasures from the sea. It had been seen in the untouched lands of the West, where the pioneer had been pitted against the natural world in a primary and engrossing contest, often to conquer, in the end most often to be conquered.

Perhaps *Moby-Dick* could never have been written except in a land where Puritanism had largely prevailed. The consciousness of an abstract evil—"that tangible malignity which has been from the beginning"—surely belonged to the Puritan; and Melville, who came in part from New England stock, may have been swayed by Puritan prepossessions. Yet the abstract speculation of the Puritan appears hardly at all in *Moby-Dick;* figure and fantasy make the medium through which the theme is revealed. Soliloquy, reverie, "supernatural surmisings" are mingled with outer happenings. The voyage of the *Pequod* is determined by the obsession of Captain Ahab; and the obsession spreads through the consciousness of its men, even—within the fantastic range of the narrative—giving shape and color to the natural world. It is always the mind that is dominant in this struggle and quest; bitterness exists, and rage, and even a lyrical response to beauty, but these belong to a supermundane sphere; they never become the humble human portion. Even the fate of little Pip, afloat upon the waters and then afterward forever mindless, strikes below the human or above it.

In this strange realm magnitude is created by the assembling of the strange crew, by the sense of an unknown quest, by the extended vision of the sea, by touches such as that describing the Nantucketer, who "out of sight of land, furls his sails, and lays him down to rest, while under his very pillow rush herds of walruses and whales." But the greater magnitude arises from the basic encounter of the human mind with the forces of evil. Though *Moby-Dick* borders at times upon that theatrical rhapsody abroad in the land when Melville was a youth and even while he was writing, its tone is true to its multifarious themes, which also belonged to the time; it is transmuted into poetry; the book rises to the heroic semblance. The achievement was immense, for if Melville found a native sealore at his hand there had been none of those partial transmutations of brief tales into larger poetic forms which may provide a creative impetus. In the sphere of inner fantasy Melville worked not quite alone, for Poe and Hawthorne had made adventures there: but nothing in heroic literature had contained the deep and passionate stress upon adventures of the mind.

Melville felt his book to be imperfect with something more than that profound dissatisfaction which may beset the greatest writers. He dreaded its completion. "God help me from completing anything," he exclaimed in the midst of the writing. "This whole book is but a draught—nay, but the draught of a draught. Oh, Time, Strength, Cash, and Patience!" He worked as though the book were draining his powers; he felt indeed that in *Moby-Dick* he reached an end, and he wrote in the midst of its composition to Hawthorne, "I am like one of those seeds taken out of the Egyptian Pyramids, which, after being three thousand years a seed and nothing but a seed, being planted in English soil, it developed itself, grew to greenness, and then fell into mold. So I. Until I was twenty-five, I had no development at all. From my twenty-fifth year I date my life. Three weeks have scarcely passed, at any time between then and now, that I have not unfolded within myself. But I now feel that I am come to the inmost leaf of the bulb, and that shortly the flower must come to the mold."

The end of Melville's imaginative force had indeed come with the completion of *Moby-Dick*, though complex fantasies continued to engage him, joined with moods as perverse as any conceived by Poe. These stalk through *Pierre* and rise again in shrouded outlines in the briefer tales of his later years. Almost invariably they assume the familiar shapes of legend, fable, allegory—forms which were half poetry—but they seldom attain unmistakable power. *Pierre* is the book of a man who has lost his way perhaps because its theme of incest with the implications within mind and feeling was too difficult for encompassment

199

within Melville's time, perhaps because in choosing the materials of common society he moved outside his natural mode altogether. Such a voyage as that of the *Pequod* could never be undertaken again. To have turned to the land—the western land—for heroic materials would have meant for Melville an unfamiliar element, even though a rich legendary material awaited him there. With the writing of his one great book Melville's work was finished.

6

THE heroic outline had been approached more than once, in popular comedy as on the levels of literature; the epical form seemed like a vessel waiting to be filled. Audubon had approached it, in his voluminous journals which were a wide portrait of the country, in the sequences of his *Ornithological Biography*, in his great *Birds of America*. Cooper, Bird, Simms, Thompson of Vermont, and Kennedy of Maryland, plotting out nearly every area of the older America, viewing almost every significant passage in the American past, used a scope that roughly approached the epical scale. Stilted as their narratives often were, they tended to revert to the simple and cumulative forms that had belonged to the popular stories of the taverns and the almanacs: these were tales; and one tale was piled upon another. The longer narratives ran in cycles. Strictly speaking, they were not novels but romances, with that infusion of the marvelous upon which Hawthorne had insisted. Legends were striated through them, with touches of myth, as the Indian became a figure there, or as the situations belonged to dim earlier years. Whatever their locale, they had to do with the frontier; and their living characters were comic: scouts, bee-hunters, horse-thieves, wandering ne'er-do-wells, Negroes. In the tales of Simms the Negro was drawn for the first time at full length. Bird tapped a deep fund of western comic talk and character. At times the terror and tragedy of the wilderness was drawn, as in *Nick of the Woods*, but the comic tone was insurgent, and portrayals of nobler characters grew dry or sterile. Even Simms, with his loving absorption in all phases of southern society, could give life only to such figures as had engaged the popular fancy and had been subjects for a broad popular drawing.

The groundwork of feeling in pioneer life had been seized and re-created in subtle forms by Melville, Poe, Hawthorne; the lesser writers seemed moved by a romantic nostalgia for the past. It is as if when the first dread and desperation of pioneering began to recede, when conquest seemed assured, a purpose was abroad to capture and maintain those lost elements and make of them a treasure-house, however bleak or coarse or comic they might be. Here and there literary forces from abroad had influence upon this effort; yet these gained power only as they coincided with a native intention. Romanticism had developed in Europe, but this new romanticism possessed a homely texture and sprang from the native character.

An imaginative force was loosed, powerful enough to attempt wide inclusions, but not to complete them in abundance. Large modes had been created; yet their looming outlines had often only been approached. The prevailing forms of the new American literature had remained primitive or anterior forms, the monologue, the rhapsody, the tale, the legend, the romance. They were full of astringencies and ellipses, with a tone that was archaic and young, and a conspicuous lack of color; Poe, Hawthorne, Melville, can be described in blacks, grays, cold whites, Whitman in terms of light rather than of color. Half designs, cartoons, sketches, were drawn and left incomplete. Hawthorne's voluminous note-books were a symbol, as was Whitman's perpetual re-writing of his poems, and the single great achievement of Melville. Nor did these writers attract those pursuant groups of minor artists who usually follow in the wake of a great movement and give it amplitude and variation. They stood alone; and strange hiatuses appeared within their literature. It was bound by no rich unconscious sense of the land, its contours, its beauty, its inalterable character, as English literature is closely bound. No deeply cut, enduring types were drawn, no living society fully evoked. A young people might have been expected to produce a literature greatly concerned with the present and the tangible; but this expression was often concerned with the highly intangible; it turned continually toward the illusive province of inner fantasy. Gusto it certainly showed, even in its colder moments.

The outcome was not quite a literature but the bold outlines of one, a kind of rich *ursprünglich* accumulation. Its direction was its own, in the mingling of primitive elements with the indwelling and self-aware. If it failed of direct portrayals it still belonged in a large sense to poetry. The move toward the heroic, not only once, but in a whole aspect of expression, was a radical accomplishment in a modern world. Most literatures have had slowly accumulated sources upon which to draw; but the comedy which here had been a source was only broadly sketched when the first of these primary writers arose; much of their accomplishment ran parallel to the expansion of a comic poetry. It was only Melville and Whitman, coming last, who could touch this with unconscious freedom; even they fairly matched it in point of time. None of these writers could be deeply grounded in a popular lore as other literatures had been grounded in such sources. Their quick drafts, the breathless haste, may have been a final cause of incompletion. Yet comedy had deepened on the levels of literature. The touch of revolution in popular comedy was there, in the purpose to find new convictions voiced by Emerson and Whitman, in the preoccupation with strange or rebellious types who left tradition behind, belonging to all these writers. Hawthorne had it even when his approach was somber; Poe and Melville were obsessed by it. A homogeneous world of the imagination had been created in which popular fancies and those of genius were loosely knit together.

VII. FACING WEST FROM CALIFORNIA'S SHORES

PLACE had been a living force in New England, in the West and South, and along the Mississippi. The vanishing horizon had all but created a fundamental national temper. When the rim of the continent was reached in California, when at the same time an enduring human hope was realized, that for treasure trove, exultation rose with a new sense of union. Whitman felt it; allusion to the new rich empire on the Pacific runs through his poetry, curving beyond his pervasive sense of the Great Valley. Something more complex came into his consciousness, for the conquest of California meant not only a final American migration but a final human migration toward the home of races.

Facing West from California's shores,
Inquiring, tireless, seeking what is yet unfound,
I, a child, very old, over waves, toward the house of maternity, the land of migrations, look afar,
Look off the shores of my Western sea, the circle almost circled;
For starting westward from Hindustan, from the vales of Kashmere,
From Asia, from the north, from the God, the sage, and the hero,
From the south, from the flowery peninsulas and the spice islands,

Long having wander'd since, round the earth having wan-
  der'd,
Now I face home again, very pleas'd and joyous,
(But where is what I started for so long ago?
And why is it yet unfound?)

The query of the last lines was to remain unanswered, but
the sense of national enlargement was profound.

Such experiences have always affected the creative imagination. The whole outflowering of the American tradition came in those first brief years of acquisition and discovery. Melville—always facing west—Whitman, even
Hawthorne, wrote their greater works in the small span of
hardly more than half a decade after the conquest of California; and national legends took new forms. It was then
that the mythical Crockett went west and to the South
Seas, and that the strangest scattered tales of far islands,
verging upon the supernatural, crowded the almanacs. A
sense of national union was created which may have been
more binding than that forced union, often considered primary, that followed the Civil War. "I linger yet by the
shores of the vast Pacific," wrote Horace Greeley in 1859,
"for I feel that the general mind is still inadequately impressed with the majestic promise that impels the resistless
tendency of our Gothic race toward the sands of that
mighty sea." But the general mind was deeply impressed.
The new empire haunted the popular imagination, this was
the greatest of the nomadic adventures. In the East, the
music halls and variety and minstrel shows were filled with

songs and stories about California for at least two decades. The American impulse toward autobiography sprang to life in California, and innumerable narratives of personal adventure poured from the press, to be eagerly seized by eastern readers.

The national mind was knit into fresh coherence by ties of fancy, of curiosity, of emotional alliance. Once more the idyllic background of the pioneer experience became clear. "I never felt a more thorough, exhilarating sense of freedom than when first afloat on these vast and beautiful plains," wrote Bayard Taylor to the *Tribune* in '49. "With the mule as my shallop, urged steadily onward past the tranquil isles and long promontories of timber; drinking with a delight that made it a flavor on the palate, the soft, elastic, fragrant air; cut off for a time from every irksome requirement of civilization, and cast loose like a stray, unshackled spirit on the bosom of a new earth, I seemed to take a fresh and more perfect lease of existence." Such serene pleasures were echoed in California newspapers of the cities and the mining camps. The more delicate flowers, the more reticent and wayward scenes, were noted. Instead of the brilliance of sky and water, of red soil and glittering rock, these shyer aspects claimed attention as if a quiet mood lay beneath the extravagant invasion.

But for the new Californians the return journey was bounded—in those quick configurations that make so deep an impress upon the fancy of peoples—by the high Sierras and the long way back by sea. Here was not only a last rim of the continent but a breaking of bounds, a final empire and a release. Hunger, desperate effort, the harsher emotions, were also composed within the scene. Again, as in the Ohio valley when wild bands of river boatmen made their loud rejoinders, the idyllic touch receded or was overlaid by a rougher expression. Again the American hurried with apparent heedlessness over the prints of an older race, bent upon obliterating these, yet accepting certain of their forms. In gross shapes the older life, that of the native Spaniard, was transmuted. Gaiety was now hardly ceremonious: yet gaiety was essential among this new people, with something of the opulence of Spanish days. A mingled procession of highly expressive types marched up and down the new land, drawn from all nations, "one of the most heterogeneous masses that ever existed since the building of the tower of Babel," as one of the great crowd of Californian self-portraitists wrote in '49. Again the theatrical strain in the American character sprang into a many-sided existence. Costume was rich and flamboyant. The theater came into abundant life with the landing of the first gold seekers.

The whole ritual of the pioneer experience was repeated with new intensity and with salient differences. Tolerance now marched with excitement, sophistication with violence. These combinations were not perfect, it is true: racial outbreaks occurred against the Mexicans, the Chileans, the Chinese; but in a closer measure than had been known elsewhere a mixed population milled over the new land with ease and freedom. The English invasion in California, like the solid onset of the French, might have provoked the old nationalistic bias when rivalry over claims grew fierce, but the familiar obsession seemed to have vanished. It was wiped out even from the theater. "There is a sort of independence and liberality here, which with the excitement attending the rapid march of the country . . . must make one who returns from hence to his old beaten path at home feel insignificant, and sad," wrote a California miner in 1855. With all the vociferation of the time and place, patriotic bombast found no outlet; it may be sought in vain even on the likely hunting-ground of political speeches. Nor did the revival take shape; the new settlements developed without the camp-meeting as a basic institution. Mormonism made a brief invasion, but leading Mormons had a way of altering their standards when they reached the gold camps. They built hotels and theaters, and staked out new claims, and gave their humble followers useful tasks.

A fantastic mood was abroad that took closely colored and earthy forms. Bull- and bear-fighting remained as from Spanish days or from other frontiers. Dancing grew primitive and bizarre. A wild hilarity prevailed without the familiar check, without the familiar descent into other communal emotions. That dark intensity, familiar to the wilderness, which had been part fear of the unknown and part the pressure of an ancient faith, seemed to have been lost on the long journey out or to have disappeared in a genial climate. Yet an almost frantic emotionalism was present: too much was at stake for these adventurers to achieve a quiet level. Personal ties had been cut: a deep sentiment, a vast sentimentalism, overflowed along with hilarity. But the terms were elementary, as if the experience of the pioneer had reached its primitive core.

The current mood in California was purely native; and it was comic. With all the vicissitudes, the heartbreak, the losses, the abundance of human failure, the comic mood arose irresistibly. Quickly the curve of theatrical interest ran up from romantic tragedy to extravaganza. Nameless humorists appeared in the new cities and the mining camps; and at least one, Squibob or John Phoenix, achieved a lasting reputation that spread beyond California, as he used grotesquerie and the hoax, ridiculing the pomposities of serious travelers in the new land.

2

IN TWO cresting waves the tide of this farthest frontier rose, in the first rush of '49, and in Washoe as fabulous quantities of gold and silver were discovered in its bleak mountains. In Washoe, with the guns of the Civil War immensely remote, Mark Twain began the renewal of the American comic legend. A touch of this appeared in one of the early letters from Carson, as he wrote of "a *river*, twenty yards wide, knee-deep, and so villainously rapid and crooked that it looks like it had wandered into the country without intending it and had run about in a bewildered way and got lost in its hurry to get out again before some thirsty man came along and drank it up."

At Virginia City, crowded with fortune-seekers from all over the world, Mark Twain outdid the miners in roughness of costume, joined the adventurous spirits on the *Enterprise*, and became "one of the Comstock features that it was proper to see, along with the Ophir and Gould and Curry mines." It was an ugly place at its wildest moment, where characters appeared and disappeared who were more consistently theatrical than any on the California stage. Artemus Ward came to stay three days, and remained three weeks that were a continuous holiday, ending in a lurching procession over the iron roofs of the town, and with Ward making a gibbering speech in blackface at one of the melodeons. Ward too was pictorial: a New Englander, he looked like the rural Yankee of the fables, a caricature of Uncle Sam, or the familiar cartoons of Jack Downing. He was born with the inalienable Yankee countenance, or contrived it. Later when Mark Twain went to San Francisco he encountered other characters of the same histrionic kind.

Bret Harte was there, wearing Dundreary whiskers. Joaquin Miller drifted in, picturesque as a prophet and full of windy rhetoric. Another oracle was added to the group, Orpheus C. Kerr, attached to the highly projected Adah Menken. There were days and nights of uproarious story-telling, and a loud banter which resounded along the Pacific and was continually flung toward Virginia City and back again. "Comedy rolled in shouting under the divine protection of the Son of the Wine-Jar," said Meredith, "never one of the most honored of the Muses." But the comedy which began in that time was sufficiently honored up and down the highways leading out from San Francisco to the Sierras and over the country.

It is a mistake to look for the social critic—even *manqué* —in Mark Twain. In a sense the whole American comic tradition had been that of social criticism: but this had been instinctive and incomplete, and so it proved to be in Mark Twain. Like the earlier humorists he was rich in notation; from *Roughing It* to *The Gilded Age* he contrived to enclose the color of a period with a thousand details of manner, ambition, lingo. But as he turned toward the inclusive or penetrative view he was invariably blocked by some preposterous extravagance that seemed to mount visibly before his eyes. He was primarily a *raconteur*, with an "unequaled dramatic authority," as Howells called it. He was never the conscious artist, always the improviser. He had the garrulity and the inconsequence of the earlier comic story-tellers of the stage and tavern; and his comic sense was theirs almost without alteration.

He summed this up, as they had never done, in *How to Tell a Story*. "The humorous story is American, the comic story is English, the witty story is French. The humorous story depends for its effect upon the *manner* of telling; the comic story and the witty story upon the matter." He had defined the native quality which he had made his own. His stories were oral and histrionic: manner was everything. "The humorous story is told gravely; the teller does his best to conceal the fact that he even dimly suspects that there is anything funny about it." Here was the tradition for the mask, and for the long procession of dull-looking, unlikely oracles. "The humorous story is strictly a work of art, high and delicate art, and only an artist can tell it; but no art is necessary in telling the comic and witty story, anybody can do it." Even the touch of national exaltation was familiar. But the art was hardly high and delicate, as Mark Twain proved by an illustration that was a vast oral practical joke, inducing the jolt of surprise through fright.

Born in the precise era when the American comic sense was coming to its first full expression, in 1835, Mark Twain had grown up in a small town on the Mississippi, in a region where the Crockett myth had taken shape and the tall tale had grown in stature. As a young printer he must have read newspapers of St. Louis and New Orleans that overflowed with the familiar comic narratives; he must have caught the full impact of that spirit of burlesque flourishing so broadly up and down the Great Valley. He could remember—as his tales of the Mississippi show—a crowd of wayward figures given to comedy, troupers, minstrels, itinerant preachers, wandering adventurers from the other side of the world: the variegated lot of migrants who could be seen anywhere in that period moving along the river or toward the plains.

In the compact encirclement of California with its renewal of pioneer life these elements flooded to the surface. Every essential aspect of his talent became articulate there; even his lecturing began in the West, the lecturing which was not truly lecturing at all but the old, spacious form of the theatrical monologue. His first two conspicuous efforts were hoaxes, in the vein which had become familiar thirty years before: after the gory *Dutch Nick Massacre* came *The Petrified Man*, which wore the old air of mythology, and permitted only the slowest recognition of the fact that the fabulous relic had its thumb to its nose. The tale which first gave him nation-wide fame, *The Jumping Frog of Calaveras*, called by Howells "one of his most stupendous inventions," was in fact a tall tale current in California before Mark Twain went there. His Colonel Sellers of later years seems to have been modeled on a slight sketch of the rascally Simon Suggs impersonating an opulent Colonel Witherspoon of Kentucky: Suggs too had soared like a kite as his fancy was loosed.

Again and again Mark Twain went back to that era of the river boatmen which had been a vanishing era in his youth. "I remember the annual procession of mighty rafts that used to glide by Hannibal when I was a boy—an acre or so of white, sweet-smelling boards in each raft. . . . I remember the rude ways and tremendous talk of their big crews, the ex-keelboatmen and their admiringly patterning successors." Some of the talk he reproduced in *Life on the Mississippi*. The Child of Calamity discoursed on the nutritiousness of Mississippi water, and declared that a man who

213

had drunk it could grow corn in his stomach if he wanted to, and that as compared to the water of the Mississippi that of the Ohio was as nothing. "You look at the grave-yards: that tells the tale. Trees won't grow worth shucks in a Cincinnati graveyard, but in a Sent Louis graveyard they grow upwards of eight hundred feet high. It's all on account of the water the people drunk before they laid up. A Cincinnati corpse don't richen the soil any."

That grotesque naturalism which had often approached ancient myth lived again briefly in such glimpses, here re-calling—as in caricature—the legend of the buried Osiris, from whose body sprang the growing stalk of the corn. Once more through Mark Twain those antiphonal and primitive self-descriptions of the river boatmen were heard, which at their best gave a gross effect of poetic ritual. "Whoo-oop! bow your neck and spread, for the kingdom of sorrow's coming! Hold me down to the earth, for I don't feel my powers a-working! Whoo-oop! I'm a child of sin, *don't* let me get a start! Smoked glass, here, for all! Don't attempt to look at me with the naked eye, gentlemen! When I'm playful I use the meridians of longitude and the parallels of latitude for a seine and drag the Atlantic ocean for whales! I scratch my head with the lightning and purr myself to sleep with the thunder! When I'm cold, I bile the Gulf of Mexico and bathe in it; when I'm thirsty I reach up and suck a cloud dry like a sponge; when I range the earth hungry, famine follows in my tracks! Whoo-oop! Bow your neck and spread! I put my hand on the sun's face and make night on the earth; I bite a piece out of the moon and hurry the seasons; I shake myself and crumble the mountains! Contemplate me through leather— don't use the naked eye!"

Yankees had come to the Mississippi; Mark Twain could render the dialogue of two old Yankees bargaining over lots in the graveyard as well as any of the Yankee actors. He turned to the Yankee fable, shaping this anew in *Innocents Abroad*, which came into new and startling life, since the account was factual. The voyage of the *Quaker City* might even be called epochal, when the persistence is recalled with which the American had viewed himself in relation to the parent nations. Here at last, in this voyage of 1869, was the American exodus faintly foretold in earlier years by such creatures of the American fancy as Sam Slick and Sam Patch.

Turning to the European past an habitual and dedicated eye, Mark Twain found on this trip what a century-old and composite American, nurtured on the Yankee fables, could be expected to find, not only that its monuments were decayed, but that the European was a dastardly fellow for the most part, however the circumstance might arouse laughter in the genial newcomer. That the ancestral European had been cringing was proved by the attitude of famous artists of the past toward princely patrons. Even European topography was inferior. "It is popular to admire the Arno. It is a great historical creek with four feet of water in the channel and some scows floating around."

Mark Twain followed the cult of newness like a thousand comic prophets and serious exhorters who had gone before him. He preferred copies of masterpieces to the originals because they were brighter. In a dozen forms he repeated the old assurance that American manners need not be mended. The American could do no fundamental wrong, because he was good. The American had always been good, in the native fancy; he had always been innocent in relation to the European.

For the first time on any substantial scale Mark Twain pictured the American within the European scene. He might have drawn this provincial and untutored traveler against the accumulated riches of ages, with satire and pathos. Perhaps the theme was too new for a truly spacious approach: Mark Twain was himself one of the innocent invaders, without distance, and without perspective. But he seems to have been hampered at the outset by the old formula. He took the trip and wrote the book as though off on an inevitable tangent, when he left California. He circled around the same theme in *A Tramp Abroad;* he repeated it broadside in *A Connecticut Yankee at King Arthur's Court.* "The boys all took a flier at the Holy Grail now and then." "You can't throw too much style into a miracle. It costs trouble, and work, and sometimes money; but it pays in the end." "No soap, no matches, no looking-glass—except a metal one, about as powerful as a pail of water!" Again he took pot-shots at art. He scorned tapestries. "As for proportions, even Raphael himself couldn't have blotched them more formidably, after all his practice on those nightmares they call his 'Celebrated Hampton Court Cartoons.' Raphael was a bird. We had several of his chromos: one was his 'Miraculous Draught of Fishes,' where he puts in a miracle of his own—puts three men into a canoe which wouldn't have held a dog without upsetting. I always admired to study R's art, it was so fresh and unconventional."

In the history of the old fable these three pieces by Mark Twain stand as monuments. As the last migration westward surged toward the Pacific another smaller and more transient movement had begun toward Europe. Even in the early '50's American travelers had begun to announce their judgments on the European scene, sometimes with an acrid humor, sometimes with rapture. A considerable number began a private "pillage of the past," bringing home copies of the masterpieces, marbles, tapestries. This migration had been halted by the Civil War, but it continued in force as soon as the War was over. By the end of the '60's the long and serious quest for European culture was well under way.

The reaction of Mark Twain to this phenomenon was foreordained, steeped as he was in the native tradition and entirely untutored. As a boy he might have seen it enacted on some small western stage, establishing the image. The basic fable grew rigid in his mind, as it had grown rigid for many other Americans. The new cultural migration was contrary to an established figment. So thousands uproariously laughed at the attack and upset and triumph of these latter-day versions, enjoying the rough and tumble the more because they too, many of them, had stood perplexed before masterpieces.

The talent of Mark Twain was consistently a pioneer talent. He showed touches of that abysmal melancholy which had led the boatmen of the Ohio and the Mississippi and the miners of California to drift into lonesome ditties; he struck out, as they did, into a wild burlesque. His obscenity was also of the pioneer piece. The sentimental strain that had been thinly interwoven with the rough tirades of the pioneer appeared in his *Joan of Arc*. Emotion he seldom revealed except in travesty; one of his favorite forms of comedy was to create the semblance of an emotional scene, beguiling the reader or hearer into the belief that this might be true, then puncturing it. Thin-skinned, so sensitive that he could hardly endure a joke turned against himself, he showed the quick revulsions, the neurotic explosiveness, which for long had broken forth into a long-winded comic vein. His fun was often half perplexity, like a revolt from crowding circumstance with no secure base anywhere: the theme of perplexity enters into his humor again and again, in his hoaxes, in his yarns, in *Innocents Abroad*. The savage note sounded, with the crackling weakness of the sardonic, like the inevitable outcome of the romantic mood gone wrong. A great repository, he caught the mood of disillusionment that followed the Civil War.

Mark Twain achieved scale, with the gusty breadth

astir in the country as the Pacific was reached. *Huckleberry Finn* belongs within the scope of that epical impulse which had taken shape in the '50's: it has indeed a cumulative epical power as its main story branches off in innumerable directions under the stress of an opulent improvisation. In this book Mark Twain gave to the great flood of the Mississippi its elementary place in the American experience, with the river as a dominating fantasy, with the small human figures as prototypes of those untethered wanderers who had appeared so often on the popular horizon. Even *The Gilded Age*, in spite of its divided purpose and shambling approaches, takes on something of the same scale, moving toward the encompassment of a period and a people. Mark Twain could never yield to the mode of satire in this book, but fell back continually upon the vast burlesque that had belonged to earlier years and was his heritage. Colonel Sellers was the epitome of those earlier strollers who were fakers and believers with unbounded confidence in fantasies—himself a fantasy of the first magnitude, embodying that perennial unworldliness which mixed so oddly with prosaic qualities in the native character. He too looked afresh at the world every morning and saw a new empire. If he was not the fabulous single figure toward which the national types had tended to merge, his stride was great; he was accepted throughout the nation as its own.

In the end Mark Twain's scope was nation-wide, because of the quality of his imagination, because of the regional elements which he freely mixed, the Yankee with the Californian, the backwoodsman with both of these. The wide reach may be unimportant for judgments of intrinsic quality, but its significance may be great among a people seeking the illusive goal of unity and the resting-place of a tradition. Through Mark Twain the American mind resumed many of its more careless and instinctive early patterns. The sense of legend was continued or restored, or at least the high comic legend again commanded the native fancy. The patterns might have been richer patterns: and Mark Twain's accent of a tense relationship with the older countries may seem deplorable; and much of his comic display has gone the transient way of comedy: he both gained and lost by a primitive vigor and by his adherence to the spoken and theatrical. But all these elements—the tense relationship with the rest—had long since joined in the making of the native character: to have abandoned or lost them would have meant an essential violence and disintegration.

No other tradition could have been shaped and substituted in the chaotic years that followed the Civil War. Traditions cannot be improvised in the slow minds of whole peoples. Even if war had not come, the long labor of a closely established integration would have remained on the greatly extended scale. The conquest of California meant not only a great lift for the fancy but an immense scattering. No deeper furtherance could have been expected in that difficult time, nothing subtle, nothing of that deeply penetrating humor which is reconciliation. If this was to appear (and against all logic it did appear in those years on a wholly different level) the main tradition might still be strengthened by this strong and coarse resurgence.

3

A CONTINUANCE of the long comic tradition was seen elsewhere in these years, maintaining the old forms and a familiar tone. A cluster of new oracles appeared as Mark Twain began to write, adopting the homely masquerade of earlier years and the familiar style of the monologue. The slow still arrows of Artemus Ward struck deep into social and political absurdities; he caught the strolling life which had been almost habitual to the Yankee. His rôle of showman was a symbol—

> ime erflote, ime erflote
> On the Swift rollin tied
> An the Rovir is free

He was afloat with the actors, the circus men, the revivalists, the purveyors of new religions: his mild satire touched them all. He pretended to tell of his stay among the free lovers, spirit rappers, and "high presher reformers on gineral principles." He had known them in early years in Ohio; he met them continually on his travels as a lecturer. On the Mississippi in the '60's he rubbed against a powerful revivalist who could move whole audiences to an abysmal grief for their sins, and who failed to become a bishop because of an irresistible bent toward telling comic stories. Ward lectured to the Mormons. His long countenance was always dull and impassive as he talked. Everything he said seemed unstudied; his best lines were uttered with hesitation as if they were afterthoughts of which he was hardly sure. Yet his lectures and newspaper squibs had the outline, close and unobtrusive, which belonged to the best of the Yankee tradition. Never so large in his political inclusions as Jack Downing, he caught a wealth of comic human detail, and could communicate its effect in print as well as from the lecture platform, using the old device of misspelling to indicate the slow stops and breathings and innumerable oddities of native speech.

Petroleum V. Nasby pictured himself as "Lait Paster uv the Church of the Noo Dispensashun," though his shots were most often political—

> 1st I want a offis
> 2nd I need a offis
> 3d A offis wood suit me; therefore
> 4th I shood like to hev a offis.

Within the rough texture of his satire he was likely to keep revivalistic rhythms and the rhapsodic tone. Orpheus C. Kerr (the office-seeker of Lincoln's time) sported with that rolling and grandiose oratory which came into strong renascence during the Civil War. "The sun rushed up the eastern sky in a state of patriotic combustion, and as the dew fell upon the grassy hillsides, the mountains lifted their heads and were rather green."

Nearly all these latter-day oracles were strolling lecturers; even their writings conveyed the impression of movement over the country. Most of them came out of the West or moved toward the West by large encirclements. In themes, in tone, they belonged to the frontier. None of them was definitely localized; their lingo was far less regional than that of the oracles of an earlier day. Artemus Ward, the most skillful of them all in the sheer comedy of sound, used the Yankee speech with an overlay from the backwoods and called the product Hoosier, though it might have been spoken in many parts of the West, and seemed in fact a composite American speech. The local character was diminished, the local scene lost. The effect again was that of scale, as the new oracles moved toward a national type. Even in the midst of the disruption of the Civil War the drift toward the composite was maintained.

Mimicry and travesty belonged to them all; they caught the scattered life of the time not realistically but with preposterous inflation. They offered talk in a familiar tone, the next thing to conversation; and they were heard and read with an absorbed delight, as if their wide public transferred the burden of uncertain selves to these assured and unabashed provincials. These oracles were indeed profoundly social in their effect as they attacked abuses and foibles and idiosyncrasies of the time; most of them kept that salty and satirical view of the affairs of the nation which had belonged to the earlier figures. Sumner thought that the political value of the Nasby papers could hardly be overestimated. Lincoln pored over all that Nasby wrote and kept the pamphlets near him. "For the genius to write these things I would gladly give up my office," he said; and he read Artemus Ward's *High-Handed Outrage at Utica* as sheer comedy—as comic relief—before the members of his cabinet in 1862, when he was about to lay before them the final draft of the Emancipation Proclamation. Saturated in the story-telling of the West, Lincoln may have gained a sense of foothold as he discovered familiar ground in these monologues. This comedy belonged with his own.

4

SOMETHING more complex than mergence of national types occurred in comedy during these years. Facing west from California's shores meant the spacious view and a fresh sense of unity; it also meant the long breath taken as a last boundary was reached, and a turn toward entrenchment in local life. The lack of a purely nationalistic spirit in California had been a sign. Through Bret Harte in California the local scene was brought into fresh and penetrating consideration. He used the traditional forms: burlesque, the brief sketch, the yarn, the episode, loosely put together, and low-keyed. Indeed he used the monologue: its tone was often apparent even when the personal approach was submerged. The first of his pieces to bring him fame, *The*

Heathen Chinee, though in verse, followed perfectly the unobtrusive manner of the Yankee monologue, and celebrated the mask: its immense vogue must be attributed to the slightly surprising repetition of an old effect. His characters were all wandering adventurers: and again—in spite of appearances—they were good; they were innocent.

His color and intensifications were new. Harte's scenes were closely drawn even while he kept the undemonstrative approach; his characters were limned for intrinsic human quality. For the first time a philosophic strain was noticeable in American comedy: Harte created tragi-comedy. For the first time—barring only the submerged creations of the Negro—elements of the humor of defeat appeared. Hitherto the heroes of the comic stories had been on the high crest, but these characters were outcasts, scalawags, prostitutes, hold-up men. The humor with which they were enwrapped was at an antithesis to the high burlesque of Mark Twain, though Harte too could write superlatively fine burlesque when he chose. Satire came in thin biting understatements. "I took quite a liking to him and patronized him to some extent." "With him life was at best an uncertain game, and he recognized the usual percentage in favor of the dealer." Sentimentalism seeped into some of the tales, and humor at times gave way to pathos; but the flicker of satire constantly lit the small portraits, a satire which was often intimate and communicative as familiar elements were noted in the California scene, such as "the demonstrative gallantry for which the Californian has been so justly celebrated by his brother Californians."

These thrusts were in the traditional manner: little Hill had used them in monologues before Yankee audiences. The response too was familiar: the American had always been sensitive to satirical comment, though in the end he usually acclaimed portraiture with ardor. *The Luck of Roaring Camp* was coldly received in California, but in later years the tales seemed a rich heritage. Harte had in fact many ties with the older local comedy; he had the sense—also strong on the Mississippi in an earlier day— that the times were momentous. Disclaiming the heroic projection, calling his tales sketches, he said he hoped to "illustrate an era"—"an era replete with a certain heroic Greek poetry, of which perhaps none were more unconscious than the heroes themselves. . . . I shall be quite content to have collected here merely the material for the Iliad that is yet to be written." Harte was acutely aware that he wrote of a vanishing scene.

The heroic moment passed, it seems, or lay in the long future, and Bret Harte has been credited with having loosed a sea of local color—or discredited. Yet with all the local picturing that followed, some of it plainly modeled upon effects which he had created, it cannot strictly be said that Harte was a primary influence in this direction. As he was writing on the Pacific Coast a further New England localism came like a dramatic rejoinder in writings of Whittier and of Mrs. Stowe. *Oldtown Folks*—now too little known—was ostensibly a novel but actually a crowd of small, episodic sketches on a colorless string of story, full of pawky humor and packed with the spare hard back· ground out of which that humor had sprung. Whittier, even in the elegiac mood, could portray local character trenchantly, and kept a low-keyed native satire, writing of

> Church-goers, fearful of the unseen Powers
> But grumbling over pulpit tax and pew-rent,
> Saving, as shrewd economists, their souls
> And winter pork with the least possible outlay
> Of salt and sanctity.

In both these writers the impulse toward localism had been of slow growth, as it was in Harte, who went to California in the early '50's and spent more than ten years there before he began writing of the California scene.

The move toward localism was not new; localism had been the very base of the comic in America, even as continual forces of dispersal tended to draw it away from that base. But the tendency to look backward with nostalgia upon the narrow local scene was new; Whittier and Mrs. Stowe as well as Bret Harte saw this as from a distance; they were bent upon a recovery of the past, upon saving the vestiges of a tradition.

It is hardly fanciful to consider that this impulse deepened on both coasts because of the great fulfillment in the West. Dispersal was to continue for many years, if it was ever to be concluded, but ultimate boundaries were at last defined. With all the continuing migrations a distinct flow back to a native regional life had begun, in terms of the imagination. Retrospect, recovery, the ample possession, were to have their long day. The years beginning in the late '60's and culminating in the '80's, so often considered an arid waste so far as creative expression is concerned, were in fact alive with a consistent purpose. It was as if a people were trying to bury itself in its deeper resources. "The great dialectic tracts," as Henry James called them, were explored. John Hay wrote comic ballads of the West, borrowing lingo and spirit. Crockett came to life on the stage, and characters from the interior of Arkansas who had been briefly pictured in the backwoods theater. "The Arkansas Traveller" perpetuated the story of the man who wouldn't mend his roof when it rained and needn't when it didn't. Cable's *Old Creole Days* appeared in 1879; later followed his revival of Creole music. In 1880 the animal fables of Uncle Remus joined with remnants of that Negro minstrelsy which had taken shape fifty years earlier. Out of the South came *In Ole Virginia* with a stringent local assertion, and from the Ohio valley the warm and mellow stories of Eggleston. In belated recognition, the *Journal of American Folk Lore* was founded; and Howells began to talk on the American language.

Even when pathos was added, the main level of this retrospect was comic, as if the resilient mood had survived the heavy surge of an outward movement and its return. The main set was toward primitive figures and primitive phases of American life. Tales of homely circumstance, like

Eggleston's, singled out archetypal figures for commemoration, such as the circuit rider. They were all likely to wear the air of legend. Through the new version of *Rip Van Winkle* the tall tale lived again in a transmuted mythology of death and dream and thunder. Still incomplete, the prolonged revival of this legend on the stage seemed only in part the result of Jefferson's impersonation. The small story had grown through fifty or sixty years in a dozen experimental versions; it had hardly been off the stage during all this long period. It was now revived and re-created, partly, it seems, for the beauty of its local fable, partly because the meaning of that fable met the current feeling by picturing the sudden gulf of years. It was far from being great drama, though it contained the elements of great drama; indeed the story of Rip Van Winkle has never been finished, and still awaits a final imaginative re-creation.

Literature did not arise as an outcome of this concerted effort to recover the past; nothing appeared to compare with American writing of the '50's. This was a homely movement, deliberate and unspectacular, unearthing rich materials rather than creating these anew in final forms. It found a transient resting-place in the theater; it employed the short story. In these years the short story took shape as an essential American form. The tale had always been part of the pioneer mode; and the comic impulse had tended to emphasize a sudden surprising thrust at the end. Poe had perfected the tale within the narrow range of his materials. Eventually the pattern was to grow rigid; the short story was often to seem hardly more than a carefully prepared ejaculation. But it is hardly true, as one argument has it, that the short story has had its prodigious vogue in America because the audience has been incapable of sustained attention. That audience was continually being scattered; the brief tale, the yarn, the sketch, the monologue, could gain a hearing when the long handling of unknown materials could find no place for lack of common knowledge; it was a form of communication. In an early day the Yankee exclamation "Do tell!" or the equally urgent "I want to know!" had been proof of an unsatisfied curiosity and an invincible wish; and the answer had been in kind. It still was; Lydia in *The Lady of the Aroostook* with her "I want to know!" was a symbol in the '70's and '80's as well. The abyss which lies between the short and the longer narrative is to be measured by more than length. It can be traversed only by means of a great accumulation of social knowledge and by the rich and solid rearing of a tradition. American stories of this whole period were short because only a fragmentary knowledge of native life and the native character was at hand.

The movement toward a recovery of the past represented an arduous effort, and offered proof of a new maturity. A war of words has been waged over the relative youth or age of the American nation; but whether one chooses the landing of the Pilgrims or the Revolution as the beginning of the national life, surely a single circumstance is plain. The young lack memory. Memory is one of the possessions of

230

age. The older individual, race, or nation has the great store; and the communal memory must necessarily be a long-established affair; many people, of many generations, must join to create it. In settled communities of the older countries the store grows incredibly rich, with old songs, stories, dances, proverbs, and a traditional knowledge of old events. Life takes on an habitual air; communication can enjoy breadth. It is from such stores that the writers have drawn continually for the wider scope, as in the novel. These rich local materials, transmitted by memory, are striated through the whole sequence of the English novel; they belong to the greater completions of the drama and of English poetry.

By this test the American mind must be counted young; nor is it sufficient to say that individuals or even small clusters of individuals have had a rich remembrance and a heritage. For the race or the nation this must be deep, widespread, cumulative, and not only abundant but super-abundant so that a *largesse* of memory is offered from which to draw. But in America none of that repose necessary for the deepening of memory had been possible. Communal memory could hardly exist when ties with the past were constantly being broken, and vestiges of remembrance brought from the older countries quickly disappeared. Whittier wrote of the English custom, surviving in New England, by which the bees were told of a death in the house; but he told of this as a rarity. Old usages were lost; and even the brief accumulations of new local habit were quickly broken as migration began. One generation of change sufficed to wipe out all but the strongest heritage.

Inevitably, then, the retrospect of the '60's, '70's, and '80's took the form of a brief notation. The accumulations of this period, in fact, though invaluable as traces, though immensely suggestive now to the creative imagination, were a small fund against the losses of time, thinly scattered as they were over many localities. Nor was the view often the long backward view captured a generation before in a more deliberate era by such writers as Bird and Simms. Memory was of the short length, mostly of a single generation. The purpose too was wholly conscious, and warped at times by regional assertiveness; memory in other peoples has grown unconsciously and has become richer for that reason. But the vanishing American scene hung like a bright mirage before many eyes, the purpose to recapture it was clear.

The purpose was stubborn, even heroic, since the cause seemed in a sense a lost cause. Time was not the only antagonist. Every large force in the nation seemed set against this effort. In the late '60's and early '70's primitive comic tales were springing up as if the era of youth for the nation would never be ended. The Negro myth of John Henry was sung in the Carolinas, where it was to endure for many years, spreading far, celebrating a "natural man" whose hammer rang like silver, shone like gold, who blew down mountains, and achieved other lesser and comic exploits. The precise origins of the lumberjack stories of Paul Bunyan can perhaps never be fixed, but they must have begun within this period; they swept through great stretches of forest from Maine to California, with the familiar mock heroic outline, with magnification penetrated by a sly and concealed humor and by a naturalistic magic. Both cycles followed the long-established pattern of the tall tale; both partook of the generalizing tendency; neither was deeply localized. Nor was the great spate of comic or comic-melancholy ballads which arose out of the West localized —the cowboy ballads, hobo ballads, ballads of the mountains and the plains. Local touches appear and at times a local lingo, but they belonged to a widening region. With feet in the saddle, head in the sky," a generic American rides through many of them.

Primitive tendencies were still dominant; and the forces of dispersal seemed unbroken. In the '70's and '80's migration was steadily moving to the western plains, and constantly breaking the fabric of local traditions. Perhaps the Civil War strengthened the sense of the local heritage in a measure, since a conscious sectionalism was a factor in its making; but the War had overturned one of the strongest of localized traditions, in altering the balance of southern and southwestern life. The violence of the War, which had been consistent with the violence of the frontier, where the local heritage had been continually forgotten, seemed to extend the large nomadic pattern.

Memory might not strongly endure; maturity, if it came, might be enriched through other channels. Yet something permanent emerged from the antagonistic movements of the local and the nationalistic. All this tacit warfare had taken place before. It had begun as soon as the first great local figures had been sharply defined in the late '20's or early '30's. On a larger scale familiar forces were being renewed, of penetration and expansion, drawing with them tendencies in the native character. If a lasting antithesis existed, it was no sterile energy which could attempt the legendary figure in *The Gilded Age* and produce the small close regional color of Bret Harte's tales. In the same period another wide continuation appeared in the novels of Henry James.

VIII. THE AMERICAN

THE Civil War has been considered a prime destructive agent in the life of the nation, warping or even destroying a native culture. But the literature of the '50's had never been truly complete. Uncalculating digressions might have followed even though there had been no catastrophe. In spite of the disruption of the War a determined experiment continued through the '60's, '70's, and '80's. The international scene became a great American scene, even in a sense *the* great American scene.

Few ideas had disturbed the American mind more acutely than those which had to do with the European relationship. In the '60's the early commentaries of European travelers still rankled: Tuckerman gathered them into a compendious volume, with rejoinders. But the old fable had undergone a change. In its last notable version, *Our American Cousin*, the nationalistic hero had exhibited his character and enjoyed his adventures in England, and possessed an English heritage. He was in fact one of those "dispossessed princes and wandering heirs" of whom Henry James was to write. In spite of the burlesque the gesture of disseverance had grown less positive in Mark Twain's long skits. The American went abroad, often to stay; sentiment overspread his return to "our old home," and that preoccupation with art

which had been satirized in *Innocents Abroad* became one
of his larger preoccupations.

This was mixed with a consideration which had long
since been borne in upon the American mind by British
criticisms. Culture was an obvious proof of leisure, of long
establishment, of half a hundred desirable assurances that
had been lacking in American life; it even seemed to re-
solve the vexing problem of manners. Culture was sought
abroad as a tangible emblem. The resultant "pillage of
the past" was to mount to monstrous proportions, and to
include the play of many unworthy instincts—ostentation,
boredom, a morbid inversion of personal desires; often, no
doubt, it represented a natural response to the fine accumulations of time. Yet surely on the wide scale it was something more than these. Fumbling and fantastic, the restless
habit seemed an effort to find an established tradition, with
the solidity, assurance, and justification which traditions
may bring. The American wish for establishment had often
seemed a fundamental wish, with all the upheaval.

Many Americans continued to make the extravagant denials of *Innocents Abroad*, but the exodus was unbroken,
and found an interpreter in Henry James. His talk of "dispossessed princes and wandering heirs" was not without a
personal connotation. As a young man, considering Europe,
he had wondered how he was to come into his "own." "The
nostalgic poison had been distilled for him," he declared,
speaking of himself. James became indeed, as Van Wyck
Brooks has said, "an immortal symbol." Strangely enough

236

in this connection, he was something more: an American artist who worked within native sequence.

Henry James has been pictured as a troubled evasionist without a country; and the charge has been turned to a militant charge against American civilization. Yet this theory can hardly account for the long engagement of a major talent. Such talent usually has only one great subject; the choice of that subject will be instinctive, resting upon innumerable elements of heritage and of intimate experience. The consciousness of the European relationship had been binding in America. Given favoring observation, some considerable artist was bound to use the international scene and to find its richest content.

But even a major talent will need the impetus which may come from other imaginative approaches. As formal literary expression of the time is scanned nothing arises to account for the scope and intention of James. He had none of those slightly inferior forerunners in his own medium by which the great writer is often heralded. He wrote as from a fresh impulse; yet the way for his achievement had been opened by a popular vanguard with whose efforts he had some contact. As a small boy he frequented Barnum's, where the Yankee farces were often performed, where the whole American legend was racily sketched, with the backwoodsman and the minstrel as occasional figures, and with melodrama well to the fore. *Our American Cousin* achieved its first great success when James was a lad of fifteen; the play created an immense volume of talk, and was continued for many years. During James's boyhood the streets of New York were alive with the color of the California adventure, with its outlining of the composite American character.

Somewhere James has spoken of the novelist's aptitude for judging the whole piece by a small bit of pattern. Such hints as those abroad in New York during the '50's could go far with a sensitive young mind like his; and others existed to complement them, in the London magazines read before the fire in the New York house, in the visits of Thackeray there, in the glimpses of the great foreign world afforded by the constant voyaging of the family to Europe. James never lost the sense of romance with which his youthful apprehensions of Europe were tinged. He was to write of the European scene with warmth and luster and enchantment; even his dull passages have their inner glow. But he began on humble, even primitive ground in his consideration of the American character as this appeared within the European scene; and he kept throughout his life convictions which he must have drawn from the fund of a common native experience.

2

JAMES was bent upon a purpose that had absorbed many American fabulists, that of drawing the large, the generic, American character. Deliberately, it seems, he abandoned the portrayal of local figures, though for this he had a singular genius: in regions familiar to him he caught the local speech, the manner, the inevitable effect of background. Barring the characters in *The Europeans* and *The Bostonians* and a scattering few elsewhere, his Americans are nomadic and rootless; even when they are seen on American soil they belong to no special locality; they are the composite type; the broad lineaments are unmistakable. He wrote of an American "confidence that broke down . . . a freedom that pulled up nowhere . . . an idyllic ease that was somehow too ordered for a primitive social consciousness and too innocent for a developed." In drawing Roderick Hudson, with his "instinctive quickness of observation and his free appropriation of whatever might serve his purpose," James seemed to have in mind something more than a character: his young sculptor becomes a national type. "His appetite for novelty was insatiable, and for everything characteristically foreign, as it presented itself, he had an extravagant greeting; but in half an hour the novelty had faded, he had guessed the secret, he had plucked out the heart of the mystery, and was clamoring for a keener sensation. . . . The boy was living too fast . . . and giving alarming pledges of ennui in his later years. . : ."

James was candid, as the early fabulists had been candid. He wrote of Americans who treated Europe "collectively, as a vast painted and gilded holiday toy, serving its purpose on the spot, but to be relinquished, sacrificed, broken and cast away, at the dawn of any other convenience." Using the familiar symbolism of the comic name, he pictured the conquering Mrs. Headway, who by a gross energy and with impenetrable surfaces achieved an external European triumph.

He pictured Mr. Leavenworth, "a tall, expansive, bland gentleman, with a carefully brushed whisker and a spacious, fair, well-favored face, which seemed somehow to have more room in it than was occupied by a smile of superior benevolence, so that (with his smooth white forehead) it bore a resemblance to a large parlor with a very florid carpet but no pictures on the walls." Mr. Leavenworth was in fact the pretentious consummation of a dominating American idea. "You may be sure that I have employed a native architect for the large residential structure that I am erecting on the banks of the Ohio," he said to Roderick Hudson. "In a tasteful home, surrounded by the memorials of my wanderings, I hope to recover my moral tone. I ordered in Paris the complete appurtenances of a dining-room. Do you think you could do something for my library? It is to be filled with well selected authors, and I think a pure white image in this style"—he pointed to one of Roderick's statues—"standing out against the morocco and gilt, would have a noble effect. The subject I have already fixed upon. I desire an allegorical representation of Culture. Do you think now," Mr. Leavenworth inquired, "you could rise to the conception?"

These questing Americans—James showed some of them full of an eager pathos, others as indifferent and lost, moving about the world for lack of another occupation. He made an inclusion that went far beyond the efforts of any

American before his time, except that of Hawthorne in *The Scarlet Letter*. He drew American women at full length. With the exception of Christopher Newman and Roderick Hudson and a few others the most significant of James's characters are women: it is they who engage in disastrous encounters abroad, they who embody diverse and contradictory American elements. Isabel Archer, Milly Theale, Mary Garland—their number could be extended: their close and delicate portraiture seemed James's greatest preoccupation. Some of his lesser feminine figures reveal hardy American habits; it is they who most often indulge in the monologue. "I don't apologize, Lord Lambeth," said Mrs. Westgate; "some Americans are always apologizing; you must have noticed that. We've the reputation of always boasting and 'blowing' and waving the American flag; but I must say that what strikes me is that we're perpetually making excuses and trying to smooth things over. The American flag has quite gone out of fashion; it's very carefully folded up, like a tablecloth the worse for wear. Why should we apologize? The English never apologize—do they? No, I must say *I* never apologize. You must take us as we come—with all our imperfections on our heads. Of course we haven't your country life and your old ruins and your great estates and all that. . . ." On she went at immense length, this pretty lady, then and later, "with a mild merciless monotony, a paucity of intonation, an impartial flatness that suggested a flowery mead scrupulously 'done over' by a steam roller that had reduced its texture to that of a drawing-room carpet."

The true heroines of James usually possess a bias of temperament which had appeared more than once in the fable of the contrast and casually elsewhere: Poe had stressed it. "Morella's erudition was profound." "I have spoken of the learning of Ligeia: it was immense—such as I have never known in women." The shadow is not deep in James's novels, but it exists. Mrs. Westgate's sister was little Bessie Alden, a great reader, who united native inquisitiveness with a sturdy integrity. There was Mary Garland, a prim and pretty bluestocking. The young women in *The Europeans*—the true Americans—appear against a background of high thinking; and those in *The Bostonians* form a galaxy absorbed in esoteric knowledge. When these women are not directly absorbed in books they are likely to fulfill the general intention by a definite leaning toward the arts: Isabel Archer walked blindly to her fate because of her belief in the fine accumulations of time. Occasionally James pictured the child of nature—fully feminine at last—as in Daisy Miller or Pandora Day, thus following another tradition; but in the main the women with whom he was most deeply engaged took the aloof, the conscious, the slightly studious part.

Portrait after portrait becomes clear in the great range of his novels and short stories. An entire gallery of characters is created to which Americans may well turn for knowledge and social experience and enlargement, or even for a sense of renewal. They are more than types: they are a whole society of typical individuals: they appear with narrow aggressions and an insular nobility, a careless honesty, a large and delicate purpose. Their ambitions are often blind, or have grown hard and unerring. This society of migratory Americans was a provincial society, transcending provincialism only by fine character. Race, history, even a sense of the future, is upon these people; they still remain singularly inclusive. They offer indeed a legible critique of the American character for those who care to read it; and in the end they reveal more than one unmistakable bias which had appeared in earlier years.

The wilderness and the farm had gone: only their faint traces were discernible in these narratives. James noted in Mr. Westgate a face of toil, a voice of leisure; he remarked a peculiar blankness on the faces of older women who may have belonged to a pioneer society. But for the most part the level has changed; these are people of leisure; they are distinctly urban. The range was wide, the innovation profound; the accomplishment of James, who began to write soon after the Civil War, seems little short of miraculous when set against the spare and simple portraiture of earlier years. Yet his illumination of the American character may have grown bright and deep because he accumulated energy from that portraiture, because he possessed the momentum which a tradition may give. He was grounded in the Yankee fable; his basic apprehension of the American character was that which had been drawn there. He was acutely sensitive to foreign criticism, as a long line of popular writers had been before him.

"It was not in the least of American barbarism that she was afraid," he wrote of Lady Barberina. "Her dread was all of American civilization." The satirical recognition included the familiar foreign charge. In *Pandora's Box* the German envoy was on his way "to explore a society abounding in comic aspects"—an American society comic to the European. Repeatedly James set the wickedness or subtlety or deceit of Europeans against American innocence. The contrast is clear in the small encounters of *Four Meetings;* it lies at the basis of *An International Episode;* it is dramatically posed, with all the implications of a wounding British scorn, in *The Modern Warning.* Even such fine characters as Kate Croy and Merton Denssher reveal an ancestral blackness, against which is drawn the touching and exquisite nobility of Milly Theale, an American.

In later years James denied that the innocent Americans in *The Wings of the Dove* and *The Golden Bowl* were exhibited as Americans; yet the contrast remains. James never presented its opposite terms with imaginative force; and the pattern was repeated too often to be anything but the outgrowth of a profound conviction. He was captivated by the vision of American innocence. In *The Europeans* the American characters appear as the very perfection of a delicate and straitened purity—those indigenous Americans who were being contrasted with vagrant others born and bred in Europe. They were "charming," these true characters, as Felix said, "in a style of their own. How shall I describe it? It's primitive; it's patriarchal; it's the *ton* of the golden age." In one of his later prefaces James wrote with an almost hysterical emphasis of "the comparative *state of innocence* of my country folk."

Truly enough, this preoccupation may have been strengthened by influences outside the old view. The endowment of innocence for heroes and heroines alike had been present in the English novels of his period in a fanciful extreme, and it was not unnatural for the son of the elder Henry James to be concerned with moral and ethereal qualities. Truly enough too, his portrayals often reach far beyond simple effects of contrast and comprise a revelation of moral beauty transcending national considerations altogether; and the pattern was often broken by gross contradictions and incongruities. Yet innocence as drawn by Henry James remains rooted in an established idea. In *The American* he wrote the complete fable, with an altered ending.

3

EVEN the title was a fulfillment. Who ever heard of a significant English novel called *The Englishman* or an excellent French novel called *Le Français?* The simple and aggressive stress belonged to an imagination perennially engaged by the problem of the national type. The name Newman had significance, faintly partaking of that comic symbolism by which a hero in one of the Yankee fables was called Jedidiah Homebred.

At the opening of the story, as Newman strolled through the Salon Carré examining masterpieces, James declared that no one with an eye for types could have failed to perceive that he was an American. "Indeed such an observer might have made an ironic point of the almost ideal completeness with which he filled out the mold of race. . . . He had the flat jaw and firm, dry neck which are frequent in the American type. . . . Long, lean, and muscular, he suggested an intensity of unconscious resistance. . . . His usual attitude and carriage had a liberal looseness; but when, under a special intensity of inspiration, he straightened himself, he looked like a grenadier on parade." Newman was of the familiar build; he had the familiar consciousness of costume; in an ensuing scene he appeared in a blue satin cravat of too light a shade and with a shirt front obtrusively wide. But according to James it was the eye, of a clear cold gray, that told the final story: "an eye in which the unacquainted and the expert were singularly blended"—the innocent and the shrewd. "I can't make you out," said Mrs. Tristram, "whether you are very simple or very deep."

Newman's local origin was never given; though he stemmed from the Yankee, he was not of New England, certainly not of Boston. The Pacific Coast had been the scene of his financial successes; and these were fixed as occurring before 1868, that is, during the period of the gold rush. He might have been in San Francisco or Virginia City with Mark Twain; he had habits of the time and place. "He had sat with western humorists in circles around cast-iron stoves and had seen tall stories grow taller without toppling over, and his imagination had learnt the trick of building straight and high." Young Madame de Bellegarde said that if she had not known who Newman was she could have taken him for a duke—an American duke, the Duke of California. "The way you cover ground!" said Valentin de Bellegarde. "However, being as you are a giant, you move naturally in seven league boots. . . . You're a man of the world to a livelier tune than ours."

Fabulous stories were told about Newman. At the great ball given by the Bellegardes he was presented to the Duchess, whose nodding tiara and triple chins and vast expanse of bosom troubled him, and who looked at him "with eyes that twinkled like a pair of polished pin-heads in a cushion." "With her little circle of admirers this remarkable woman reminded him of a Fat Lady at a fair." "I've heard all sorts of extraordinary things about you," she said, fixing her small unwinking gaze upon him. *"Voyons,* are they true? . . . Oh, you've had your *légende.* You've had a career of the most chequered, the most *bizarre.* What's that about your having founded a city some ten years ago in the great West, a city which contains today half a million inhabitants? Isn't it half a million, messieurs? You're exclusive proprietor of the wonderful place and are consequently fabulously rich, and you'd be richer still if you didn't grant lands and houses free of rent to all newcomers who'll pledge themselves never to smoke cigars. At this game, in three years, we're told, you're going to become President of all the Americas."

"He liked doing things that involved his paying for people," said James; "the vulgar truth is he enjoyed 'treating' them. . . . Just as it was a gratification to him to be nobly dressed, just so it was a private satisfaction (for he kept the full flavor of it quite delicately to himself) to see people occupied and amused at his pecuniary expense and by his profuse interposition. To set a large body of them in motion and transport them to a distance, to have special conveyances, to charter railway-carriages and steamboats, harmonized with his relish for bold processes and made hospitality the potent thing it should ideally be."

Newman preserved a negligent air in such enterprises just as he casually gave an order for copies of half a dozen masterpieces to Mademoiselle Noémie in order to provide money for her *dot*. But he clearly saw the direction of Mademoiselle Noémie's purpose when she announced to him that her paintings were daubs in the hope that her candor might bring her a more considerable profit. He passed over her declaration with his customary blankness, dropping into some hidden cavern of his mind the revelation that his taste had been at fault. "You've got something it worries me to have missed," said Valentin. "It's not money, it's not even brains, though evidently yours have been excellent for your purpose. It's not your superfluous stature, though I should have rather liked to be a couple of inches taller. It's a sort of air you have of being imperturbably, being irremovably and indestructibly (that's the thing) at home in the world. When I was a boy my father assured me it was by just such an air that people recognized a Bellegarde. He called my attention to it. He didn't advise me to cultivate it; he said that as we grew up it always came of itself. . . . But you who, as I understand it, have made and sold articles of vulgar household use— you strike me—in a fashion of your own, as a man who stands about at his ease and looks straight over ever so many high walls. I seem to see you move everywhere like a big stockholder on his favorite railroad. You make me feel awfully my want of shares. And yet the world used to be supposed to be ours. What is it I miss?"

Newman's reply was resounding, and might have been taken out of many an American oration of the past. "It's the proud consciousness of honest toil, of having produced something yourself that somebody has been willing to pay for—since that's the definite measure. Since you speak of my washtubs—which were lovely—isn't it just they and their loveliness that make up my good conscience?"

"Oh, no; I've seen men who had gone beyond washtubs, who had made mountains of soap—strong-smelling yellow soap, in great bars; and they've left me perfectly cold."

"Then it's just the regular treat of being an American citizen," said Newman. "That sets a man right up."

The tone, as one knows Newman, was jocose, with an admixture of serious conviction. It was the comic belligerent tone that had spread through the assertive nationalism of the Yankee fables; and James seemed to enjoy the mixed quality. He glossed over nothing, writing with gusto of Newman's early preoccupation with money, which had also been dominant in Yankee swapping and bargaining. He admitted that his hero considered "what he had been placed in the world for was . . . simply to gouge a fortune, the bigger the better, out of its hard material. This idea completely filled his horizon and contented his imagination. Upon the uses of money, upon what one might do with a life into which one had succeeded in injecting the golden stream, he had up to the eve of his fortieth year very scantly reflected."

"I cared for money-making, but I have never cared so very terribly about money," Newman told Madame de Cintré with expansive confidence, launching into self-revelation. As he sat in her drawing-room he stretched his legs; his questions had a simple ease. "Don't you find it rather lifeless here," he inquired, "so far from the street?" "Your house is tremendously old then?" he asked a little later. When Valentin had found the date, 1627, over the mantelpiece, Newman announced roundly, "Your house is of a very fine style of architecture." "Are you interested in questions of architecture?" asked Valentin. "Well, I took the trouble this summer to examine—as well as I can calculate —some four hundred and seventy churches. Do you call that interested?" "Perhaps you're interested in religion," answered his host. Newman considered for a moment. "Not actively." He spoke as though it were a railroad or a mine; and he seemed quickly to feel the apparent lack of nicety. To correct this he turned to Madame de Cintré and asked whether she was a Roman Catholic.

Satire invaded the portrait—a deep satire—but James loved Newman. Toward the end of his life he spoke of his young "infatuation", with his subject, and though by this he particularly meant an artistic absorption, his personal devotion was likewise plain. He revealed his hero as a man whom Madame de Cintré could love—that creature "tall, slim, imposing, gentle, half *grande dame* and half an angel; a mixture of 'type' and simplicity, of the eagle and the dove." It was Newman's goodness which drew her; but this alone would not have sufficed for the daughter of an old race if goodness had not been joined with an essential dignity.

But while Madame de Cintré and Valentin perceived the genuine stature of Newman others of his family remembered their prejudices. When Madame de Bellegarde first received Newman, knowing his wish to marry her daughter, she sat small and immovable. "You're an American," she said presently. "I've seen several Americans." "There are several in Paris," said Newman gaily. "Oh, really? It was in England I saw these, or somewhere else; not in Paris. I think it must have been in the Pyrenees many years ago. I'm told your ladies are very pretty. One of these ladies was very pretty—with such a wonderful complexion. She presented me with a note of introduction from some one—I forget whom—and she sent with it a note of her own. I kept her letter a long time afterwards, it was so strangely expressed. I used to know some of the phrases by heart. But I've forgotten them now—it's so many years ago. Since then I've seen no more Americans. I think my daughter-in-law has; she's a great gadabout; she sees every one."

Even the gentle Madame de Cintré furthered the critical note, perhaps from a mild notion that Newman would be amused. "I've been telling Madame de la Rochefidèle that you're an American," she said as he came up to her in her salon. "It interests her greatly. Her favorite uncle went over with the French troops to help you in your battles in the last century, and she has always, in consequence, wanted greatly to see one of your people. But she has never succeeded until tonight. You're the first—to her knowledge—that she has ever looked upon." Madame de la Rochefidèle lifted an antique eyeglass, looked at Newman from head to foot, and at last said something to which he listened with deference but could not understand, for Madame de la Rochefidèle had an aged and cadaverous face with a falling of the lower jaw that impeded her utterance. Madame de Cintré offered an interpretation. "Madame de la Rochefidèle says she's convinced that she must have seen Americans without knowing it." Newman considered that she might have seen many things without knowing it; and the

French visitor, again speaking in an inarticulate guttural, said that she wished she *had* known it. This interchange was followed by the polite approach of a very elderly gentleman who declared that almost the first person he had looked upon after coming into the world was an American, no less than the celebrated Doctor Franklin. But he too, in the circumstances, could hardly have known it.

The animus of James, who has so often been pictured as a happy expatriate, mounted as such episodes recurred. At the great reception given by the Bellegardes for Newman after the announcement of his engagement to Madame de Cintré, he was introduced to their friends by her elder brother. "If the Marquis was going about as a bear-leader," wrote James stormily, "the general impression was that the bear was a very fair imitation of humanity." James even made a comment on worldly society which might have derived from one of the early wise, wandering Yankees; its like had been heard in *Fashion*. "Every one gave Newman extreme attention: every one lighted up for him regardless, as he would have said, of expense: every one looked at him with that fraudulent intensity of good society which puts out its bountiful hand but keeps the fingers closed over the coin." Nearly fifty years later James could betray an enduring bitterness. "Great and gilded was the whole trap set, in fine, for his wary freshness and into which it would blunder upon its fate."

When the catastrophe came, when the Bellegardes broke their word and Claire was commanded to withdraw from her engagement, Newman was rejected and publicly humiliated because he was American: they found themselves unable to tolerate that circumstance in relation to their family. He was rejected on the score of manners—the old and vexing score. He should have known that to ask the old Marquise to parade through her own rooms on his arm the evening of the ball would be almost an affront. When the journey was accomplished and she said, "This is enough, sir," he might have seen the gulf widening before his eyes. His commercial connections were held against him; and James pointed the irony of the objection. The Bellegardes were shown as sordidly commercial; in shrewdness they far outdistanced Newman. He was beaten indeed because he was incapable of suspecting the treachery accumulating against him. At the end Newman was unable to maintain his purpose of revenge against the Bellegardes; he destroyed the scrap of evidence which would have proved their earlier inhuman crime. His act is not overstressed; a deep-lying harshness gave stringency to Newman's generous impulses. But the contrast is firmly kept.

With all the preordained emphasis these characters are rounded and complete. The integrity of Valentin was placed against the unscrupulous coldness of his older brother. Claire, with her lovely purity, lights the black picture created by the Marquise. If the balance seems to be tipped down by the inclusion of Mademoiselle Nioche and her deplorable father, there is always Mrs. Bread. As a great artist James had moved immeasurably beyond the simple limits of the original fable. A genuine tragedy was created whose elements were tangled deep in inalienable differences. At the last Newman was unable to understand either the character or the decision of the woman he so deeply loved. Circling across the sea and the American continent, he returned again to Paris by an irresistible compulsion, and at twilight one evening, a gray time, walked to the convent of the Carmelite order in the Rue d'Enfer and gazed at the high blank wall which surrounded it. Within, his beloved was forever enclosed, engaged in rites which he could never understand, withdrawn for reasons which he could not fathom. He could never pass beyond that wall, in body or in spirit. The image was final, and became a dramatic metaphor: in the spelling of the old fable the outcome had changed from triumph to defeat. Defeat had become at last an essential part of the national portraiture.

4

ALMOST invariably the opening moods and even the later sequences of James's novels were those of comedy. He instinctively chose the open sunny level; the light handling of his early *Confidence*, uncomplicated by the international situation, shows what he could do in maintaining this when his materials permitted. He ran indeed through a wide gamut of humor, from that of the happy and easy view and a delicate satire to a broad caricature and irony. Social comedy appeared in Henry James. For the first time an

American writer drew a society and infused his drawing with an acute sense of human disparities. Yet the aggregation of his novels does not spell comedy, but a kind of *tragédie Américaine*, which was in large part a tragedy of manners. "I have the instincts—have them deeply—if I haven't the forms of a high old civilization," Newman told Claire de Cintré; but the instincts, if he possessed them, were not enough. *Daisy Miller*, bringing down a storm of angry reproof upon James's head, was a classic instance which he multiplied with variations of subtlety and range.

Defeat for the American adventurer was new, at least in wide transcription. Triumph had hitherto been the appointed destiny in American portraiture, except for vagabonds and common adventurers. Yet with all the tragic implications the ultimate ending of these latter-day fables was not that of tragedy. In the midst of his final encounters with the forces of opposition Newman gathered his energies; his spirits rose. When he confronted the Marquis de Bellegarde he "had a singular sensation; he felt his sense of wrong almost brim into gaiety." He could laugh during the momentous interview with Mrs. Bread; at one moment in their plotting his face "lighted with the candor of childhood." The mood was unreasoning, beyond reason: it was a typical mood, that of resilience under opposition or criticism. Finally, after all the conflict, after his searching and baffled effort to understand inscrutable forces, this mood was resolved into something subtler and more enduring than resilience. When Newman stood before the wall that forever enclosed Claire de Cintré "the barren stillness of the place represented somehow his own release from ineffectual desire." Touching the nadir of despair and disillusionment, he was "disburdened"—free at last from those dark personalities by whom he had been cruelly wronged. He reached a moment of profound recognition, not perhaps of the inner character of the forces that worked against him —these he could never understand—but of his own final plight. He achieved that laden balance of mind and feeling from which an enduring philosophical comedy may spring. As one sees Newman beyond the end of the book he has become a far graver character, but for him something of humor might play quietly once more.

Again and again James pictured this low-keyed humor of defeat. For Isabel Archer more than one way of escape lay open; fronting these possibilities, she made the choice which meant renunciation; and the outcome is not tragic, for all the wrench which it produces at the end, since James has revealed that free poise and nobility of her character which made renunciation inevitable and acceptance of her lot tolerable. Even *The Wings of the Dove* cannot be called tragedy. Milly Theale learned the worst there was to know of those to whom she was attached, their betrayal, their base purpose; yet with knowledge she still could keep a magnanimous love. James repeated this stress again in the recognition which finally lay between Kate Croy and Milton Denssher. Each had plumbed a deep and even dangerous knowledge of the other; yet an indissoluble accept-

257

ance remained between them; and their final alliance had a touch of the secure upward swing which belongs to comedy.

In comedy reconcilement with life comes at the point when to the tragic sense only an inalienable difference or dissension with life appears. Recognition is essential for the play of a profound comedy; barriers must be down; perhaps defeat must lie at its base. Yet the outcome in these novels was in a sense the traditional outcome, for triumph was comprised in it; but the sphere had altered from outer circumstance to the realm of the mind and spirit; and triumph was no longer blind and heedless, but achieved by difficult and even desperate effort.

In this outcome James transcended the nationalistic altogether—that obsession which had had so long a history. Yet in the aggregate of his novels he repeated a significant portion of the old fable. He showed that the American was in truth what the belligerent Yankee had always declared him to be, a wholly alien, disparate, even a new character. In the end the primary concern of James was with that character; and he kept a familiar touch of the fabulous in his narratives. "I had been plotting arch-romance without knowing it," he said of *The American;* and by romance he meant what Hawthorne had meant, life with a touch of the marvelous, an infusion which can be apprehended only imperfectly by the sense of fact. Romance appeared in the generality and scale which James gave to his characters and to his situations. Such titles as *The Wings of the Dove* and

258

The Golden Bowl suggest a poetized conception completing the romantic character of the themes; and his handling is kept free from complicated circumstance. Poetry indeed overspread much of James's writing. Like that of the popular fabulists, it was packed with metaphor. "The morning was like a clap of hands." "She carried her three and thirty years as a light-wristed Hebe might have carried a brimming wine-cup." His figures could also be ironical; the romantic feeling is constantly enclosed by a close drawing. Recognition is fundamental in all of James's portraiture; yet a basic poetry of outline and expression remains clear, most of all in his later novels. Few writers have had so deep a sense of the poetry of character; and his poetical penetration was the rarer achievement because his approaches were not those of the primary emotions.

In commentary James once spoke of one of the women whom he had drawn as "unaware of life." Elsewhere he wondered "what it might distinguishably be in their own flourishing Order that could *keep* them, the passionless pilgrims, so unaware?" "Passionless" surely was not meant to include his major characters; yet even they could not be called passionate in the sense that the characters in *Wuthering Heights* are passionate; it is significant of his obsessions that elsewhere James could give the attribute "passionate" to a pilgrim in quest of the past. For the most part emotion in these Americans in his wide gallery is frustrated, buried, or lost. Instead, renunciation, tenderness, pity, are likely to be dominant among them. The finest of these feelings do not belong to the primary emotions; they are restrained or delicate or withdrawn. These characters indeed are of an established native mold; this diminution had prevailed elsewhere. In a fashion James himself revealed the same qualities; a profound tenderness suffuses the greatest of his writing, but not the compulsion of a deep and natural, simple emotion. He gains power by integrity, by a close intensity of view, often by intensity of the mind. His portrayals gain every possible concentration from the high art by which they are revealed. "Dramatize! dramatize!" he said again and again; and the dramatic quality belonged to his writings at every point, in the ready immediacy of the talk, in the swift juxtapositions, in swift and daring ellipses, particularly in his later novels. At one point he considered that the drama was his true form. "I feel at last as if I had found my *real* form, which I am capable of carrying far, and for which the pale little art of fiction, as I have practiced it, has been, for me, but a limited and restricted substitute." James failed in writing drama; nothing of true dramatic expression had appeared in American literature, and he was not to transcend its tendency. He necessarily failed, lacking a depth of simple emotion; the approach to the drama had been made before without completion, perhaps for the same reason. James returned to the novel, and kept the dramatic organization.

The highly conscious artist was uppermost in Henry James; and he joined in the traditional bias toward the inward view. Strangely enough, though he had no New

England ancestry and was likely to be positive in his declarations to the contrary, he came closer than any of the earlier American writers to that introspective analysis which had belonged to the Puritan, closer even than Hawthorne. His scrutiny of motives, while delicate, was intense. He never used that direct revelation of elements in the stream of consciousness which had been ventured by Whitman and Hawthorne before him; yet his later novels are full of the unsaid and understated; they are full of complex moods and states of inner feeling revealed by the slightest and most ephemeral of notations. Whether or not James was subject to some untraceable Puritan influence, whether he touched popular sources, whether perhaps he gained greatly from the initial experiments of Hawthorne and Poe, his novels vastly amplified this new subject of the mind lying submerged beneath the scope of circumstance, which had long engaged the American imagination.

5

NEARLY always the mark of that era in which an artist is young will in some way lie upon his work, however far he may advance into the future. Henry James bore the mark of that deeply experimental era which came to a culmination in the late '40's and early '50's. Like Poe, Hawthorne, Melville, Whitman, he performed that difficult and elliptical feat by which a writer both invades a province and occupies it. Like them he was in a sense a primary writer.

No American before him had made a full imaginative approach to living characters and the contemporary scene; the view hitherto had been mainly the retrospective view. He greatly extended the areas of native comedy; he all but created a new subject for the novel in his stress upon the inward view; he discovered the international scene, as Van Wyck Brooks has said, "for literature." There is irony in the fact that so wide and subtle an accomplishment should have been produced within a tradition that still bore the print of the pioneer. There is a further irony in the circumstance that the American character should first have been fully realized within the European scene. This remoteness has been considered a flight and a loss; and truly enough to have perceived that character with equal amplitude against the native background would have meant an immense gain in imaginative understanding. Yet James's choice fulfilled the consciousness of a fundamental relationship; only the denial had been abortive.

The great experimental writer is like to betray signs of incompletion, to cover more than one era, to show hesitation as well as an unmistakable security. James showed some of these signs. They are apparent in the great division between his later and his earlier writing, and in the incalculable abysms of his later style. In a strange fashion after the middle of his career he showed a partial reversal of his sense of language, which took on an extreme gentility even while it attempted that colloquialism which had been part of the American tradition. He strove for elegances like a minor writer of the '30's who sought to prove that Americans too could enter the stately domain of English literature. He used quotation marks to set off such phrases as "detective story," and the attempted grace of his movements through the great morass of his words was often elephantine. In his final revisions of the earlier novels he often emasculated a vigorous speech. The result was a form of writing which was neither English nor American in character. Yet few experimental writers have maintained so fine an artistry or encompassed with that artistry so great a scope. His failures are minor failures within a great original accomplishment.

Howells was the only other measurable American writer of this time to employ the novelistic form; the concerns of Howells were largely regional; he was engaged by small portions of the American scene and of the American character; he never fused these into an unmistakable and moving whole. The real situation in *Silas Lapham* lay between the Yankee and the Bostonian, between Lapham and the Coreys, between Penelope and young Corey. Here were elements of social comedy or tragedy, which Howells pictured in one scene which remains a high scene in American humor, full of comedy indeed, full of pathos and hurt— the scene of the Coreys' dinner-party. But Howells evaded the full scope of the indicated differences, packing Lapham off to Vermont and Penelope and young Corey to South America. He made the same evasion in *The Lady of the Aroostook*, never showing Lydia in any prolonged contact

263

with the superior Americans with whom her destinies were linked, never exploring the social situation beyond its superficial aspects, and again at the end sending his two major characters to far parts, where the manners and speech of the country girl need trouble nobody, and where Howells at any rate was not troubled by ensuing complications.

In spite of lapses in local observation, Howells had a striking aptitude for seizing essential elements in the native tradition: he knew the Yankee, the backwoodsman, the itinerant revivalist. His narratives are full of prime comic sketches, full of a racy contemporary and local speech. They reveal too that acute and expressive awareness with which the American constantly viewed himself, his fellow countrymen, his nation. His young men are always theorizing about America, and often have superior attitudes. "What a very American thing!" exclaims one of them when he heard Lydia saying "I want to know." "It's incredible," he continued. "Who in the world can she be?" The American quarrel with America, the product of a long self-consciousness, was beginning.

Howells had it in his power to draw social comedy of breadth and the first order, for disparities of background were included within his view; he was grounded within the comic tradition. He might have been the great artist to picture the American against the native scene, complementing the portrayals of James abroad. He had all the gifts except a passionate concern with his subject. Whether from lassitude or from a fundamental lack of imagination he never truly explored his materials; not one of his novels can be put beside *The Portrait of a Lady* or *The American*. He veered from one theme to another, from one locale to another. His novels were in the end not novels at all but an invaluable collection of minor notations on the American character.

Henry James stands alone in his time, not wholly to be accounted for, not in any immediate sense productive as an influence. He began writing in the '60's; his work was hardly a force among other writers for nearly half a century. In later years other American writers have followed him in using the international scene; yet his other great achievement, that of portraying the inner mind, cannot be said to have given any notable impetus to the American novel. It is abroad that the implications of his work have been pushed to their furthest boundaries. Proust and Joyce, Dorothy Richardson and Virginia Woolf, may or may not have been influenced by James; but they have carried the whole stress of an American intention far beyond anything achieved by American writers, in their portrayal of the inner consciousness.

The fate of Henry James has been that of other primary writers within the American tradition. Each of these had stormed some battlement without a following sequence of writers. The prolific energies that create an entire literature were lacking in this long period, though a widely flung pattern had been created which had freshness and even magnificence.

IX. ROUND UP

THE pattern created for an American literature had been touched with poetry again and again; it had often been grounded in a primitive poetry. The exultant "I" appearing at the very center of popular comedy had promised the sudden narrow intensity of the lyric; and here and there the lyric fragment had appeared. But the pure lyric rests upon that final freedom by which the single mind loses association with the crowd at least for the intense moment; and in America the individual had often seemed nearer to the crowd than to himself; among highly emotional talents expression was likely to be public and general, running to oratory. Social preoccupations seemed to prevent that deep arrogant convergence of personal feeling and experience by which the lyric is produced. Poe wrote a few flawless lyrics, but he too was constrained to follow the bent of the time and formulated in prose the emotions which had been part of the communal experience, or else ventured into that other province toward which the American temperament had consistently turned, that of inner fantasy.

Emily Dickinson was not predictable; yet the comic sense, widely abroad, upsetting many stabilities, was bound at last to break that tie holding the poet within the bondage of social preoccupation. Emily Dickinson was not only a lyric poet; she was in a profound sense a comic poet in the American tradition. She possessed the sense of scale and caught this within her small compass. A little tippler, she leaned against the sun. The grave for her was a living place whose elements grew large in stone. Purple mountains moved for her; a train, clouds, a pathway through a valley became huge and animate. Much of her poetry is in the ascending movement, full of morning imagery, of supernal mornings: seraphim tossing their snowy hats on high might be taken as her symbol. Her poetry is also comic in the Yankee strain, with its resilience and sudden unprepared ironical lines. Her use of an unstressed irony in a soft blank climax is the old formula grown almost fixed, yet fresh because it was used with a new depth—

> Faith is a fine invention
> For gentlemen who see;
> But microscopes are prudent
> In an emergency!

She could cap tragedy with tragi-comedy.

> Drowning is not so pitiful
>   As the attempt to rise.
> Three times, 'tis said, a sinking man
>   Comes up to face the skies,
> And then declines forever
>   To that abhorred abode
> Where hope and he part company—
>   For he is grasped of God.

The Maker's cordial visage,
    However good to see,
Is shunned, we must admit it,
    Like an adversity.

She was concerned with eternal verities; yet her elastic and irreverent rebellion broke forth again and again—

"Heavenly Father," take to thee
The supreme iniquity,
Fashioned by thy candid hand
In a moment contraband.
Though to trust us seem to us
More respectful—"We are dust."
We apologize to Thee
For thine own Duplicity.

Occasionally her wit turned mordantly upon earthly matters: "Menagerie to me my neighbor be." She saw the small and futile motions in a house to which death had come. And she could double ironically upon herself as well as upon the Deity. In the end—or at least in the composite, for the end is hardly known—she contrived to see a changing universe within that acceptant view which is comic in its profoundest sense, which is part reconciliation, part knowledge of eternal disparity. If she did not achieve the foundation of a divine comedy she was at least aware of its elements; its outlines are scattered through the numberless brief notations of her poems.

Like Poe and Hawthorne and Henry James, though with a simpler intensity than theirs, Emily Dickinson trenched upon those shaded subtleties toward which the American imagination long had turned. "I measure every grief I meet with analytic eyes." Anger, hope, remorse, the weight of the past, the subtle incursions of memory, the quality of despair, and fear, cleavages in the mind, all came under her minute scrutiny—

> One need not be a chamber to be haunted,
> One need not be a house;
> The brain has corridors surpassing
> Material place.

Even her glances toward an exterior world at their finest are subjective. Her poetry was indwelling in a final sense; she used that deeply interior speech which is soliloquy, even though it was in brief song.

She never lost a slight air of struggle; this appeared persistently in her sudden flights to new verbal and tonal keys, in her careless assonances which still seemed half intentional, in the sudden muting of her rhymes. She verged toward the dramatic, as others in the tradition had done before her; almost invariably her poems concentrate upon a swift turn of inner drama: yet like the others she sheered away from pure drama. Her language is bold, humorously and defiantly experimental, as if she had absorbed the inconsequence in regard to formal language abroad during her youth in the '50's when Whitman was writing; yet often she achieved only a hasty anarchy in meaning and expression, and created hardly more than a roughly carven shell.

She seemed to emerge afresh as from a chrysalis in each lyric or even in each brief stanza; and the air was one which had been evident before in the sequence of American expression. Emerson had it, as Santayana noted, in everything he wrote. Whitman had it, and was aware of the quality: it was that of improvisation. In one way or another every major American writer had shown its traces, except perhaps Henry James in the broad spaces of his early novels, but he too turned toward experiment in the end. Emily Dickinson was another—perhaps the last—of those primary writers who had slowly charted an elementary American literature; and she possessed both the virtues and the failings of her position. Her poetry has an abounding fresh intensity, a touch of conquering zeal, a true entrance into new provinces of verbal music; but incompletion touches her lyricism. Often—indeed most often—her poems are only poetic flashes, notes, fragments of poetry rather than a final poetry. Yet like the others who had gone before her—Whitman, Hawthorne, Emerson, James—she set a new outpost, even though like them she had no immediate effect upon American literature. It was not until ten years after her death that the early poetry of Edwin Arlington Robinson appeared; and the space widens if the '40's are remembered as formative years for Emily Dickinson, the '80's for Robinson. Nor does he show any perceptible trace of her influence. But if not by her power, then by some profound stress in the American character, the gates were being slowly opened for an ample poetry.

2

FOR more than a century the poetic temper had been dominant in the country, nourished by a sense of legend. The American imagination had invested the commonest preoccupations and homeliest characters with an essential poetry. Now as the areas of a literature were fairly defined the poetic strain arose as the major strain. For nearly twenty years after the publication of *The Children of the Night* in 1896, poetry comprised the only notable American literature.

The appearance of Robinson marks a turn, not only because he was the first of a group of poets and even of a new literary movement, but because he has used American traditions with freedom and fullness. For companions in the legendary village of Tilbury Town he has chosen types recurrent throughout early American comedy, ne'er-do-wells, liars, the quirky, the large-hearted and lost, spendthrifts of time and money and love. Robinson is master of that unobtrusive irony that has belonged to the Yankee; like the older Yankee he turns constantly to a dry metaphor—"an old vanity that is half as rich in salvage as old ashes." He has all but created a new form of blank verse; and not the least of the elements which have gone into its making is the rhythm of a taut, yet slowly moving Yankee speech. Burlesque appears in his use of rolling measures for mock romance; understated comedy lies beneath many of the shorter poems—"He missed the medieval grace of

271

iron clothing." A reticent humor runs through much of Robinson's poetry, so quietly as to pass unnoticed by many readers, yet producing a constant lighting and relief and change, with a balancing of forces against the impending tragedy. Tragedy has become his great theme; he uses that groundwork of defeat which had come slowly into the American consciousness: yet the outcome is not always wholly tragic; it is likely to be neither death nor destruction but a stripped acceptance of fate: within this range comes the great play of Robinson's perception of character.

Character had always been the great American subject—character enwrapped in legend, from the Yankee of the fables and the fabulous Crockett to the novels of Henry James. Character is of course Robinson's great subject, seen in legendary aspects, though the nationalistic bias, which had often warped an earlier approach, is now gone. His main concern has been with those elements of the mind which have made an almost continuous American preoccupation. For a poet he is singularly unengaged by the outer world: the look of his people, like his touches of landscape or other effects of setting, is drawn in a few brief, intense passages: his genuine subject is fantasy, the evocation, the obsession, the complex and indwelling emotion. He has placed the psychological narrative within the realm of poetry in a new and modern sense, and is an heir of both Hawthorne and Henry James, following too that homelier tradition for the monologue verging upon soliloquy which had long been part of the popular tradition. Even though his longer poems enclose a narrative—most often a highly dramatic narrative—they have the air of soliloquies, not in the single mood but in many moods. Conflicts take place within the mind or among a group of minds—as in *Lancelot*—or move into the realm of "supernatural surmisings" far beyond common experience, as in *Cavender's House* and *The Man Who Died Twice.*

At the same time Robinson has laid an English ghost. That haunting sense of English standards which had taken so many obsessive forms in an early day both in and out of the realm of literature had by no means died by the latter end of the century: small groups of minor writers were still appearing who sought to imitate English writers; American literature was still, at the most hopeful, regarded as a province of English literature. Robinson is the first American poet to make free and unembarrassed use of English traditions as if these were part of a natural heritage, even while he keeps an unmistakable American groundwork. His poetry could never be mistaken for English poetry by any sensitive reader; the tone, the idiom, the latent sound of the voice are American.

Before Robinson only Henry James had used both a literary and a popular American tradition; and in James the signs of an American literary heritage were scant; he belonged to the small vanguard who were creating a literary groundwork. In a profound sense Robinson is also an originator; only a poet of fresh power could have emerged from the minor poetry of the '80's and '90's as he did with *The*

Children of the Night. But in feeling and intention he is essentially a traditional writer; and the change which he embodies has great significance in the history of the American imagination. It is only when traditions are deeply established that a whole literature can be created. After slow and even reluctant ventures, a period of fulfillment seemed to begin. The change was marked; it grows clear in the work of other poets who followed Robinson in time. Lindsay, Frost, Masters, Sandburg all have revealed characters, fantasies, and patterns of mind or feeling that appear in an early comic folk-lore.

Lindsay is a latter-day gamecock of the wilderness who betrays at times a genteel cast, which he seems to have learned from the literary dilettantism mentioned by Emerson long ago. Fays are likely to appear in his poetry, along with Johnny Appleseed or John Brown or Andrew Jackson; and he has kept a primitive nationalistic feeling.

Andrew Jackson was eight feet tall.
His arm was a hickory limb and a maul.
His sword was so long he dragged it on the ground.
Every friend was an equal. Every foe was a hound.

Andrew Jackson was a Democrat.
Defying kings in his old cocked hat.
His vast steed rocked like a hobby horse.
But he sat straight up. He held his course.

He licked the British at Noo Orleans;
Beat them out of their elegant jeans.
He piled the cotton bales twenty feet high,
And he snorted "freedom," and it flashed from his eye.

And the American Eagle swooped through the air,
And cheered when he heard the Jackson swear:—
"By the Eternal, let them come.
Sound Yankee Doodle. Let the bullets hum."

And his wild men, straight from the woods fought on
Till the British fops were dead and gone.

The piece ends with a bellicose assertion which could hardly have been matched in the days of the red-white-and-blue Yankee; and it is prefaced by a futile rallying-cry for the renascence of American traditions: "It is for us to put the iron dog and deer back upon the lawn, the John Rogers group back into the parlor, and get new inspiration from these and from Andrew Jackson ramping in bronze replica in New Orleans, Nashville, and Washington, and add to them a sense of humor till it becomes a sense of beauty that will resist the merely dulcet and affettuoso."

With his belligerent assertion of the noisier and cruder phases of the American inheritance Lindsay seems a throwback to some of the earlier comedians of the last century. He is often oratorical, theatrical, evangelical. But when he began to write, about 1910, that fundamental past had receded farther away than the Revolution; bringing this into view, he may be counted one of those writers who sustain a tradition and in large measure re-create it, for at his best he succeeds in finding a fresh poetry. In the first two movements of the *Booker Washington Trilogy* and in *The Congo* he has caught enduring Negro rhythms within a simple pictorial style of genuinely primitive largeness and force; he overflows with the exuberant story-telling of the West; and

275

he has achieved a bold lyricism in *The Broncho That Would Not Be Broken*. Scattered through his immense and unchecked abundance are brief, deeply moving lyrics like *Heart of God*. Then he has turned, like the earlier comic poets, toward the creation of new myths, as in his *Bryan* and *General Booth Enters into Heaven*. Lindsay appears as a slightly conscious reincarnation of the early fabulous era; he has the fathomless good humor and the inconsequent air of surprise that belonged there. Fantasy—a wild comic fantasy, infusing many materials—belongs to his poetry, in the extravagant oral style of the past.

Untroubled by the effort to establish a tradition, Robert Frost has used familiar elements as his own, by the slightest, surest indications rather than by transcription. Old patterns of speech appear, in the familiar Yankee rhythms, unobtrusive and slow; old voices are heard, as in *The Generations of Men*, and bits of regional remembrance. Character is drawn in the habitual Yankee fashion, almost always with an indirect beginning, scant emphasis, a slow unraveling. "Never show surprise!" says one of the characters in *North of Boston*, "this book of people." Frost has kept the native humor, often deepened to a bitter irony, but delicately infused; most of his humor, like that of the early Yankee tradition, is so deeply inwoven with his further speech as to be almost inseparable from it. There is no touch of frontier coloring here, only furtherance of a tendency which had been implicit in the Yankee monologues, that toward soliloquy. Frost's lyrics are soliloquies, as are his drawings of people. This is a poetry which is acutely and sensitively self-conscious, turning to deep account the old self-consciousness that had been constant in the American mind and character, finally moving beyond the local, beyond New England people, New England pastures, or snowy roads, or houses black with rain, into sensitive human revelation.

Something of antiphony was sounded as Lindsay spoke out of the West after the far quieter voice of Robinson had been heard; it sounded again as the *Spoon River Anthology* was placed against the New England poems of Frost. In the long and many-sided poem of Masters are drawn elderly children of those loud-spoken backwoodsmen who belonged to the small river towns and villages of the '30's and '40's; the people of Spoon River keep the habit of the monologue, even in death. Perspective grows through death and its decisions; defeat is upon these people; humor is turned to irony and joined with that tenderness that had belonged to Whitman and often seems to replace stronger emotion in American writing. Freedom of form in the *Anthology* came through Whitman, with a revelation of a basic living speech like that in Robinson, Lindsay, Frost, which derives from a race of talkers and oral story-tellers. For all the brevity of the single speeches the scale is the legendary scale; again—as in popular comedy and in an early literature—it is less the single character that is evoked than the village, the aggregate type, a way of living.

277

Again in the poetry of Carl Sandburg speech is dominant, taking free poetic forms; his poetry loses from merely visual reading. Like that of Whitman it is often improvisation, containing notations for poetry rather than poetry itself; but Sandburg's rhythms are his own; they spring from the speech of a late day and a mixed people. No other poet has given such direct glimpses of the immediate American scene—of the land, its look from the Shenandoah Valley to the Ohio and the Great Lakes, from the mid West to the coast of California, its cities and prairies, its weeds and flowers and cornfields, backyards and birds, rains and winds and people. The notations are brief; again and again they make a "little album." Humor pervades them, an exhilarated, inflated humor that belongs to the West, as in *Many Hats*, or an elementary overflowing good humor, or a simple irony—

The lavender lilies in Garfield Park lay lazy in the morning sun.
A cool summer wind flicked at our eyebrows and the pansies fixed their yellow drops and circles for the day's show.
The statue of Lincoln, an ax in his hand, a bronze ax, was a chum of five bluejays crazy and calling, "Another lovely morning, another lovely morning."
And the headline of my newspaper said, "Thirty dead in race riots."
And Lincoln with the ax, and all the lavender lilies and the cool summer wind and the pansies, the living lips of bronze and leaves, the living tongues of bluejays,

278

all they could say was, "Another lovely morning, another lovely morning."

This freshly caught observation is newer than it sometimes seems; the character of the land—the look of the broad scene—had never been appropriated by American writers; it had been revealed in the briefest notes, often only in the single metaphor, or in generalization; even Whitman had generalized it. Only one other American had attempted observation on a broad scale; this was Audubon—the Audubon who was the wandering backwoods adventurer, strolling through the wilderness and along the rivers, playing the flageolet, making comical notes, painting portraits, or decorations for river steamers, drawing birds, moving at last up and down the whole breadth of the land. Sandburg is akin to this errant adventurer. His sense of scale—more benign than Audubon's—has a touch of similar mischief. He often uses the highly American form of rhapsody, and breaks at times into the pure lyric. But for the most part his inclusions are too wide for the lyric, his emotion communal rather than individual. The print of the pioneer lies deep upon his poetry, the pioneer who knew the land, and was forever captured by fresh scenes, moving toward them.

3

IT IS a gauge of the national temper that the first modern approaches to character and the native scene should have been made in poetry rather than in that form which has most commonly contained them, the novel. Strictly speaking, the novel has not developed in America. Above all the novel is a copious form, copious in its handling of the human theme, copious for the most part in its sequences; the English novel has developed in group after foliated group, embracing multitudes of characters, many and variable scenes. This abundance has always been largely concerned with an immediate era, with immediate materials; often it has sprung from provincial life and has remained embedded in provincial life, though its finer residuum may have nothing to do with time or place. But the single real novelist whom America had produced, Henry James, had turned away from the immediate scene; in more than one sense his view was the far view; he was bent, as were his characters, upon establishing a relationship with the European past. That local literature which began with the conquest of California and continued through the '70's and '80's had also been largely concerned with retrospect. When retrospect was not dominant something generalized had taken its place, manifest in the long sequences of comic myth-making, which was grounded in the immediate and circumstantial but moved quickly into the typical and fanciful.

These tendencies have remained unbroken; the distant, the retrospective, the legendary have prevailed even in the new period. It is not the novel which has developed but the romance, the cumulative tale, the saga, even the allegory. A touchstone for the writing of Willa Cather exists in the fact that it is easier to compare her with poets than with novelists. As a regional writer she may be linked with Frost, though her themes belong to the West and the farther Southwest. Fine craftsman as she is in prose, her narratives are shaped to those simple, close outlines which belong to the basic forms; her characters never abound either in numbers or in closely packed experiences as in the older novel; and her prevailing intention is one which has belonged to legend: enshrinement of the past. In *O Pioneers* and *My Antonia* the figures—human as they are—become all but prototypical in the backward look upon pioneer life of the prairies. In *A Lost Lady*, with all the clear focusing upon character, it is equally a lost phase of American existence, a cluster of people who are also types, and a way of living, that are recovered and remain unforgettable. In *The Professor's House*, within the portrayal of an intricate and sensitive mind, it is something quite outside human relations that leaves the last print, the little city in stone high up on the mesa. In *Death Comes for the Archbishop*, with characters who already belong to legend, the theme widens into a primary retrospect of spiritual adventure in a strange and beautiful land. All these narratives disengage and capture some primary element in a past existence; the touch of a distant magic is upon them. With a modern view of character, a modern sense of circumstance, they are romances. Rölvaag's *Giants in the Earth* possesses the same legendary quality within a single large compass; and his characters take on legendary stature. A deeply possessed native experience—the pioneer experience —that has been woven into the common consciousness, is here evoked by familiar elements, the journey, the quest for a home, the contest with the land, with hunger, storms, and heat.

This latter-day legend-making seems hard-won, like many another aspect of American literature; only rarely has it come into full and beautiful form. But the legendary or fabulistic temper persists, plain in the long sequence of Cabell's allegories and romances, appearing even in *An American Tragedy*, in which Dreiser attempted to create a sweeping allegory out of materials that could rightly lend themselves only to the working out of a few narrow destinies. In that flood of books written by newcomers in the land who have tried to crystallize some fresh aspect of American existence, the impulse has been toward the autobiography rather than the novel. The portions which have enduring worth in these narratives are almost invariably those which have to do either with an anterior life in an older country, retreating into the glamorous or legendary, or with early passages of a new existence in America, that retain a simple and elementary force. Scattered through contemporary literature are innumerable other narratives that seek to recover the past, that of New York of the '50's or New Orleans of an earlier day, of the Kentucky wilderness or of Indian life; they are not historical novels in the sense that *Esmond* is a historical novel; their purpose is to recover if possible the essence of the past, some lost quality, a vanished stream: with all the stress upon a warping circumstance their mood is that of glamour.

Retrospect has deepened in these narratives, spreading over a wider area than in the '70's and '80's, finding closer human values; fancy has taken new forms. The comic is no longer the single prevailing impulse, but has receded to a simpler and more casual, perhaps a more natural place, as in the later poetry; the harsh emotions of an early day are mingled with others of more varied character. But even with the widening range, which might seem to permit the easier and more direct view, the immediate scene has not been penetrated with imaginative force and fullness. With one exception none of those definitive novelists have appeared who make an aspect of contemporary life their own and leave it with the color of their imagination upon it forever afterward.

The exception of course is Sinclair Lewis; he possesses the copious touch; and people of the present day fill his pages. Yet with all his grasp of an immediate life, Lewis remains within the older American tradition; he is primarily a fabulist. In *Main Street* he stresses his intention at the outset. "On a hill by the Mississippi where Chippewas had camped two generations ago, a girl stood in relief against the cornflower blue of Northern sky. She saw no Indians now; she saw flour-mills and the blinking windows of skyscrapers in Minneapolis and St. Paul. . . . A breeze which had crossed a thousand miles of wheatlands bellied her taffeta skirt in a line so graceful, so full of animation and moving beauty, that the heart of a chance watcher on the lower road tightened to wistfulness over her quality of suspended freedom. . . . The days of pioneering, of lassies in sunbonnets, and bears killed with axes in piney clearings, are deader now than Camelot; and a rebellious girl is the spirit of that bewildered empire called the American Middlewest."

Even occasional digressions from immediate circumstance in *Main Street* have the fabulous touch, like the wind that blows a thousand miles, or the eras of history brought to bear upon the Kennicott's courtship. Later in the book Lewis changes his definition of the pioneer, declaring that the farmers—"those sweaty wayfarers"—whose lands surround Gopher Prairie and stretch into the farther distance, are pioneers, "for all their telephones and bank-accounts and automatic pianos and co-operative leagues." In the end Gopher Prairie itself takes on aspects of a pioneer existence, half shaped, inarticulate, pressed against an uncertain void. Then once again the theme enlarges, and Main Street becomes a national street, its existence a pervasive American existence.

This is that highly circumstantial fable-making which had been a characteristic American gift; and the prevailing tone is one which had appeared within the whole line of American fabulists, particularly those of the frontier. The material is prosaic, the mood at bottom romantic; gusto infuses the whole, with an air of discovery. Even the derision is not a new note; this had appeared again and again in American attitudes toward American life, and is part of the enduring native self-consciousness; it is seen here, as before, in a close tie with the comic. Lewis uses homely metaphors that might have been spoken by Yankee Hill, describing "an old farmer, solid, wholesome, but not clean—his face like a potato fresh from the earth." The familiar biting understatement appears, and the inflation; the western strain is as strong in Lewis as the Yankee. "She sat down as though it were a gymnasium exercise." "He was always consulting John Flickerbaugh, who handled more real estate than law, and more law than justice." The American gift for comic mimicry seems concentrated in Lewis, and his people seem to possess the unfailing native passion for the monologue: flood-gates of their talk are opened at a touch. Sights, sounds, the look of things and of people, as well as speech, are crowded against one another with tireless fluency. Nothing halts this movement in *Main Street;* nothing halts the cumulative intention; episode is piled on episode. The movement lengthens, and finally becomes in the large flow sagalike. The outcome is to portray the generic; the human situation steadily diminishes in force. At the beginning it is clear that the division between Carol and Kennicott is emotional, not civic: but the human circumstance is pushed aside by an urgent intention to reveal a comprehensive aspect of American life. The preoccupation is the familiar social preoccupation.

Lewis displays a detachment which never belonged to

285

the early fabulists. Babbitt's shrewd traction dealings are seen with an appraising eye instead of with that exhilaration by which earlier artists had been carried away, viewing similar triumphs. An unmitigated nationalism is slit by the same penetrative view; and that primitive desire for cohesion which had risen strongly through early comedy is shown to have become the crudest of mass instincts. Lewis turns his abundant fables into critiques and challenges, but the transcendent effect is the traditional effect: the American portrait, a comic portrait once more, has been drawn in amplitude. Babbitt takes a place beside the archetypal Yankee; and for the first time an archetypal native scene is drawn in Main Street. The response too has been the habitual response. Bitterly as the direct seizure of American life has been resented, it has offered the portrait; the mirror was upheld, and the American with his invincible curiosity about himself could not fail to gaze therein.

There is a sense in which Lewis may be considered the first American novelist. In his unflagging absorption of detail and his grasp of the life about him he suggests Defoe; and it may be that like Defoe in England he will prove to have opened a way for the development of the novel in America. The impact of his scrutiny lies all about; the American scene and the American character can never slide back into the undifferentiated state of an earlier view. Yet the novel may not develop at all in America in the older sense. In England it arose out of an immensely long preparation even before Defoe; for a century its growth was gradual; in the Victorian period it came to a great completion. If the word Victorian means anything on the English side it is a rich and settled stability within which traditions, long rooted, could come into bloom; the outlines of the Victorian period were not straitened but hospitable, so that the most divergent motives and movements found comfortable quarters there. No mere spatial invitation of a continent could offer the same breadth or depth. No such accumulation of effort and tradition has been possible in the short and broken cycle of American life; traditions are even now only beginning to take a coherent shape. Part of the vexing judgment of American literature has come from the expectation on the American side, born of an exhilarated fancy, that American literature could match English literature.

Whether or not it can ever do so, the pace of each, and perhaps the direction, has been wholly different; the movement of each has necessarily been conditioned by profound differences in the national history. Perhaps the great stability that produced the Victorian novel will never be repeated, either in England or elsewhere. The English novel in the past has dealt for the most part with societies or distinctly outlined social groups; and everywhere these seem to be breaking up; in America they have hardly existed. By one of those ellipses which sometimes occur in the life of nations as well as in that of individuals, a stage may have been omitted in American development, that which would have allowed a slow accumulation and enrichment. American expression has always moved toward the theatrical or the dramatic; it may be that these rather than the fuller courses of the novel will become a characteristic American form. Perhaps, as Virginia Woolf has suggested, the older novel will disappear, moving toward poetry. The American narrative has at least verged toward the poetical, though its poetry is not yet a poetry of contemporary life.

A full and imaginative penetration of contemporary life would seem to be required if maturity in literature is to be reached; but the glance backward, beginning early, continuing long, holds no implication of flight or evasion; it need not suggest that a present existence is too ugly or too difficult for the imaginative view. The mood of retrospect seems indeed the soundest of possible instincts, fulfilling a purpose against which almost every large force in the country seemed to war upon, that to take root. The ellipses created by migration and change may never be filled; much of the past is now gone forever; yet through retrospect and the legendary approach a basis may be created out of which an ample sense of the present may at last spring.

4

POPULAR fantasies in familiar patterns still exist in abundant strength in America. The popular oracle has never died. In the wake of the stage Irishman of earlier years and the later Gallagher and Shean, or lesser figures, came

Mr. Dooley: "Well, sir, afther a long argymint between th' dhriver an' the horses, conducted I thought, with an onnecessary display iv temper be Mike, but with th' ca'mness iv ripe ol' age be the horses, these chargers consinted to dhraw us away fr'm th' railroad property befure we cud be run in as threspassers. It was plain that th' horses did not want to go back to th' hotel, although they did not take their meals there. Annyhow we dashed on an' on an' up an' down, through th' heart iv th' city, an' at a place which I guessed must be the spinal colyum Mike cried 'Ho,' yanked frantically at th' reins, an' applied th' brakes. But too late. Th' horses had already stopped, an' we found oursilves in front iv a buildin' that I instantly recognized fr'm th' pitcher be what Mike told me as th' Wild Waves hotel; but O! how changed fr'm th' time whin it set f'r its photygraft. It was th' same hotel, but th' blush had fled fr'm its shingles. Th' flags flew no more, but had flown. Th' lake had gone back three miles an' its site was occypied be a coalyard, th' tennis coort had moved around to th' back yard an' was full iv clotheslines, th' little girl with th' hoop had grown up, got married, an' wint to Sheboygan to live, an' th' prancin' bays pranced no longer. On th' spacyous veranda, or front stoop, th' on'y s'ciety lady I cud see was wan iv about me own age an' figure who was settin' in a rockin' chair rockin'. . . ."

For a brief space in the '80's the oracle had gone into a partial eclipse, but in Mr. Dooley he rose again as if this homely figure stirred a deep-seated popular passion. In the

American short memory the earlier oracles were forgotten; the Yankee, Hoosier, and backwoods ancestors slipped from the general view. Like many another creature of the American fancy he seemed—for a time—new born. But a change had come over this oracle and the others who have come after him; except for brief excursions such as that to the Wild Waves Hotel many of them are sedentary; they no longer rove over the country in person or in fancy. Mr. Dooley's monologues were delivered to Hennessey inside a shop. This may mean the beginning of the end of their homely sway, or the opposite—a fresh lease on life and a subtler wisdom. The subjects are the old subjects, national foibles, "peace and war," and politicians; and the audience has been national.

After Mr. Dooley came a flock of Jewish caricaturists, with further oracles like Abe and Mawruss, and finally Mrs. Feitlebaum on domestic topics, whose linguistic accomplishments outstrip those of any exponent of the early dialectic tracts. "Nize Baby, itt opp all de rize witt milk so momma'll gonna tell you a Ferry Tail from de Pite Piper of Hemilton. Wance upon a time was a willage from de name from Hemilton. So it was ronning along avveryting smooth witt Ho K—accept wot it was one acception: Was dere a hobnoxious past from rets. Hm! sotch a pasts wot dey was de rets."

Will Rogers, rover, lecturer, cowboy, showman, is an adviser in high places, a hundred years after Jack Downing. Blackface entertainers have appeared in duologue with the patter of minstrelsy which occasionally runs to the oracular and keeps the monologue of one speaker to the fore. The speech of country oracles is still syndicated in papers of the smaller towns throughout the country, even though the character presented is fast disappearing. In the larger cities the columnists have come forward, highly urban, the sharpest and most irreverent of social critics, keeping the monologue. The comic monologue seems as settled a convention as the Greek chorus; and it still embodies a familiar habit, that of the complete revelation which tells everything, tells little, and unfolds the outlines of a character.

In a different vein Ring Lardner has pictured purveyors of this full, free, but blank self-portrayal, among baseball players, caddies, song-writers, wives, the nurse in *Zone of Quiet*. In one of his tales two of these talkers meet, each trying to drown out the other, the beaten one seeking a possible silent listener. Most of these people could talk indefinitely; the stories are only loosely seized sections of their talk, snatches of their ceaseless voices: the continuing overtones can be heard even when the story is finished. "Well girlie you see how busy I have been and am libel to keep right on being busy as we are not going to let the grass grow under our feet but as soon as we have got this number placed we will get busy on another one as a couple like that will put me on Easy st. even if they don't go as big as we expect but even 25 grand is a big bunch of money and if a man could only turn out one hit a year and make that much out of it I would be on Easy st. and no more hammering on the old music box in some cabaret. . . ."

After the long sway of the mechanized short story Lardner has turned back to prime materials in their old and sprawling personal form. His mimicry, like that of Lewis, is in the native tradition, close and truthful, yet with a leaning toward large rhythms and typical effects. He commands verbiage in the old style, jargon and the American delight in jargon, and the flattest Yankee manner. "Maysville was a town of five thousand inhabitants, and its gas company served eight hundred homes, offices, and stores." He even uses the favored mode of comic misspelling in the monologue which goes back to the almanacs and was perfected by Artemus Ward. "Well he swang and zowie away went the ball pretty near 8 inches distants wile the head of the club broke off clean and saled 50 yds down the course."

Like the characters of the early comic tales, his people are nomads. They have just moved into a neighborhood and are soon to move away; they lack backgrounds, they are only seen in pairs or trios, seen without families often, or with only a boresome friend. Old couples out of their native habitats sun their bones among other old couples just as homeless along the curbs or in the parks of Florida winter resorts. Even those tales which have to do with a group are projected against a void, or against some transitory scene like a hotel, a train, a baseball park. Here indeed are familiar subjects, familiar turns of story-telling, with intensifications of mood and a considerable difference in the effect of final character and the sense of character. The earlier wanderers of comedy were always foot-loose. These, their descendants, are continually netted by circumstance, by baseball contracts, importunate hostesses, or old age. Their orbit is far smaller; and the colored, the local background of an earlier time is gone: none of the interwoven look and feeling of place belongs to them, as it belonged to the comic figures of an earlier time. That process of amalgamation which has seemed a determined purpose of the comic sense might have wreaked its worst upon them. These people might be a final product of a humor that had worn away idiosyncrasies, taking with it all the edged elements of character. They are American; they are nothing but American, and essential to all parts of the country. That is the single outcome; that is the triumph too of Lardner's portrayal.

All his stories turn on humor; practical jokes make the substance of many situations as in an earlier day, but in the end the brutality which underlies them is exposed. That innocence which once was made a strong strain in American portrayals is seen uncombined with shrewdness and revealed as abysmal stupidity. At times the old comic ferocity appears, as in *Hair Cut;* but this has grown several-sided and in the end more human, for it is subjected by understatement to a withering blast of. feeling. Lardner has pushed the monologue or the brief comic tale to an ultimate revelation by a series of negations; his tie is with that Yankee art which gained its effects by negation and a pervasive underlying theme. Derision becomes an outward shell covering a multitude of submerged emotions, rage, fear, bewilderment, an awkward love; the blank formula takes on intensity; emotion is still inarticulate, as earlier under the comic sway, but it surges toward the surface.

Elsewhere the same amplitude appears in the monologue, as in the tense and bitter humiliation revealed by Anderson's *I'm a Fool*, whose form is that of comedy, whose outcome tragi-comedy. A latter-day story-telling seems to have returned to the older and freer mode, and is at its best either in the monologue, or the brief tale that has the air of remembrance or improvisation. Often indeed these modern tales are flawed, as by the torment of a style in Dreiser's *Lost Phoebe*, a beautiful and deeply moving story, touched by that tenderness which seems an American gift, particularly among writers handling homely materials. In Sherwood Anderson's stories, incomparable as they are for remembrance or for significant phases of mid-western life and character, infused too at times with tenderness, there is almost always the unwarranted personal intrusion—the vestiges of the monologue where the monologue has no place. Yet these tales of Anderson and Dreiser possess a human warmth that has been lacking in many American narratives; they press toward emotion, when emotion has been insufficiently expressed. Humor plays through them; and they restore an element which had been dominant in the long American tradition, that of speech: their air of improvisation is not accidental; many of them are told as if spoken. Some of them could easily belong to the theater. Lardner's *Travelogue*, with its defeated hero who has had a tooth pulled and points to the cavity and tells how long the roots were, obviously belongs to the theater. *I'm a Fool* could be spoken there. The monologue as soliloquy has invaded the contemporary stage in *Strange Interlude*, joining with a long tendency in American imaginative expression, that which explores inner fantasies.

Many familiar intentions are seen, with changes of mood or stress. The Jew is moving out of caricature into the realm of humanized drawing, on the stage and in the narrative. After a long submergence the Negro has come into a broad portrayal. In the main the Negro had appeared as a comic character in the stories of the '80's; but gradually other elements have been added until a many-sided and diversified type has been evoked, with a few richly drawn characters, often overtaken by tragedy. The change seems all but inevitable; it has occurred in literature before. A figure enters as comic; then gradually, when the full light of comedy has been cast upon him, human lineaments begin to appear, and he is included in a larger realization. In early American comedy this blaze of light was intense, so that tragi-comedy was often an immediate element there. Now after a long lapse that ample scrutiny seems to be returning with freedom.

For the most part these alterations have taken place

within the tale or on the stage. Occasionally drama has been achieved, but not in sufficient abundance to fulfill the promise of a folk-theater which would be indeed not one theater but many, focusing and illuminating the many-sided native character, drawing upon the diverse strains in the American tradition. The lighter theater is still a deeply ingrained American form, fresh and characteristic, a place of overflow and experiment, revealing as in primary sketches many a large turn of the American character, the effervescences of the moment, current obsessions, popular reactions, momentary phases of humor. It is gay, and full of the "lively arts"; triumphant humor still survives there. It has become immensely accomplished, particularly in dancing and broad impersonation; yet it has not used the long and many traditions which lie behind it; it has not commanded that light, full, authoritative handling which means that the imagination is soundly at work. With all its accumulation of a brilliant technique and an illusory finish the lighter theater is still for the most part an affair of changing fragments; its most complete accomplishment is likely to be in the realm of burlesque, which leans upon the established production. It has borrowed sophistication, but it is seldom really sophisticated. This theater has remained primitive without falling into those strongly marked and simple patterns which belong to a primitive theater. Its tireless vigor and kaleidoscopic exterior changes seem a phase of young experiment. New fantasies, rough drawings of character, juxtapositions of native feeling, come out of it, perhaps to be drawn upon as in the past by other arts of expression.

5

HUMOR has been a fashioning instrument in America, cleaving its way through the national life, holding tenaciously to the spread elements of that life. Its mode has often been swift and coarse and ruthless, beyond art and beyond established civilization. It has engaged in warfare against the established heritage, against the bonds of pioneer existence. Its objective—the unconscious objective of a disunited people—has seemed to be that of creating fresh bonds, a new unity, the semblance of a society and the rounded completion of an American type. But a society has not been palpably defined either in life or in literature. If literature is a gauge, only among expatriates has its strong semblance existed, without genuine roots, and mixed with the tragical. The other social semblance which has come into the common view is that of Main Street.

Nor has a single unmistakable type emerged; the American character is still split into many characters. The comic upset has often relaxed rigidities which might have been more significant if taut; individualism has sometimes seemed to wear away under a prolonged common laughter. The solvent of humor has often become a jaded formula, the comic rebound automatic—"laff that off"—so that only the uneasy habit of laughter appears, with an acute sensitivity and insecurity beneath it as though too much had been laughed away. Whole phases of comedy have become empty; the comic rejoinder has become every man's tool. From the comic the American has often moved to a cult of the comic. But a characteristic humor has emerged, quiet, explosive, competitive, often grounded in good humor, still theatrical at bottom and full of large fantasy. The note of triumph has diminished as the decades have proved that the land is not altogether an Eden and that defeat is a common human portion. Humor has moved into more difficult areas and has embraced a subtler range of feeling; exaltation of the common American as the national type has been deflated. Yet what must still be called a folk strain has been dominant; perhaps it is still uppermost; the great onset of a Negro art, the influence of Negro music, and popular responses to the more primitive aspects of Negro expression suggest that the older absorption in such elements is unbroken. If the American character is split and many-sided at least a large and shadowy outline has been drawn by the many ventures in comedy.

A consistent native tradition has been formed, spreading over the country, surviving cleavages and dispersals, often growing underground, but rising to the surface like some rough vine. This ruthless effort has produced poetry, not only in the sense that primitive concepts are often poetic, but keeping the poetic strain as a dominant strain. Not the realistic sense, which might have been expected of a people who call themselves practical, but the poetic sense of life and of character has prevailed. With all the hasty experiment this tradition has revealed beauty, and wry engaging human twists. It has used subtle idioms, like the quieter Yankee idiom; it has contained the dynamic serenity of Whitman and the sensitive discovering genius of Henry James. With all the explosions its key has often remained low; this tradition has shown an effect of reserve, as if in immediate expression and in its large elements something were withheld, to be drawn upon again. It has produced two major patterns, the rhapsodic and the understated, whose outlines may be traced through the many sequences of popular comedy and through American literature; regional at first, they have passed far beyond the regional.

Clear courses have been drawn, yet these have been full of the vagaries that come from complex experiment. New themes have often been upturned and penetrated only in part. The epical promise has never been completely fulfilled. Though extravagance has been a major element in all American comedy, though extravagance may have its incomparable uses with flights and inclusions denied the more equable view, the extravagant vein in American humor has reached no ultimate expression. The comedy of Rabelais provides a gauge, or that of *Ulysses*. On the other hand little equability has appeared, only a few aspects of social comedy; and emotion remains, as earlier, submerged, or shaded and subtle and indwelling. T. S. Eliot has voiced an insistent mood.

Well! and what if she should die some afternoon,
Afternoon gray and smoky, evening yellow and rose;
Should die and leave me sitting pen in hand
With the smoke coming down above the housetops;
Doubtful, for quite a while
Not knowing what to feel or if I understand. . . .

Set against this self-consciousness and disillusionment are
further primitive elements of American life, showing themselves in the continuance of the cults, in lodges, parades,
masquerades, as in earlier years, in shouts like "Hallelujah!
I'm a bum!" and in a simple persistent self-portraiture not
unlike that to which the American was first given. He still
envisages himself as an innocent in relation to other
peoples; he showed the enduring conviction during the
Great War. He is still given to the rhapsody, the monologue, the tale, in life as in literature. Of late has come one
of those absorptions in homely retrospect to which the
American mind has periodically been devoted; common and
comic characters, pioneers, orators, evangelists, hoboes,
hold-up men, have come to the fore with a stream of old
story and song, often engaging the same Americans who
turn to Eliot or Robinson or Henry James.

These oddly matched aspects of the American character
are often at variance. Together or separated, they have
found no full and complete expression. Who can say what
will bring fulfillment? If this comes it may be conditioned
by many undetermined elements in the national life and
character, by outside impingements even—since Americans
are acutely aware of these—like that which weighed heavily

in earlier years, the burden of British opinion. Its effects are still not altogether resolved; it has been noted that the sharp critiques offered in an earlier day by visiting foreigners are now defined by Americans, often as though they had merely borrowed the attitude. The involvement with the older countries is genuine; and the task looms for literature of absorbing traditions of the older world as part of the natural American heritage. The alliances must be instinctive or the fabric will be seamy. In general the American creative mind has lacked the patience and humility to acquire them, or it has been fearful of alienation from American sources.

Against full use of the native tradition many factors are set. That nomadic strain which has run through all American life, deeply influencing the American character, is now accented by the conditions of modern life; and the native character seems to grow more generalized, less specially American. Within the space of a lifetime Henry James saw something of the kind happen; in later years he remarked of the heroine of *Pandora's Box* that she could no longer "pass for quaint or fresh or for exclusively native to any one tract of Anglo-Saxon soil." Yet the main outlines of the American character still persist; American types can be found far from their native habitat and unmistakable in outline, homeless Yankees in Nebraska or frontiersmen in Monte Carlo, and others who may show an erosion due to alien places so that the original grain has grown dim, but who show that grain.

For the creative writer the major problem seems to be to

know the patternings of the grain; and these can hardly be discovered in rich color without understanding of the many sequences of the American tradition on the popular side as well as on purely literary levels. The writer must know, as Eliot has said, "the mind of his own country—a mind which he learns in time to be much more important than his own private mind." A favored explanation for the slow and spare development of the arts in America has lain in stress upon the forces of materialism. But these have existed in every civilization; they have even at times seemed to assist the processes of art. The American failure to value the productions of the artist has likewise been cited; but the artist often seems to need less of critical persuasion and sympathy than an unstudied association with his natural inheritance. Many artists have worked supremely well with little encouragement; few have worked without a rich traditional store from which consciously or unconsciously they have drawn. The difficult task of discovering and diffusing the materials of the American tradition—many of them still buried—belongs for the most part to criticism; the artist will steep himself in the gathered light. In the end he may use native sources as a point of radical departure; he may seldom be intent upon early materials; but he will discover a relationship with the many streams of native character and feeling. The single writer—the single production—will no longer stand solitary or aggressive but within a natural sequence.

BIBLIOGRAPHICAL NOTE

BIBLIOGRAPHICAL NOTE

F EW materials are more important for a view of American humor than those provided by the comic almanacs during the period from 1830, when they began to appear, to 1860, when they had grown less local and flavorsome. These fascinating small handbooks yield many brief stories and bits of character drawing not to be found elsewhere; more than any single source they prove the wide diffusion of a native comic lore. To list adequately those used for this study would be to compile a small book, if the intricacies of imprints were to be unraveled and descriptive notes added. In general it may be said that the rich collection of comic almanacs in the Library of the American Antiquarian Society has been examined, including numbers of *The American*, *The Old American*, *The People's*, *Finn's*, *The Rip Snorter*, the many almanacs put forth by the tireless and sprightly Elton, such as his *Whims Whams* and his *Tragical and Piratical Almanac*. The comic grist that poured forth from New York in the '40's and '50's under many titles is well represented in this collection, and has been considered, as have the highly important Crockett almanacs published in Nashville and other places, even in Boston. These too bore many titles, sometimes carrying the name of Crockett's mythical companion, Ben Hardin, or suggesting a large number of other characters, as in *Sprees and Scrapes in the*

305

West; Life and Manners in the Backwoods and Exploits and Adventures on the Prairies (1841), which contains brief tales of many kinds.

Serious almanacs have been scanned over a period which begins some years before the Revolution and includes the long sequence opening with the first number of *The Old Farmer's* in 1793. Humor was often contained within the pages of these staid pamphlets; they foreshadow comic effects to be found in more complete and striking forms in later years. They have proved invaluable in suggesting popular preoccupations even when these were not strictly comic. The connotations of *The Old Farmer's* have been discussed with a wealth of learning by Professor George L. Kittredge in his *Old Farmer and His Almanac* (1924).

In most of the joke-books before 1840 only the faintest traces of a native humor can be discovered. The preface to *The Chaplet of Comus* (1811) declares that "the reader will find in this collection more specimens of *American humor* than in any other publication. The palm of wit has been unjustifiably withheld from our countrymen by foreigners, and even some of our own writers have intimated that no good thing of a humorous kind can come out of New England." But the title hardly suggested American humor; and the promise was not fulfilled in the text. The *Aurora Borealis, or Flashes of Wit* (1831) contains a slight tale about a Yankee peddler and a few other localized stories; but for the most part this, like other joke-books of these years, reveals brief tales or episodes that are unmistakably

English, with a sprinkling of others that go back to Aesop. The early Joe Miller joke-books were often taken over bodily from the English issues. But in 1833 one of the comic almanacs pictured a tombstone bearing the legend, "Here lies Joe Miller"; and though the name survived, these famous little books—some of which Lincoln saw— contained thereafter an increasing bulk of humor that can be distinguished as American. They are now rare; a few of them have been seen for this study, and occasional others like the *Nonpareil*.

A more direct and important source has been *The Spirit of the Times* (New York) from 1831 to 1861. Its files have proved a compendium of native tales, notes, comic theatrical items, and lively allusions to current attitudes. Scarcely an aspect of American humor is unrepresented there. This sporting and theatrical journal, edited by a Yankee, William T. Porter, is particularly rich in the humor of the Mississippi Valley and the frontier.

William Jerdan's *Yankee Humor and Uncle Sam's Fun* (London, 1853) has yielded Yankee and Southwestern humor as seen in England, with glimpses of English attitudes toward comic representations of the American character. Other English reactions have been found in the files of *The Spirit of the Times*, the New York *Mirror*, in clippings from London papers in the Harvard Theatre Collection, and in notices incorporated in early biographies of American comedians.

An important contemporary view of the early Yankee is

307

offered in Royall Tyler's *A Yankee in London* (1811). Papers by Albert Matthews on *Brother Jonathan* (*Publications of the Colonial Society of Massachusetts*, 1902), and on *Uncle Sam* (*Proceedings of the American Antiquarian Society*, 1908) have contributed to the study of the early Yankee, as has Oscar G. T. Sonneck's *Report on the "Star Spangled Banner," "Hail Columbia," "America," and "Yankee Doodle"* (1903). "Corn Cobs Twist Your Hair," a version of "Yankee Doodle," appears in sheet music (1836) and was apparently first sung on the stage by Yankee Hill. Such periodicals as *The Yankee* (1828-29) and *Yankee Notions* (1852-60) have added stories or bits of discussion about the Yankee character. John Neal's *The Down Easters* (1833) and other early literary portrayals of the Yankee have been considered.

Plays embodying the Yankee character and Yankee humor have been surveyed from *The Contrast* onward, including the popular pieces of Woodward, Logan, Kettell, Jones, Bayle Bernard, and Stone. G. H. Hill's *Scenes from the Life of an Actor* (1853) has been substantially drawn upon for Yankee portraiture of the lecture platform and the stage, as have Northall's *Life and Recollections of Yankee Hill* (1850) and Falconbridge's life of Dan Marble. Outlines of the figure of Sam Patch appear in the latter biography, with descriptions of the Sam Patch plays. Other brief allusions to Sam Patch have been found in the Downing papers, in *The American Joe Miller* (1840), and in contemporary notes on the Yankee character. Perley I. Reed's

Realistic Presentation of American Characters in Native American Plays Prior to 1870 (1924) has been a helpful guide for the less accessible Yankee plays.

Ample studies of the Yankee oracles appear in J. R. Tandy's *Crackerbox Philosophers* (1925), in M. A. Wyman's *Two American Pioneers: Seba Smith and Elizabeth Oakes Smith*—which contains an invaluable bibliography disentangling the authentic Downing papers from those of the many imitators—and in V. L. O. Chittick's *Thomas Chandler Haliburton* (1924), which is particularly rich in its handling of Sam Slick and his times.

The darker legends of New England have survived only in fragments. Hawthorne's tales and his notebooks have been a source for these, as have Whittier's *Legends of New England* (1831) and his *Supernaturalism in New England* (1847).

Since the trail of the Yankee led into the backwoods, studies of his character have often included references to the backwoodsman; and at times the two seemed inextricably mixed. The title of Falconbridge's life of Dan Marble, a Yankee actor, may stand as indicative of this mergence: *The Gamecock of the Wilderness, or the Life and Times of Dan Marble* (1851). In addition to such mingled sources, backwoods or frontier character and humor have been derived from Flint's *Recollections of the Last Ten Years* (1826), Hall's *Legends of the West* (1832), his *Harpe's Head: A Legend of Kentucky* (1833), *Tales of the Border* (1835), and *The Wilderness and the Warpath* (1846);

from Hoffman's *A Winter in the West* (1835) and his *Wild Scenes in Forest and Prairie* (1839), from Drake's *Discourse on the History, Character, and Prospects of the West* (1834); from Mary R. Mitford's *Stories of American Life* (London, 1830), which contains material not easily found in other forms; from Irving's *A Tour of the Prairies* (1835), and from *The Life of John James Audubon* by Lucy Audubon (1869), *The Life and Adventures of John James Audubon, the Naturalist*, by Robert Buchanan (1869), and Audubon's *Ornithological Biography* (1831-39). Herrick's *Audubon the Naturalist* (1917) has been useful. Rusk's admirable *Literature of the Middle West Frontier* (1925) and Venable's *Beginnings of Literary Culture in the Ohio Valley* (1891) have supplied clews to material on the backwoodsman.

Outlines of the Mike Fink legends have been drawn from Field's *Drama in Pokerville* (1847), Thorpe's *Hive of the Bee-Hunter* (1854), from western almanacs, and from *The Spirit of the Times*. Franklin J. Meine's provisional bibliography of Mike Fink material has been an invaluable guide. Only a few fragments of boatmen's songs have survived. *The Boathorn* by William O. Butler may be found in *The Western Review* (Lexington, 1821).

The larger portion of the tales about Crockett in this study have been drawn from the western almanacs; in addition, the familiar *Narrative of the Life of David Crockett of the State of Tennessee* (1834) and the *Sketches and Eccentricities of Colonel David Crockett of West Tennessee*

(1833) have been used, as well as *An Account of Colonel Crockett's Tour of the North and Down East* (1835). Since the plays based on the character of Crockett—and indeed the entire group of early backwoods plays—have disappeared, their general substance has been derived from notices in contemporary theatrical journals, biographies of actors, and travels. Such a purely fictional work as Carruthers' *A Kentuckian in New York* (1834) has furthered the effect of localized character and of acute interaction between American types.

For the homelier stories of the old Southwest Watterson's *Oddities of Southern Life and Character* (1882) provides important critical notes. A large collection of tales about corncrackers and rapscallions of this region will be found in Franklin J. Meine's *Tall Tales of the Southwest, 1830-60,* (1930), which contains an excellent brief bibliography. Longstreet's *Georgia Scenes* (1835), Baldwin's *Flush Times of Alabama and Mississippi* (1853), Field's *Drama in Pokerville* (1847), Harris's *Sut Lovingood* (1867), Thompson's *Chronicles of Pineville* (1845) and *Major Jones's Sketches of Travel* (1847), Hooper's *Adventures of Simon Suggs* (1845), and *The Big Bear of Arkansas* (1845), *A Quarter Race in Kentucky* (1846), edited by William T. Porter, have comprised the principal materials from which conclusions have been drawn as to the less inflated tall tales of the Southwest.

The literature on early minstrelsy is extremely slight. An important work is still to be done in discovering and de-

311

scribing those extant minstrel songs which bear unmistakable traces of Negro origin. For this study a considerable body of sheet music bearing early imprints has been scanned, in the American Antiquarian Society and the Widener Library; songs by Rice, Emmett, Foster, and some less-known writers have been thoroughly considered. Emmett's walkarounds—"Dixie" was a walkaround—are particularly significant as suggesting Negro origins. In addition, minstrel songs in pocket song-books of the '40's and '50's, usually printed without music, have supplied interesting variations; the imprints have proved the wide diffusion of such songs. Minstrel plays or sketches, which often indicated the accompanying songs, in the Widener Library and the Chicago University Library, have been used, including such early pieces as *O, Hush, or the Virginny Cupids*, *The Mummy*, and *Bone Squash* by T. D. Rice. For comparisons between minstrel songs and the spirituals, *The Slave Songs of the United States*, compiled by W. F. Allen, C. P. Ware, and Lucy McKim Garrison (1867, 1930), has been considered, with other recent compilations of spirituals. Krehbiel's *Afro-American Folk-Songs* (1914) has been invaluable for its discussion of the character of Negro music and the origins of the spirituals.

Photographs of minstrel players over a long period, in the Harvard Theatre Collection, have provided evidence that early minstrelsy attempted a close impersonation of the Negro, most often of the plantation Negro; the early photographs show a marked contrast with those of later years with their highly stylized figures. Notes in *The Spirit of the Times* and in contemporary theatrical memoirs describe the characterizations of Jim Crow Rice and his successes throughout the country and in London. Galbraith's *Daniel Decatur Emmett* (1904) has been useful as offering Emmett's own version of his sources, and as indicating the influences which led him to use Negro melodies, choruses, and animal fables. LeRoy Rice's *Monarchs of Minstrelsy* (1911) contains biographical sketches suggesting regional alliances of many early minstrels, with notes on their impersonations. Cable's *Creole Slave Songs* in *The Century*, April, 1886, has been used for this study.

Theatrical histories, memoirs, and accounts of travel by strolling players have supplied a considerable bulk of material; these writings all but match the almanacs in importance as revealing popular humor, popular preoccupations, and evidences of the national character. Actors were concerned first of all with idiosyncrasies, since these added to their art; they seldom seemed to possess strong prejudices; and they often had a gift for concentrated mimicry and description. The writings of John Bernard, Dunlap, Rees, Wemyss, Northall, Cowell, Vandenhoff, Sol Smith, Ludlow, Tyrone Power, Leman, Hackett, Wallack, Jefferson, have yielded materials on the Yankee, the backwoodsman, the Negro, the minstrel, as well as on theatrical history. Other similar sources include the anonymous *The Actor, or A Peep Behind the Curtain* (1846), Alger's *Life of Edwin Forrest* (1877), Pyper's *Romance of an Old Playhouse*

(1928)—on the Mormon theater—and materials on the California theater of the gold rush, collected mainly from newspaper sources, for the author's *Troupers of the Gold Coast*. Josiah Quincy's *Figures of the Past* (1924) contains interesting references to Mormon theatricals at Nauvoo.

Contemporary pamphlets, tracts, sermons, biographies, memoirs, considered for another study, have been drawn upon for an interpretation of the strollers of the cults and revivals. For the passages on burlesque oratory and on the American language Thornton's *An American Glossary* (1912), Mencken's *American Language* (revised edition, 1923), and Krapp's *The English Language in America* (1925) have been used, as well as miscellaneous contemporary writings. Sandburg's *American Songbag* (1927) has proved admirable not only for its rich collection of surviving popular songs but for the notes on regional backgrounds or connections. Esther Shephard's *Paul Bunyan* (1924) and other scattered stories have provided the outlines of the Bunyan cycle. *John Henry: Tracking Down a Negro Legend* by Guy B. Johnson contains an excellent summary.

First editions and prefaces, miscellaneous writings, journals, and letters have yielded materials on the literary figures considered in this study. For the most part these general sources are indicated in the text. Hervey Allen's *Israfel* (1927) has established facts in Poe's early life suggesting immediate influences of his time. Lewis Mumford in *The Golden Day* (1926) has pointed out that terror and cruelty dominated Poe's mind, as they dominated many phases of pioneer expression. Apart from its thesis, Joseph Wood Krutch's *Edgar Allan Poe: A Study in Genius* contains an abundance of suggestion as to the play of inner fantasy in Poe's tales. Franklin J. Meine has discovered Poe's review of Longstreet's *Georgia Scenes* in *The Southern Literary Messenger*, March, 1836, thus proving a point of contact between Poe and current Southwestern humor. *The Pilgrimage of Henry James* by Van Wyck Brooks (1925) has proved highly stimulating, even though the present conclusion that the international scene is a natural and even traditional American subject is at variance with that of Mr. Brooks. Perhaps no one can read Bergson's *Laughter* without being influenced by its definitions; some of these have entered into the present interpretation. Meredith, Max Eastman, Freud, and other writers on humor have also been considered; but an effort has been made to describe American humor and the American character without attachment to abstract theory.

BIBLIOGRAPHICAL ESSAY

W. T. Lhamon, Jr.

CONSTANCE ROURKE was famous for tracking down sources ruthlessly and displaying them scrupulously in her after-notes. Thus the annotating bibliographer need not measure her thoroughness but only indicate where subsequent scholars have followed her clues, argued with her theses, or worked materials that have emerged since her time.

Of the two books directly about Constance Rourke, the last is the least: Samuel I. Bellman, *Constance M. Rourke* (Boston: Twayne-G. K. Hall, 1981). This introduction to Rourke is frequently misleading about *American Humor* (expanding Rourke's mythic trio to five "colorful performers," for instance); and Bellman ignores earlier scholarship that had already established his points, for example, Bluestein's connection of Rourke to Johann Gottfried von Herder. Fortunately, Joan Shelley Rubin's *Constance Rourke and American Culture* (Chapel Hill: University of North Carolina Press, 1980) usefully locates Rourke's ideas in her familial, political, and educational backgrounds – respectively, matriarchal, Progressive, and midwestern Deweyesque, then Vassar (where she also taught, 1910-15). Rubin's enthusiasm for Rourke is sometimes tepid: "Rourke plays no original part in the theoretical discussions of culture and myth among her contemporaries" (xiii). Thus she slights the importance of Rourke's theory, making her out to be more a scholarly drone than a shaper of the hive. Rubin is in many other ways severely corrective, however, especially in revealing through Rourke's correspondence her contemporaries' dependence on her work. Rubin's bibliography is excellent – the fullest list of Rourke's own journalism and scholarship, as well as the secondary commentary on her.

317

Gene Bluestein's chapter on *American Humor,* in *The Voice of the Folk: Folklore and American Literary Theory* (Amherst: University of Massachusetts Press, 1972), shows how Rourke applied Herder's insights to American culture. Uniquely, Bluestein has followed her understanding of black culture, as well as her selective adaptation of the Cambridge myth critics to the American experience.

The publication of *American Humor* placed Rourke squarely at the foundation of the "usable past" school of criticism. That phrase derived from the famous essay in 1918 by Van Wyck Brooks, "On Creating a Usable Past," first printed in the magazine *The Dial* and since reprinted many times, most conveniently in *Van Wyck Brooks: The Early Years; A Selection from His Works, 1908–1921,* edited by Claire Sprague (New York: Harper Torchbooks, 1968), pp. 219–26. Probably the most famous of the early books in this mode is by Lewis Mumford, *The Golden Day* (New York: Boni and Liveright, 1926). It is the classic, oracular account of the 1830–60 flowering of American letters, which F. O. Matthiessen would establish fifteen years later as the *American Renaissance: Art and Expression in the Age of Emerson and Whitman* (New York: Oxford University Press, 1941). Rourke's *American Humor* came between them and stands with both. Part of a series Mumford did with other books on architecture and the arts in general, *The Golden Day* was to represent "spiritual form." But its evanescent topic increased Mumford's diaphanous rhetoric and, especially next to Rourke's and Matthiessen's work, *The Golden Day* reads like bell-ringing. We need, wrote Mumford at the end, "a criticism of the past, which will bring into the foreground those things that have been left out of the current scheme of life and thought.... It is nothing less than the effort to conceive a new world" (282–83). His project was so vast and his labor so divided that one misses in each volume the connecting web. Thus the plain integration of *American Humor* is even more appreciable.

Rourke's economy is also apparent against the massive proportions of Matthiessen's study. And it is also worthwhile to compare the relevant sections of Matthiessen's work, such as "American Demigods" (635–45), to *American Humor*. Matthiessen tells stories there as well as Rourke, drawing on slightly different sources and quoting more directly than Rourke, who tended to renarrate by conflation. But lively as Matthiessen is in these sections, he implicates the material less than Rourke did, draws fewer connections, and shows little intention in the lore. For him it is background to literature – the "frontier soil" (638) from which Twain grew, for example; it is not art in itself. Matthiessen gave his deeper commentary to Emerson and Whitman, Twain and Melville, rather than spreading it also across George Washington Harris and the anonymous Davy Crockett almanackers.

A wonderful book in Rourke's discipline of the usable past school is *Mark Twain's America*, by Bernard De Voto (1932; Cambridge, MA: Riverside, 1960). Like Rourke, De Voto is positive about the folk heritage in American literature, demonstrating how Twain's "literary intelligence was shaped by the life of the frontier" (240). Pages 91–99 contain a succinct summary of frontier humor, stressing more than Rourke did its violent, lusty, coarse, and unpleasant aspects. De Voto is unusually frank about his connection to Rourke. Scholars at some remove, however, have overlooked her significance. For instance, see the essays on Lewis Mumford and the usable past in a special issue of *Salmagundi* 49 (1980). Also, Richard Ruland has performed the notable feat of writing a study of the usable past idea in American literary criticism while ignoring Rourke – *The Rediscovery of American Literature: Premises of Critical Taste, 1900–1940* (Cambridge: Harvard University Press, 1967); he also quotes but neither names nor cites his eponymous *The Re-discovery of America* (1929) by Waldo Frank (with *Chart for Rough Water* [1940], New York: Duell, Sloan and Pearce, 1947).

319

A clutch of scholars have worked in the areas that Rourke pioneered. Not strictly matriculating in the usable past school, they nevertheless have recreated for the present much of the past. Walter Blair is among these and his *Native American Humor* (1937; San Francisco: Chandler Pub. Co., 1960) shows his obvious debt to Rourke. It is the best introduction to several folk and popular sources for American literature, with the last half of the volume devoted to an anthology and a fine annotated bibliography. Although Blair silently drops minstrel humor from Rourke's canon, there are black literary critics now on the scene beginning to redress this characteristic ellipsis. See particularly *Black Literature and Literary Theory,* edited by Henry Louis Gates, Jr. (New York: Methuen, 1984), and *Blues, Ideology, and Afro-American Literature* by Houston A. Baker, Jr. (Chicago: University of Chicago Press, 1984). Adequate accounts of the effect of black culture on the largely white mainstream have yet to be written.

Folklorists have, of course, a continuing interest in the kinship of lore and literature, but the field remains as complex as when Rourke harrowed it in 1931. For an overview of the history of professional attitudes toward folk tales, see Linda Degh, "Folk Narrative," in *Folklore and Folklife: An Introduction,* edited by Richard M. Dorson (Chicago: University of Chicago Press, 1972, pp. 53–83); Degh provides a reasonable version of the positions John M. Ellis undercuts in *One Fairy Story Too Many: The Brothers Grimm and Their Tales* (Chicago: University of Chicago Press, 1983). For an introduction to the plethora of ways in which scholars connect American literature to general folklore, see "Studying Folklore and American Literature," by Sandra K. D. Stahl, in *Handbook of American Folklore,* edited by Richard M. Dorson (Bloomington: Indiana University Press, 1983, pp. 422–33). Alan Dundes is the current folklorist closest to Rourke's insistence on transcending collection with analysis of a wide range of folklore. In *Interpreting Folklore* (Bloomington: Indiana University Press, 1980) Dundes reprints many of his articles. He does not address Rourke's comic trio, or any of her explicit engagements, but he does share her interest in folk character: "I submit that the folk should be put back into folklore. I am interested in folklore because it represents a people's image of themselves" (viii). Similar uses of folklore are evidenced in Robert Darnton's *The Great Cat Massacre and Other Episodes in French Cultural History* (New York: Basic Books, 1984) and in Laurence W. Levine's *Black Culture and Black Consciousness* (New York: Oxford University Press, 1977). These two books by historians care for recent folklore scholarship and are imaginative in their reconstruction of the mindsets of the French peasant and the modern Afro-American. Rourke was their forebear, too.

The ingenious sketching of the Yankee in *American Humor* has remained definitive. Richard Dorson, in *Jonathan Draws the Long Bow* (Cambridge: Harvard University Press, 1946), extends but does not contradict her picture of the lore of the Northeast. His full notes indicate repositories of colonial folklore as well as the creative research Dorson did to find them. His first chapter, "New England Storytelling," is a good introduction to the fertile relationship between oral and printed tales.

The coarse and vital lore of the frontier – Rourke's Gamecock – has attracted much research. Walter Blair and Franklin J. Meine have twice coedited the same material, first in *Mike Fink, King of the Mississippi Boatmen* (New York: Henry Holt, 1933), second in *Half Horse Half Alligator: The Growth of the Mike Fink Legend* (Chicago: University of Chicago Press, 1956). The books represent two stages in the presentation of folklore. The first is a running narrative that the editors recreated from the authentic fragments that the second displays in their actual discontinuity. Blair and Meine believed they had to pique interest initially, then much later

321

provide the scholarly facts that most concerned them. Ironically, had they waited a little longer with the second volume they could have incorporated the Disney revival (and revision) of Mike Fink in movies and television in the late fifties.

The essential book on frontier legends since *American Humor* is Richard Dorson's *Davy Crockett: American Comic Legend* (New York: Rockland Editions, 1939). Dorson reveals here his early indebtedness to Rourke, whose own *Davy Crockett* (New York: Harcourt, Brace, 1934) he cited as revealing the richest lodes of Crockett almanacs (166) and whom he said "superbly unraveled the deeper implications of the pagan comedy of the frontier, its creation of the national self-caricatures of the Yankee and the backwoodsman" (164). Note he did not mention the minstrel. At the end of his career, Dorson changed his evaluation, disparaging Rourke's methods as "confusing folklore with subliterature" (*Folklore and Fakelore* [Cambridge: Harvard University Press, 1976], 95). Despite the infighting, Dorson's selection from the Crockett legends is invaluable because it reveals the painfully high levels of racism, misogyny, and anti-intellectuality – the "full-bodied legendary personality" (xxv) – at the heart of American legends in the nineteenth century. Blair, Meine, even De Voto (to a lesser extent) soft-pedaled this dimension, and Rourke deflected it into theory. To laugh at the strange or xenophobic threat, she had implied, was for the American to approach and avoid it simultaneously. Still, the aggression of these deep anxieties is shocking to face straight on, which Dorson's selection allows us to do.

An indispensable resource for further reading on American minstrelsy is *Afro-American Folk Culture: An Annotated Bibliography of Materials from North, Central, and South America, and the West Indies,* compiled by Roger D. Abrahams and John Szwed (Philadelphia: Institute for the Study of Human Issues, 1978). It has substantial, but not foolproof, cross-referencing of minstrel research and memoirs;

for instance, though they list Hennig Cohen's article on proto-minstrel folk play among slaves, the authors do not reference it under minstrelsy ("A Negro 'Folk Game' in Colonial South Carolina," *SFQ* 16 [1952]: 183–84).

A rule of thumb in studies of minstrelsy is that the more they account for the phenomenon as a theater show, the more they insist it grew from white, northern fantasies of Negroes. But when the analysis is of lyrics, music, or dance, per se – that is, of the show's elements – then the insistence returns to the southern, black, folk origins that Rourke theorized. Similarly, the more one stresses early minstrelsy, as opposed to the later formulaic show, the more one agrees with Rourke. In her bibliography, she remarked on this change herself: "the early photographs show a marked contrast with those of later years with their highly stylized figures" (312–13). A synthetic conclusion might thus be that the elements were black and the formal properties white – though even the form seems to be implied in Cohen's report of the South Carolina slave play. Thus Robert C. Toll, in *Blacking Up: The Minstrel Show in Nineteenth-Century America* (New York: Oxford University Press, 1974), and G. D. Engle, in *This Grotesque Essence* (Baton Rouge: Louisiana State University Press, 1978), present what has become the orthodox, "travesty" theory. They analyze the shows through theater history, in the first case, and by scrutiny of surviving playscripts of late nineteenth-century minstrel shows, in the second. There is disagreement in the ranks, however, because theater historian Richard Moody, whom Engle cites (xv) as proof of racial fantasies, actually disagrees with him. In *America Takes the Stage: Romanticism in American Drama and Theatre, 1750–1900* (Bloomington: Indiana University Press, 1955), Moody wrote nearly the opposite of what Engle maintained. Moody said, "many characteristics of the real-life Negro unavoidably appeared in the minstrel-stage Negro. . . . Without the peculiar background of American Negro slavery, the minstrel show would never have been founded" (33). Hans Nathan is authoritative in *Dan Emmett and the Rise of Early Negro Minstrelsy* (Norman: University of Oklahoma Press, 1962). Stressing the early period of minstrelsy, he focuses on printed song lyrics and their illustrations. He corroborates the conclusions of Rourke and Moody that minstrelsy had racially mixed roots. Nathan includes a full bibliography of Emmett's work and an 180-page anthology of the songs attributed to Emmett, with their music. C. F. Wittke's *Tambo and Bones* (1930; New York: Greenwood, 1968) is the best specialized study from Rourke's era; it also acknowledges Negro origins for the form.

Marian Hannah Winter takes the life of William Henry Lane as an exemplary career in her discussion of minstrel dance, its sources, and the position of blacks in minstrelsy: "Juba and American Minstrelsy" in *Chronicles of the American Dance,* edited by Paul D. Magriel (New York: Henry Holt, 1948, pp. 38–63). Also see Lynne Fauley Emery, *Black Dance in the United States from 1619 to 1970* (Palo Alto, CA: National, 1972).

The single most provocative recent commentary on American minstrelsy is in Ralph Ellison's essay "Change the Joke and Slip the Yoke," which appeared originally in *Partisan Review* (25 [1958]: 212–22) and has been reprinted in Ellison's collection *Shadow and Act* (1964; New York: NAL-Signet, 1966, pp. 61–73). Arguing with the critic Stanley Edgar Hyman, he claims that minstrelsy, as it has come down to the contemporary artist, is a debasement of black culture. But, "as Constance Rourke has made us aware," he wrote, the issue was "too serious to be dealt with in anything less than a national art. The mask was an inseparable part of the national iconography" (63–64).

Let two final items affirm both the mask and its inseparable place in the American image bank. First, Walker Evans included two photographs of minstrel posters peeling off brick walls, dated 1936, in his *American Photographs* (1938; New York: East River Press, 1975, pp. 72, 88). The way he sequenced these images among courting whites and desolate blacks, white males bonding and a lone Negro miner masked with coal dust (instead of burnt cork), corroborates the burden of significant double meaning that minstrel shows still bore in the early-modern years of *American Humor.* Second, "The Artificial Nigger," a story by Flannery O'Connor at the outset of the next literary generation, centers the minstrel figure in her important collection, *A Good Man Is Hard to Find* (New York: Harcourt, Brace, 1955). Especially apparent here is the profound ambiguity of the title figure in the story and the way white characters misinterpret it. By this late date, the iconic Negro has come so far in the American imagination that it is entirely divorced from reality. O'Connor's "Artificial Nigger" statue shows blacks to be inscrutable to whites—just as "invisible" to them, in fact, as Ellison suggested in his novel *Invisible Man* (1952; New York: Vintage, 1982). But O'Connor also showed the minstrel figure to be totemically life-changing, one of the hard-to-find good men of her collection's title. No longer a faithful drawing of blacks, by the middle of the twentieth century the minstrel man nevertheless usurped the charisma of both the gamecock and Yankee unto itself, bearing the entire weight of the previous comic trio on his own thin mask.

INDEX

INDEX

INDEX